BOOK of

CW00456744

Andrè RavenSkül Venås

Copyright 2020

ISBN: 9798628742174

Contents

1. Freyja; the Goddess

Freyja the most worshiped of the Norse Goddesses, quickly became my go to for prayer and daily worship. Of course, Þòrr and Óðinn

were the first Gods I gave oath too, I soon
learned that one of the characteristics I was in
search of was the power and wisdom of Óðinn's
magick, which I soon learned was taught to him
by Freyja. As a Norse Vitki it is my
responsibility to connect as closely as I can to
the Gods, and Freyja having taught Óðinn the
magick of the Völva, so it seemed the obvious
choice to study, pray and worship her. Freyja is
an embodiment of the Sacred Feminine but also
a symbol of strength, she is a strong woman and
balances the masculine and feminine aspects of
herself and in return will help to build on the
Masculine and Feminine in all of us, as long as
we stay true and focused in our worship. This
balance in the Magickal world is one of the most
important aspects in the Spirit and Physical
world. So now I pray to Freyja, that is what I feel
and focus most of my attention on, first and
foremost, the importance of our sacred feminine
that we sometimes forget. And beauty as well,
the world is filled with many beauties and must

not be overlooked and Freyja is the most beautiful of them all .

A morning prayer to Freyja.

"Hail Freyja. Keeper of Brísingamen,
Wielder of Seiðr, Teacher of Magicks.
Goddess of beauty, love and lust.
Ruler of Fólkvangr, Mistress of the Slain.
With your fiery hair and sky-blue eyes,
Guide me and my fellow kinsman, so
that we may be strong in times of struggle.
Let us not forget our sacred Feminine, or
Masculine. May we bring new beauty to this
world? May you use me as your instrument?
And teach me the powers you hold sway.
-   Hail Freyja."

Freyja, Vanir Goddess of great power and magickal knowledge. Mistress of cats, leader of the Valkyries; a shape shifter. Inspires all sacred poetry. Love, beauty, animals, sex, enchantment, witchcraft, gold, wealth, trance, wisdom, magick, childbirth, horses, foresight, long life, fertility, music, poetry, writing, protection, luck, the moon, death, the night and the sea.

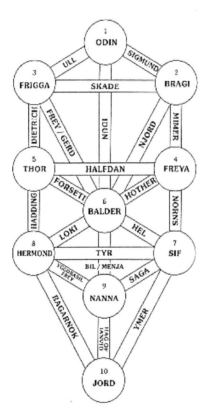

The Norse Pantheon applied to the Tree of Life.

Freyja the most important of all the goddess' in Norse Mythology. Her father was Njordr in Noatun, god of the sea. Her mother was Nerthus or Skadi in Thrymsheimur, daughter of the giant Thjassi. Freyja's brother is Freyr, god of fertility. Freyja's husband was Ottr, who has left her a long time ago and she sometimes cries tears of amber because she misses him so. She roamed all the nations searching him out and she often traveled under various guises; Mardoell, Hoern, Gefn and Syr are some of the most popular. Freyja has only one daughter, Hnoss, with Ottr, who is so beautiful that whatever is valuable and lovely is named "treasure", after her. Freyja lives in Fólkvangr in Asgardr, in her beautiful home, Sessrumnir. Her chariot is drawn by two cats (according to the Viking Answer Lady were named Bygul and Trjegul) that were given to her by Þòrr and of course, the priceless Brisingamen necklace, which she paid the highest of prices, the Norse still refer to Brisingamen as the Milky Way.

One of Freyja's powers is the mastery of material manifestation, the infusing of the physical world with the spiritual. Freyja not only masters the senses; she revels in them and shows that physical existence itself is a wondrous thing. Freyja also discovered the powers of the material world and how to control and shape them. Freyja is a mediator between peace and violence, and the Queen of fallen heroes. Riding her chariot pulled by Bygul and Trjegul through battlefields, she picks up half of the dead, and leaves the other half for Óðinn and takes their souls to her hall, Sessrumnir, in Asgardr. Sometimes she also rides the boar Hildisvini, who is her faithful companion.

"Fólkvangr it is called,
And there rules Freyja.
For the seats in the hall
Half of the slain
She chooses each day.
The other half is Óðinn's."

She loves music, spring and flowers, and spends much time with the fey. She is seen wearing a cloak of falcon feathers, which allows the wearer to change into a falcon and fly between the worlds, she once lent it to Loki Laufeyjarson when he needed to get to Jötunheim. Soon after she went to live with the Æsir as a hostage, she taught Óðinn Seiðr.

A bit about Seiðr,

Nordic mythology is rich in mystery and symbolism. Stories of Óðinn and the Norse Gods are directly related to life's struggles in a multitude of mysteries and mystic practices. The

Magick that Óðinn the All-Father uses is called Seiðr meaning string or cord. It is a form of shamanism that was commonly practiced through-out northern Europe, being most prevalent among woman. It was the practice of Seiðr that bestowed the ability upon Óðinn to traverse up and down Yggdrasil with his steed Sleipnir, and between worlds in the pursuit of wisdom and immortality.

Hidden within the mythos, tradition and poetry of the Norse are the symbols of the Seiðr. The Norns are masters of the practice of Seiðr, but it was Freyja who introduced it to the Gods, in particular, Óðinn. Alongside one another, Óðinn and Freyja both hold sway on the feminine and masculine deities of Seiðr.

However, the Norn remain outright masters, as it is their responsibility to weave the destiny of the worlds, Gods and mankind into the tapestry of time. It is believed that Freyja, a

Vanir and chief maiden of the Valkyries, first learned the art from the Norn, and in turn taught it to the Æsir. When Freyja's Valkyries advance their knowledge of Seiðr, they, in return, become Norn themselves. On Midgard this form of magic was mostly practiced by woman, who acted as seeresses and priestesses. They were known as the Völva or Seiðkona. These mystics would travel between towns and provinces providing services of their practice in exchange for hospitality and payment. Men also practice the art of Seiðr but were often ridiculed as being 'Engi', meaning unmanly. Even Loki accused Óðinn of being 'Engi'. Regardless, the practice of Norse Seiðr survives to this day for Masculine and Feminine alike. And it is continuously growing throughout today's society.

Somewhat like other schools of Magick, philosophy and religion, the macrocosm in Norse mythology is depicted by means of a tree. This is the mighty ash tree Yggdrasil, the world or cosmic tree. With nine worlds within its roots, trunk and branches the tree is surrounded by a tenth realm or cosmic egg. The tree symbolizes both the macrocosm (creation) and the microcosm (human), along with their hierarchies, realms and laws. Yggdrasil, the Sephiroth, the Tree of Knowledge, the ash tree of Greek mysteries and many more depict this very same concept.

Óðinn sees through one eye and councils with his two ravens Hugin (thought) and Munin (memory). These ravens soar the skies of Midgard and then return to Óðinn to whisper what they have witnessed. In some circles, the ravens represent the conscious and sub-conscious minds. Mastery of this duel relationship between conscious and subconscious mind is a requirement for any spiritual or practitioner of Magick. In the case of Hugin and Munin, this is very likely as their names directly refer to conscious thought and subconscious memory.

Beneath one of the three roots of Yggdrasil, lies Mimir's well of wisdom where Óðinn sacrificed an eye for the right to drink from it. Óðinn's sacrifice of plucking out his right eye in order to gain wisdom from Mimir's well represents the ability to perceive through one eye. This symbolizes the third eye which is commonly found in religious, philosophical and mystic branches. This is perhaps the most well-known of all mystery symbols and likewise universal in its meaning. The third eye represents perception from a higher perspective. This eye is able to see past all and into other realms in order to find knowledge, truth and wisdom. Óðinn's thirst for knowledge led to further self-sacrifice when he hung himself from Yggdrasil, stabbed himself with his spear Gungnir and hung for nine days refusing aid from others, peering down into the Well of Urd.

The practice of Seiðr, like any other
arcane art is a means of manipulating the nature
of reality, manifesting reality at that. From
Yggdrasil to Hugin and Munin, a connection
can be made to understand fully what is hidden
beneath the art and poetry of Norse history and
the magick we weave from the Universe. To this
day its power is strong enough to ensnare those
who look into it, ensuring its survival far into our
future...

Freyja, queen of the Valkyrie,

Freyja, the goddess of Beauty, youth, and of Earth, having golden-red hair (sun) and sky blue eyes (sky) is represented as a woman dressed in her feather armour and falcon helmet, carrying a shield and spear, and flowing skirts or dresses. She was born in Vanaheimr, as the goddess of the Vanir and came to Asgardr when Njord offered her in the prisoner exchange for a truce between the gods and giants.

When she reached Asgardr, the gods were so taken by her beauty and grace that they bestowed upon her the realm of Fólkvangr and the great hall Sessrymnir. Freyja was also known as Valfreyja, Queen of the Valkyries, and often led the Valkyrs down to the battlefields. The fallen warriors were transported to Folkvang, where they would be entertained for eternity.

Pure maidens and faithful wives were also allowed to enter the hall so they might enjoy the company of their lovers and husbands after death. This belief was so strong that often a wife or lover, seeing her love being slain on the battlefield, would run out into the battle hoping to receive the same fate, even throwing themselves on their own lover swords. Failing to die on the battlefield, sometime the wives and lovers would throw themselves on the funeral pyre of their love ones.

Freyja is so loved by her worshipers that Freyja' day, was carried into the English language as Friday. Her last known temple was destroyed by Charlemagne in Magdeburg, Germany.

Freyja has a reputation as a flirt. She enjoys love poetry and uses her love lore on many gods and creatures of the underworld. The trickster god Loki has accused her of having an incestuous relationship with her brother Freyr.

Her most prized possession is the necklace Brisingamen, allegedly there are no magical attributes linked with this piece of jewelry. Therefore, vanity alone caused her to treasure it. When the All-father had Loki take it away from her, Freyja started a war in retaliation.

The Valkyries are closely related to the cult of Freyja because she is considered the bride of all fallen heroes, as well as the bride of the early kings. Like Óðinn, Freyja is a leader of souls as well as a sorceress. She is known as a priestess who taught prophecy to the Æsir.

An address to Freyja:

"Vanir Bride, Hail Vision-Giver! Capped in
Cat-Fur, Cloaked in Feathers, Drumming for
The Dance of Dreams, You Haste to Hunt
Out Hidden Things. Scant Now the Screen
That Hinders Sight; Let Us Learn the Lore
of Trance-Work."

2. The Witches' Rune

"Darksome night and shining moon East, then South, then West, then North Harken to the Witches' Rune. For here I come to call you forth! Earth and Water, Air and Fire Wand and pentacle and sword, work you all to my desire Hark you all unto my word! Cords and censor, scourge and knife, Powers of the Witch's blade, wake you all now unto life, come now, as the charm is made! Queen of Heaven, Queen of Hel, Horned Hunter of the Night, lend your power unto my spell, Work my will by magic rite! By all the power of Land and Sea, by all the might of Moon and Sun, As I do will, so mote it be! Chant the spell and be it Done!

Runes of Freyja

 ehu...

Ar Y/J Freyja Both Green Earth Year Passing Time
Kaun K Freyja Feminine Red Fire Freyja's Rune Light Knowledge

Inguz* NG Freyja Both Green Water Fertility
Astral Plane

Freyja's symbols:

Sows, Daisies, Garnet, Amber, Cats, Honey,
Mead, Berries of all kinds, strawberries in
particular.

Herbs of Freyja:

Cowslip, daisy, primrose, maidenhair, myrrh,
strawberry, mistletoe, cherry.

Uses of the runes

Three to Summon and Speak with Spirits.
Three to Find a Lifemate. Three to Attract a
Lover. * Use for Turning a Curse back on its
Sender. Three to Break Bonds. These are
Runes of Healing. Use these Runes to Banish
Sorrow and ease Anguish.

Potential lessons Freyja can teach:

Seeking soul mates

Relationship issues

Working with the dead or ancestors

Learning self-worth and self-esteem

Recovering from abuse

Magic/Sorcery

Sex magic

Sacred Sexuality

Protection for pets and other animal

companions.

3. Rituals for Freyja

While many people petition Freyja for
love, she is also a powerful sorceress and diviner.
Keep in mind Freyja is a Goddess of the North,
and therefore if you ask Her for her help, you

must be willing to give Her something back in return! Never leave it open for interpretation or you may find yourself bound to a task you don't want to do. You could promise to use your abilities to benefit Freyja herself, or could dedicate a week of service to Her, or donate money to an animal shelter.

Friday is the best day to do this working, preferably on a waxing moon:

One candle, gold or red
Offerings of rose petals, berries, white wine or a bit of honeycomb
Fresh flowers if possible, depending on season.
Seal of Freyja below drawn on cloth or cleansed paper with ink containing your blood.

Try to make sure everything is organic or as pesticide-free as possible - Freyja is an agricultural deity and therefore will not appreciate anything chemical-laden. Cut the

Fehu rune into the candle with a dull knife, chanting the following.

"Freyja, Lady of Seiðr, she who sees far,
Teacher of Galdr, your words are power.
Grant me your gifts in Seiðr,
Grant me your gifts in Galdr
So, I may serve well."

Light the candle and take some time to meditate before the flame, giving the offerings to Freyja and giving Her time to accept them.

Invoking Freyja (Lokkr)

Anoint blood onto the seal from your left
hand and then the candles. Visualize the seal glowing
gold before burning it on the left side candle. Fix the
seal in your mind as it burns and call upon Freyja.

"Hailsa Freyja, Goddess of love and beauty
Ruler of Fólkvangr, lady of the slain
I call upon you here and now to join me
And grace me with your presence
Hailsa Freyja'

Then keep your eyes and mind open to Her reply.

Thank Freyja when closing the ritual

4. The Tale of Æsir and Vanir

Fehu

The Æsir lived in Asaheimr quite happy in their knowledge that they ruled over all in the chief city of Asgardr soon after the creation of the Universe. One glorious day mighty Óðinn was sitting staunchly upon his golden throne Hlidskjalf in his great hall Vlaskjalf searching the

Worlds of Yggdrasil for evil and keeping check on his ever curious Æsir. Something far in the distance hidden in the branches of Yggdrasil the world tree, something had caught his eye, but he couldn't quite make out what it was. As he stared intensely trying to focus on what he couldn't quite see, Heimdallr, his son rushed into the throne room skidding to an abrupt halt afore his father and spake.

"My apologies for disturbing you, all mighty All-Father, while at my post upon Bifrost I caught a glimpse of what seems to be other Gods, like us but not just quite."

As he paused to catch a deep breath, the All-Father Óðinn spake.

"I've been quite aware of something in the distance which has been troubling me, but I've been unable to make any sense of it. Now as I look even harder, I can see you're most correct. I know now that these other gods are the Vanir and their land in the distance is called Vanaheimr, also known as Uhland or Upphiminn, high atop the great tree Yggdrasil. They are bright and shining and are born of the purest upper air. They believe not in combat, war, or the glorious-nous of the fight."

"Rather they deal in witchcraft using these skills to triumph in their battles. They have a magic called Seiðr which gives them foreknowledge of the events of a battle, magically gaining information that allows them to conquer their enemies. This makes them extremely dangerous to us. We must seek out whether or not they intend to remain a peaceful race or if they would choose to be at war. They do seem far more interested in reaping the harvest than do the Æsir."

"I can feel that their ruler, Njordr, has great power indeed. He controls the movement of the great winds and the mighty seas. He has two newborn children, a boy and a girl, the result of an unnatural incestuous relationship with Nerthus his fire haired sister. Let us hope the twin offspring, Freyr and Freyja, do not become horrible monsters like their parents."

"I want you to go to them as my emissary and seek out their truths. To show our friendly intentions tell Njordr we are favouring his son Freyr the land of Alfheimr as a tooth gift since he has just cut his first tooth. Maybe his association with the delightful Ljósálfar will assure Freyr's goodwill as he ages. And here are some precious golden bracelets, necklaces and jewels for his daughter, the beautiful fiery maiden Freyja."

With his words cast towards Heimdallr, Óðinn returned his gaze and thoughts to other worldly issues. Heimdallr left in silence to forego his newest assignment.

Upon his return Heimdallr found his father supping with the Einherjar in Valhalla. He sat next to the All-Father at his great table and they discussed the intentions of the Vanir.

"They have assured me they mean us no harm, and if we keep to our ways they will keep to theirs, therefore no trouble should come about between us."

Heimdallr paused as a Valkyrie filled his gem inlaid drinking horn.

"And what of Njordr? What is he like?" demanded Oðinn.

"He's extremely handsome and glistening," began Heimdallr.

"He fairly shines, clad in his sea green tunic that shown like the brightness of the stars. He wears a crown of fish bones and shells entwined with seaweed upon his head, for his interests are of the sea. But on occasion he will also be seen adorning a lovely hat of eagle and heron plumes. His hall with it's great golden spires loom over the sea so he can bless the ships arriving and leaving for commerce from the ports. Whereas you are fond of wolves and ravens, Njordr is quite different. The sea sponge receives his special favor and is sometimes known as Njordr's glove."

Heimdallr paused as Óðinn fed Geri and Freki from his golden polished dining plate, then continued.

"His sister, as you know, is Nerthus. She too is of the sea. Their two children are growing up mighty and strong. They do not appear to be monsters as their parents do. They are both golden-fire haired with sky blue eyes and are the most beautiful of the Vanir."

At the mention of this, looks of disgust and rage came over the many faces sitting around Óðinn's great feasting table, for the practice of incestuous marriages was looked upon with great disfavor by the Æsir and all the warriors in Valhalla. Through-out the rest of the evening the only conversations that rumbled through the great hall of Valhalla centered on the Vanir and whether or not the noble Einherjar should be tested in brave combat against them.

After all had finished consuming the evening's feast, the Æsir and the Einherjar began testing their warrior skills upon each other. Clashing iron swords, spears and wooden shields, honing their battle prowess even further.

As time passed on, Heimdallr made many more visits to Vanaheimr, becoming quite popular there. And he dutifully reported the doings of the Vanir to his father Óðinn.

"They still show no animosity towards us All-Father and Freyr and Freyja are growing up to be quite beautiful and well fained towards the Æsir, as well as towards each other. They both have a talent and interest in the harvest and seem unconcerned with noble, warlike deeds." delivered Heimdallr.

Óðinn ignored Heimdallr's hints about the relations Freyr and Freyja might be having with each other or gossip which had recently been making the rounds in Valhalla about the two Vanir and some of the Æsir. He didn't reveal to his son he had also been meeting with Freyr and Freyja and had become close friends with both of them. Freyja, who was sometimes known as Abundantia, had introduced him to a disreputable magic called Seiðr, which was meant only to be practiced by women.

Óðinn, using his shape-changing abilities, would meet with Freyja and change his shape to that of a young beautiful woman so that he could receive further instructions in the mystical art. If this were to be known Óðinn would be in great disfavor with the Æsir. Yet Óðinn still risked it, for the knowledge and power he learned might be useful in every battle until the final battle at Ragnarok. Over time his relationship with Freyja intensified to the point that they had become passionate lovers. Long nights of sweat and tears of joy rolled by as Óðinn and Freyja plunged deeper and deeper into each other. Flesh on flesh, grinding on one another in absolute ecstasy, melding their sexual fluids into absolute Magick.

Angrboda a witch from Jötunheimr soon after Heimdallr's most recent visit to the Vanir, took disguise and went to Vanaheimr to insight deceit. She dwelt in the Myrkvydr's forested shadows and she was the daughter of the Hrymthursar Hrimnir. Her uncle, Hrimnir's brother, was Egther, and Egther had charge of several remarkable herds, he also owned the powerful and cherished sword of the Jötuns. In Vanaheimr she became fast friends with Freyja, but only for the purpose of war. For next to the Æsir, the Jötuns hated the Vanir most. Over time their friendship deepened, or so Freyja was led to believe, until she had complete trust in Angrboda. So it was without fear she followed Angrboda into Jötunheimr, where normally she would be loathed to go.

Once in Jötunheimr, Angrboda threw off the guise of friendship turning back to the witch she really was. Freyja was caught, trapped in the hands of the Jötuns. Locked up in a dank dark tower cell. She was the Goddess of fertility and fecundity. After her departure from Vanaheimr all this began to diminish. This was true not only in Vanaheimr, but also in Asgardr and Midgardr, crops wilted and refused to grow and animals, particularly swine, would not fatten and their young were stillborn, or grossly deformed and then died soon after. From high atop her mountain prison in Jötunheimr Freyja saw this happening through-out the lands.

"Please." begged Freyja,

"I will do anything for the Jötuns if only you would let me leave this place." she pleaded sobbing with tears in her eyes.

"Yes, I think we have just the favor in mind" mumbled Angrboda.

"You will travel in disguise to Asgardr and you will start a war between the Æsir and Vanir.", demanded Angrboda.

The strategy was simplistic, evenly matched the Æsir and Vanir would succeed only in destroying each other making the Jötuns the real victor without having lifted so much as a over-sized gnarled finger. Although Freyja harbored no ill will towards the Æsir she wanted her freedom and agreed for she felt it was the Æsir who would be vanquished and she would be free to return home.

And perhaps may Óðinn recognize her and realize she was being used by the Jötuns? Using her magick Angrboda helped Freyja's journey to Asgardr by disguising her as the witch Gullveig, Angrboda's sister. Gullveig was the goddess of gold and in this form Freyja was sent to corrupt the Æsir with greed and lust for this precious metal.

Not one of the Gods recognized her through the disguise as she arrived in Asgardr. She was fair to look upon; her light yellow hair, and indeed her whole glorious body, shone temptingly like golden metal. Every one of the

Æsir welcomed her as one of the Vanir. She succeeded to stir a frenzy among the Gold hungry Æsir and soon everything was being hoarded. Golden ornaments were stolen away and hidden in hastily constructed vaults, or melted down to make ring money which could be traded for things that formerly had been freely given amongst the Gods. Halls in Asgardr which had been built with gold for its beauty were raped in the night for their treasures. Value was weighed in carats and greed prevailed. Óðinn observing all this evil called a special meeting in Harr, one of his great halls.

Gullveig was escorted to this meeting.

"We welcomed you here with kindness and you have repaid us by sowing seeds of discontent. What is your defense?" Óðinn demanded with a thunderous voice.

She looked Óðinn deep in the eyes, hoping he would see through this disguise and realize she was not sincere in the words that she spake.

"I've brought nothing here that did not already exist you greedy old fool. You've used gold throughout Asgardr to show the glories of the Æsir. If not for vanity, then you would have used wood to construct your halls. It gives the same shelter and protects from winds and storms just as well."

As she began screaming of everyone's greed, Óðinn hastily cut her off.

"I believe we understand well enough what you have done here. You have presented no defense and there can be no excuse for what you have done."

Óðinn looked around to confirm the rest of the Æsir were nodding in agreement, and continued,

"I judge your actions to have been of evil intent and against what the Æsir stand for. You shall be severely punished for your crime."

Upon Óðinn's command she was spitted over the long fire like a pig. The fire pit stretched the length of entire the great hall. She spun and flames engulfed her whole but she did not die. The Æsir found out then what many know, evil is hard to destroy. Instead Gullveig was reborn and escaped. Angrboda now journeyed to Asgardr disguised as Heidr. Her attempts to renew the passion for gold first brought on by Gullveig failed. She also was taken to the great hall, Harr, where she was judged, spitted and burned. Nor was she killed on the first try. She was reborn as her true self, Angrboda, and recognized as a Jötun, whereupon she was immediately seized and burnt again. This time Loki rushed at the flames and searched through them looking for her heart. He found its half-burnt remnants and swallowed the meager meal. Thus the seed of her evil nature was planted deep inside him.

Sometime later Loki departed Asgardr for a cave in the Myrkvydr Forest where he gave birth to three children. They were in order of birth the Fenriswulf, an enormous, viscous dark grey wolf; Midgardrsormr (also known by the Jötuns as Jormungandr), the world serpent; and Hel who was half dead and half alive, half grotesque undead creature and half beautiful hellish maiden. Loki was very pleased with himself, indeed.

Despite the spitting and burning of Freyja /Gullveig/Angrboda/Heidr, the Æsir and Vanir still were not at war. A few of the Jötuns then took matters into their own hands and journeyed to Vanaheimr carrying the news of Freyja's burning to the Vanir.

"Noble Freyr we bring you this news of your sisters death at the hands of Asgardr and offer to help you seek vengeance, for the Jötuns are upset by this as well. We've always considered Freyja and all the Vanir as our friends and any injustice to the Vanir is an injustice to the Jötuns."

Freyr looked upon the Jötuns with suspicion. They rarely ever came to Vanaheimr without trouble following. But there was nothing he could do about the matter. Freyja seemed to have disappeared and had not been heard from for quite some while. The last anyone could remember she had mentioned she was going to Asgardr for a visit.

Convinced of her death, Freyr was honor bound to avenge it. With the Jötuns standing right there he had to take immediate action so as to show no weakness before them lest they entertain thoughts of conquering Vanaheimr. Freyr went to the center of Vanaheimr and called out,

"*Fellow warriors and relations both near and far, I have had news of the murder of my sister and your kinswoman the beautiful Freyja by the gods of the Æsir. We've sought to live in friendship and peace with them and have kept our part of the truce. But now with this action by them we can no longer honor that truce. I ask that all of you accompany me in an assault upon Asgardr.*"

The call to action was swift and within the remaining hours of sunlight the whole of the Vanir were journeying towards Asgardr prepared for battle. Óðinn had watched the Jötuns visit to Vanaheimr and now looked with interest as the Jötuns at the edge of Jötunheimr parting company with the Vanir. The Jötuns informed Freyr they were going to head towards the East and then quickly circle around Asgardr and attack from the other side. Freyr was not a warrior and certainly lacked training in battle strategy. So, he really couldn't disagree with their plan. And, even if he disagreed with the Jötuns, there was nothing he could do. So, he watched as the Jötuns turned towards the east. And that is the last he saw of them. They did not circle around, they did not attack Asgardr from the other side. They headed back to Jötunheimr to watch safely from atop mountains that offered them a clear view of Asgardr. To watch as their two enemies destroyed each other.

Freyr led the Vanir on to Asgardr. Óðinn called the Æsir to battle. The next morning they met with ferocity in their hearts. On one side of the field Óðinn sat atop his horse with the warriors of Asgardr behind him. Freyr with his force behind him sat astride his horse opposite the Æsir. He and Óðinn rode to the center of the field to discuss the payment of wergild for the death of Freyja, and perhaps avoid bloodshed in an honorable manner. Freyr mentioned a suitable sum. Óðinn responded sarcastically,

"I assume you would like that in gold?"

Freyr did not recognize the sarcasm and responded,

"Of course, gold would be more than fine."

Óðinn laughed and refused payment,

"The only wergild the Vanir will receive from the Æsir will be the iron from the tips of our spears and the edges of our swords, and the wood from the shafts of our arrows."

The discussion was brought to an abrupt halt when Óðinn raised his sword Notung in one hand, and flung his spear towards the Vanir with the other. A bloody battle began. The Vanir fought with Vígspa, their battle magic; the Æsir with brute force and iron weapons. Mountains and icebergs were launched as missiles – the Æsir hurling them with sheer physical strength, the Vanir projected them with magic.

At one point Njordr was able to burst Asgardr's wooden walls with his mighty battleaxe and victory seemed certain for the Vanir. But the sheer force of the Æsir were able to force their enemies almost back to the walls of Vanaheimr. The balance of the battle shifted back and forth, to and fro from Æsir to Vanir so frequently it was hard to tell which side was winning. So it came about both groups of Gods had won and lost the same number of battles, but neither was close to winning the war.

And while the Æsir and Vanir, overcome with exhaustion, rested, Njordr and Óðinn met to talk things over since Freyr wished to have no further dealings with Óðinn. In the distance they could see the Jötuns watching and waiting with more than just a little interest. Njordr spake first,

"Óðinn, our methods may be different but we are all Gods. Gods who are destroying each other, while there in the distance stand the devious Jötuns, our true enemies, ready to pick up the spoils."

Óðinn nodded in agreement, with a deathly gleam in his eye.

"What you say is true. The Jötuns will be the only winners of our battles, for it is only a matter of time before the Vanir and Æsir succeed in destroying each other. I think we should hold a Thing and discuss our differences."

So a Thing was convened with both Vanir and Æsir in attendance. Prior to the Thing Óðinn had sent his ravens, Hugin and Munin, out in search of Freyja, whom they found on roaming aimlessly in Midgardr, walking through fields of luscious grasses and smelling wild flowers. She was returned to Asgardr, where the story of how she had been used by the Jötuns was learned. The Thing devolved into a confused shouting. A loud clatter of voices arose from the Vanir. They were answered by equally vociferous voices from the Æsir. The clang and clatter of discontent went on in circular arguments that seemed would never end. Several times coming deathly close to reigniting the bloodshed.

"The first matter to be discussed is the payment of wergild for the death of the beautiful Freyja."

"But she is no longer dead," stated Óðinn contentedly.

"So we have no further obligation to pay."

"That makes no difference. You did kill her at one point."

"Who is to assume the cost for all the damage done to the Æsir?"

"Ha, your damage was nothing compared with what we suffered."

"Our walls have been shattered. You call that nothing?"

"What about the lost lives of our fellow warriors?"

"Warriors?" blurted Óðinn obscenely.

"How can farmers of suspicious personal habits be warriors?"

And it went throughout the rest of the day, the night, and the next day. Tempers raged as each side traded accusations or claimed the greater losses and suffering. If the meeting had been held other than on sacred ground the two groups would have come to blows once again. Finally, Forseti, known for his efforts at mediation and problem-solving stepped forward to speak. Of all the Æsir, the Vanir trusted him to be of fair judgement. All quieted to listen as he spake.

"It has not yet been a day since each side, deadlocked in glorious bloody combat, are now shouting complaints that because they had inflicted the greater damage to the other, victory should be awarded to them. Now each bemoans losses which far outweigh the losses suffered by the other side. From listening to the quarreling, I believe both sides' losses are fairly equal. As for those casualties suffered in battle, let us bring them back to life so there can be no further complaint about the matter. This leaves us with the final problem of a lasting peace. Our battles are too recent for us not to still distrust one another. Therefore, I propose we exchange hostages. And if either side breaks the peace then the lives of those hostages shall be forfeited."

This seemed a fair proposition for both sides and everyone immediately agreed to the terms. Then bega the arguments about whom was to be exchanged. The Vanir wanted Þòrr so he could help protect them from the Jötuns. But the Æsir immediately refused. They would never give up their greatest hero.

So finally, it was agreed that Hönir, the Aurkonungr or marsh king, and Mimir would be sent to the Vanir in exchange for Njordr and his two children, Freyr and Freyja. Freyr would also bring with him his two servants, Byggvir, his valet, and Beyla, his maidservant.

With all of their differences settled and peace established, the Thing came to an end. But before leaving, they set up a gold communal cauldron in the middle of them and all of the Vanir and Æsir spat into it as they left. This peace token was called Hraki. The Æsir took Hraki and fashioned the spittle into the form of a man whom they named Kvasir. Kvasir became the living symbol of the truce between the Æsir and the Vanir.

Because Kvasir was born full grown he lacked childhood memories. He had no reminiscences of toys or parties, no fond recollections of pretend battles with other children. And, more importantly, no childhood friends. So he set out to visit the worlds of the great tree Yggdrasil, making friends along the way. He possessed the childish wonder of discovering new things, and walked throughout the worlds of the tree, where he was always welcomed seeking the stories of others' childhoods. He was the first poet and often spoke in poetry.

Freyr and Freyja were welcomed into Asgardr and given the duties of sacrificial priestess and priest of the Æsir and were known as the Blotgodar. Great halls were built for them and they were treated not as hostages, but as friends. Many of the Æsir were particularly glad for Freyja's return, especially Óðinn.

Njordr lived in his hall, Noatun, near the sea where he stilled the mighty tempests of Ægir with his calming hand. Freyr lived in solitude in Uppsala. His palace, covered with precious gems, stood off by itself. A rose tree forest shaded it so that it was set in darkness. Freyr often stood lookout over the lake that bordered his property, staring at the white swans swimming in it, thinking about his loneliness and hoping to someday meet someone who would end it.

Freyja's domain was Fólkvangr, and her palace was called Sessrumnir. After moving to Asgardr she became involved with the Valkyries and frequently led them to battle and was known as Valfreyja when she did so.

Mimir and Hönir went to Vanaheimr. But things went quite differently in Vanaheimr. At first the Vanir looked favorably upon their two hostages. Mimir, Óðinn's uncle, was a personage of great wisdom and renown. Hönir was swift, long-legged, extremely handsome and noble in bearing. Because of this he replaced Njordr as chief of the Vanir. Although not overly intelligent, Hönir enjoyed the wise council of Mimir who gave him sound advice on all occasions. Eventually Hönir became so dependent on Mimir's council he could not reach a decision unless Mimir was standing at his shoulder whispering what to do in his ear. Hönir's pretense to knowledge could not go on forever. One day Mimir was gone when a dispute arose. It was so serious it could not be put off until Mimir's return, as Hönir demanded. A Thing was held and Hönir had to attend and give council. Fearing he would give out disastrous advice, all he would say was,

"Let the others decide."

Hœnir used this to dodge all question during the first part of the Thing pointing out others who had greater expertise in the area in question. Pressed for further decisions throughout the meeting he would only utter the same phrase,

"Let the others decide."

The Vanir began to feel the Æsir had deceived them in the exchange of hostages.

Some of the Vanir laid in wait and when Mimir returned he was set upon and his head removed. Mimir's head was then tucked under Hönir's arm, and he was sent back to Asgardr as a present for Óðinn. Óðinn received the head of his friend and uncle with sadness and decided the knowledge Mimir possessed could not be allowed to die. He immediately set about to preserve the head.

In seclusion, in form of the young woman that studied under Freyja, he performed Seiðr on the head. She first covered it with herbs and other preservatives to halt and reverse the decay. Next she chanted mystical incantations and carved runes of life on it. The head soon gained the power of speech. After he was once again changed from a woman to his old form, Óðinn carried the head back to the well of Mimir near the ashen Yggdrasil and balanced it on the stone lip of the well, away from the wind. Óðinn would be able to ask it for advice when advice was needed, for Mimir had become even wiser from learning the wisdom of the dead.

Even though the Æsir's hostages had been returned and accepted back, by rights Freyr and Freyja could return to Vanaheimr. But the three decided to remain in Asgardr, although their travel frequently took them back to their homeland. So, the War between the Æsir and Vanir was over. But what of the damage to Asgardr from the battles? Gaping holes in the battlements remained.

5. The Tale of Freyja and Ottr

Ottr the Simple as he was known, the son of
Instein, was in a dispute with Angantyr. They
both laid claim to a tremendous treasure of gold,
silver and gems. And so a Thing was to be held,

and the one with the noblest lineage would be awarded the treasure. Unfortunately for Ottr the Simple he lived up to his name and wasn't very bright. For the life of him he couldn't remember more than a couple of his ancestors.

Fortunately he had worshiped Freyja faithfully for years. He prepared a great sacrifice to her and knelt down by the fire and asked for her help. He had decided to spend the entire night praying to her. Freyja had long followed his devotion to her. She was by far his favorite of the Æsir and Vanir. So, when he asked for her help she was moved to intercede on his behalf. She appeared before him, glowing in white, the most spectacular sight his eyes had ever gazed upon. He was so startled he fell over into his fire pit and caught his sleeve on fire. He then beat out the fire vigorously with his opposing hand.

He had prayed for years to her and it had never crossed his mind she would actually appear before him. He didn't know quite what to say or how to act. This had never come up when discussing the Æsir and Vanir with his friends. Though they had prayed for it, they never actually expected to meet any of the Æsir or Vanir. So, he improvised,

"Oh great and wonderful Freyja. Um, your beauty exceeds um your, your, um, legend. I am so transfixed that I can't, ah, um, avert mine eyes. You have blessed this um, um humble um man with your presence. What can I um do for you?"

Well, he'd managed to get it all wrong. It was what could she do for him? He realized his mistake and began to correct himself,

"Or, ah um um what you can do for me er what we can do for each other um or together we can do things um together um or apart as you may want um I am your humble servant um Ottr. Yes I am Ottr." He thought to himself,

"I am sooo pathetic."

Before he could start up again Freyja raised her hand,

"Enough. I know what you're trying to say..." with quiet frustration moving over her eyes and lips.

Ottr broke in.

"Of course, you do. You are Frigg the all power um er Freyja, you're Freyja the all powerful."

"Oh, I've called her Frigg. She probably doesn't like that. I should just shut up," he told himself.

Freyja took it all in stride. She knew the affect she had on some of the Æsir, imagine the potency of that effect on a mere man of Midgardr. He bent over so low and so near the fire she was afraid he'd catch himself on fire again.

"*Arise, Ottr the Simple,*" aptly named she thought, and continued,

"*Stand on your feet before me and tell me what it is you want of me.*"

He got up and began explaining his situation,

"*I have claim to a great treasure, but I must prove my lineage is greater than Angatyr's.*" He was calming down and starting to make more sense.

"*Very well, I will help you. But, my aid comes at a price. You must fore-swear all other members of the Æsir and Vanir, and all of your love and* devotion must be only for me. You must honor me only, and no other Æsir or Vanir."

She repeated it so in his simpleness she made certain he understood. He already did this, except, maybe for a few devotions to Óðinn. Even he realized it wouldn't do to forget about the leader of the Æsir and Vanir. Yet, it was Freyja standing before him, not Óðinn. So what would it matter if he decided to worship only her? It was unlikely Óðinn would even notice he'd stopped with his small offerings. He was nobody. He was too insignificant to be noticed. Yet, a member of the Æsir and Vanir stood before him. He had been noticed. His logic was already a little faulty. Ottr agreed,

"I will worship only you and will do whatever you command me to do. And in exchange you will help me win the treasure I've laid claim to."

Freyja pressed him further just to make certain,

"And you agree to build no altars to others, not even Þórr, not even Óðinn."

Had she read his mind. He reassured her,

"Yes," he replied.

Freyja stared at him waiting. He added,

"Yes, I will build altars to no one except you beautiful Freyja."

With that she immediately changed him into a boar and rode him to Jötunheimr to visit the one person who could help them. He certainly hadn't expected this.

He was exhausted by the time they reached Jötunheimr. He hardly ever walked to the end of the road and back. Now he found himself transmogrified into a boar with Freyja riding on his back as he galloped with neither rest nor food to Jötunheimr. He wasn't prepared for the distance. And he certainly wasn't prepared for Jötunheimr's size. Every time he tried to stop and rest Freyja kicked at his sides. He ran for days. They didn't stop to eat. Nor, did they stop so he could relieve himself. So, he did the only thing he could and relieved himself as he ran. Nothing like this had ever happened to him before. He was beginning to regret his devotion to Freyja. Was any treasure really worth all this bother. Besides the fact that he was exhausted.

The Jötun Hyndla lay sleeping deep within her cave. Her dreams were not peaceful, so in her sleep she rolled about growling and snorting, flailing with her arms trying to get comfortable. No one dared enter when she was in this state lest she accidentally lash out at them, confused between what was in her dreams and what was real. For her the waking and dream worlds overlapped.

Freyja and her boar Ottr stood at the mouth of the cave listening to the rumblings from within. Freyja yelled into the darkness,

"Hyndla, Hyndla, arise. It's too late in the day to be sleeping. Come out my friend so we might talk."

The growling changed to a howling sound, like that of a wolf baying at the moon. Hyndla was yawning and stretching as she came awake. She rolled over trying to decide whether to really get up, or simply go back to sleep. She decided to go back to sleep. Freyja, sensing Hyndla was not making much progress towards leaving the cave, yelled in again,

"Wake up Hyndla. Darkness will soon be upon us and we have quite a ways to travel to reach Asgardr. You must come with me so we may sup with Óðinn tonight in Valhalla, and win his favor. Those who have his kindly attention can expect great rewards. Did he not give a magnificent helmet and war coat to Hermodr? And the bold warrior of Midgardr, Sigmundr, was given a fierce sword with which to win great treasures and kingdoms. So, do not wile away your time in a dank dark cave. Instead, come with me and wile yourself upon Óðinn."

Hyndla had sat up at the mention of possible treasures. She listened, weighing how difficult it would be to journey to Valhalla, and what she would expect in return for such an effort. Freyja knew she had her now. To further lure the Jötun out she mentioned what Hyndla loved most.

"Gold is one gift in abundance in Asgardr, and Óðinn hands it out as if the nuggets were mere pebbles. And don't forget Óðinn can award you glory in battle. Or, he might offer you a drink of the Precious Mead,"

"Although I don't think great wisdom has ever been a goal of yours. But perhaps you might like to be so skillful a speaker you could trip up your opponents in flyttings by skill rather than trickery."

"Other gifts Óðinn has to offer include fair winds to guide sailors and their ships or high tides so they might hug to coastlines rather than having to venture out over Midgardrsormr. Skalds and poets are given word skills to use in their stories so no one will fall asleep listening. But the most precious gift Óðinn gives to warriors is one that can win riches and kingdoms. It is more prized than a magical sword. It is the gift of courage and a brave heart."

Freyja listened intently, she could hear Hyndla moving towards the front of the cave. Then she continued,

"If you come with me I will woo Þórr on your behalf. Even though he thinks of Jötuns as his enemies, he has often looked fondly on Jötun women. As you know, Jarnsaxa is a particular favorite of his. You, too, could feel the rumblings of earthquakes and see the flashes of lightning that come with Þórr's lovemaking. You could become his lover and hold the power of his manhood that is lusted by all women down to the very last of the Jötuns."

Hyndla's head emerged first from the mouth of the cave. She crawled out on all fours, blinking into the late afternoon sun. Although, it was quite late even this much sun hurt her eyes, since Jötuns abhorred sunlight. In all the Worlds of the Tree but Jötunheimr the sun could turn them to stone. So they avoided it even in the protective world of Jötunheimr. Rarely had Hyndla left her cave. So most of her life had been spent bent over crawling from cavern to cavern.

She raised up as straight as her gnarled Jötun body allowed. She was dressed in coarse burlap and obviously had not bathed in awhile, if ever. She smiled at Freyja, revealing many gaps in her teeth, happy that she would be going somewhere.

So far her life had been consistently dull with each day resembling all the others. Freyja sized up the Jötun and realized her boar wouldn't be able to carry both of them at full speed.

"Call one of your wolves out so I might harness it next to Hilksuin. Although my magnificent boar could easily carry both of us back to Asgardr, I wish for us to travel as swiftly as possible. If you ride one of your wolves Hilksuin will not be overtaxed."

Hyndla looked from Hilksuin to Freyja, then back to Hilksuin. She stared at the boar's eyes and laughed at the deception she had discovered.

"You expect me to trust you when you deceive me from the start. Your boar Hilksuin could easily carry most of the Æsir fully armored to the last battle at full gallop without even becoming winded. Yet look at this panting, sweaty, beast whose back legs are brown from having soiled himself. No, this is not the famous Hilksuin. It's clear you wish to protect the strength of your lover Ottr, the son of Instein. You have conveniently changed him into a boar, though I cannot guess for what reasons. Its his eyes, they give him away. They are not the red

glowing eyes of Hilksuin. They are human eyes."
Freyja scoffed at this.

"You have sat in your cave far too long imagining
things. This is Hilksuin, my battle-boar. Look at
his carefully groomed golden bristles which glow
so he can even travel swiftly in the dark. He was
made a long time ago by the clever Dwarves
Dain and Nabbi."

Freyja's denials made Hyndla even more
suspicious. She could understand someone
turning their lover into a boar, since they were so
frequently boring. But why deny it? She smelled
Hilksuin. He did not smell like the boars she had
known. Though there was that odor about him.
She began retreating into the cave. But Freyja
had dealt with dim-witted Jötuns most of her life
and knew how to manage them. At first she tried
threatening Hyndla. But that didn't work. She

then resorted to flattery and promises of great wealth. She again sprinkled her conversation with words like gold, emeralds, precious stones, and wealth. Hyndla agreed to go to Asgardr with Freyja, but in order to save face added,

"I suppose if I don't go with you, you'll just stand outside my cave begging me until it's time for the last great battle, and I'll never get any sleep."

Freyja mounted Ottr, while Hyndla sat astride one of the largest wolves Freyja had ever seen. It was almost as large as Fenriswulf himself. Freyja looped a twin harness around the wolf so she could control both animals as they rode along, and to protect Ottr in case the wolf became a bit nippy.

Their journey was quick, and in short order they were at Valgrindr, the outer gate of Valhalla. Hyndla could see the goat Heidrun munching away at Læradr, standing on the roof, with mead flowing to Valhalla and a constant stream of urine flowing to those doomed in Elidner. Heidrun caught sight of Hyndla, became frightened and ducked behind a gable. The two rode on to the banks of the river Thund. After they dismounted, Freyja secured the two bridles to a tree at the water's edge. Hyndla protested,

"Why do you lead me away from the meal you promised me inside Valhalla. I have no desire to play on a river bank. I have not eaten in ages and want some food."

Freyja realized Hyndla was probably not exaggerating. It most likely had been ages since she had eaten. What could she have been thinking bringing such a large hungry person to Valhalla? She tried to distract the Jötun,

"I thought it would be interesting for us to talk about two mighty warriors, noble heroes who

fought bravely and won honor and fame. I speak,
of course, about Ottr the Young and Angantyr.
They were both sons of the Æsir."

Well, she rationalized to herself, Ottr the
Simple is also young, so calling him that wasn't
wrong. Technically it was true. Hyndla decided
to put up a while longer with Freyja's company,
the meal she expected to eat would more than
make up for this minor wait. Though, she
couldn't help but add,

"I have never heard of a warrior called Ottr the
Young. I have heard of a fool called Ottr the
Simple, though."

Ottr the Simple could take no more of
this and said,

"I'm right in front of you. Show some respect.
You haggard old giant!"

But to Freyja and Hyndla it just sounded like a series of grunts and wheezes. Freyja poked at Ottr to quiet him, and continued,

"The great warrior Ottr the Young once built an altar to me. And through magic those stones were turned to glass which reflected into the sky. Ottr piled many oxen onto the shards of my altar. Their blood dripped down and caught in the chinks of the glass forming little pools of sacrifice. Soon the glass was reddened with my glory. Ottr the Young never bothered worshiping Óðinn or Þórr. He preferred to sacrifice to women, and chose me above all others. Even above Frigg, Sif, or any of the others in Asgardr. And his devotion to me was greatly rewarded. But show me how smart you are Hyndla. Tell me about the great warrior families. Who are the Skjoldungr, the Skilfinrg, Othlingr and Ylfingr? Tell me about those on Midgardr? Tell me the names of those who were

firstborn, and those who were high born? Say
the names of the most noble on Midgardr."

Hyndla had not asked for this flytting,
but saw that she had no choice. She first turned
to the tethered boar. Nodding in his direction
she spoke,

"Ottr the Simple was the son of Instein, who
was the son of Alf the Old. Alf was the son of
Ulf, the son of Sæfari, the son of Svan the
Red."

Ottr, hearing his name turned his head to
listen. But nothing he didn't already know was
being said, so he swished his tale to bat away a
fly that was bothering him and returned to
drinking from the river Thund. Hyndla continued
with Ottr's family history.

"Ottr the Simple's mother wore red-golden
bracelets and other jewelry befitting the princess

she was. Her name was Hledis. Her father was Frodi. Her equally noble mother was Friaut whose mother was Hildigun. Hildigun was the daughter of Svava and Sækonung. In your boarish state, can you remember all this, Ottr?"

Freyja didn't bother to try to pretend the boar wasn't Ottr anymore. Ottr began to be caught up in his family history. Freyja was also listening intently. Hyndla continued,

"It is odd that one who has such a noble lineage would wind up slurping water out of a river and grazing on grass. But I will remind you of your other illustrious relatives. Hildigun married the noble warrior Ketil, your great-grandfather on your mother's side of the family. Frodi was the father of Kari. Hoalf was born of Hild. Nokkvi's daughter, Nanna, was then born. Her son married your aunt, your father's sister, need I continue..."

Ottr was exhibiting more interest in what Hyndla was saying. Hyndla continued,

"Your family history contains twelve berserkers who fought with the battle fury of hundreds of warriors. They ran into battle foaming at the mouth and naked, confident their warriors skills would protect them and therefore they did not need armor. The twelve were born on the island of Bolmso, the sons of Arngrim and Eyfura. Their names included two named Hadding, as well as Hervard, Hjorvard, Hrani, Angantyr, Bui, Brami, Barri, Reifnir, Tind, and Tyrfing."

Hyndla had still more to say,

"The noble Jormunrekkr sacrificed all of his sons to the Æsir. He was kinsman to Sigurdr Fafnirsbani, who slew the terrible worm Fafnir. Volsungr and Hjordis of the Hraudungs were his grandparents. Hjordis was the daughter of King Eylimi of the Othlings. Their blood also

runs in your veins. But there are more. Hvedna's
father was Hjorvard. One of her brothers was
the great warrior Haki. Aud the Profound was
the daughter of Ivar. She and Hrorek the Ring
Giver had a son named Harald War Tooth."

Suddenly Freyja yelled in triumph.

"Enough, enough."

"You have won an inheritance in gold for Ottr
the Young. He and Angantyr had a wager
concerning their lineage. The winner inherited
the entire family treasure, the loser, nothing.
Now I will give Ottr this mead of memory to drink
so when he meets Angantyr in three days he'll
be able to recite his entire family history. The
same family history you have just recited.
Because of your knowledge, Hyndla, the wealth
of Instein will go to its rightful owner."

Hyndla, realizing she had been tricked, grabbed the cup of mead from Freyja and strode over to Ottr the Simple. She bent over him and yelled curses into his ear. Pus oozed from the gaps between her teeth where once teeth had been. Her putrid breath caused Ottr the Simple to shiver. Freyja was a short distance away jumping about in triumph. Hyndla turned her glance and tongue to the Vanirasynje.

"You jump and gambol about as if you were Heidrun running around with a herd of goats in heat. But I can bring your happiness to a close. All I need do is pour this mead onto the ground. Your hero can't even remember his own name is Ottr the Simple. Without this mead of memory Angantyr, the more deserving of the two, will win the inheritance. Should you not help a warrior on merit, rather than on how blindly he worships you? Angantyr is by far the more deserving. Yet, he has not raised a sacrifice of glass to you. So,

you ignore him in favor of a fat simpleton. Have you an answer to my charges?"

Freyja ignored the question and threw her arms up menacingly,

"I will cast a ring of fire around you so the only way for you to escape is through it. Hopefully, you'll burn in the process. Give me the cup to save yourself."

Hyndla seemed not to be concerned. She taunted Freyja even more,

"And that ring of fire will cause a fine pork roast, too. I'll hold Ottr the Simple and he will not escape the flames. Where is your husband Ottr? Why has he left you? Could it have something to do with the Dwarves you slept with for a rather gaudy, showy, necklace?"

At these words flames shot up around Hyndla and began closing in on her. Hyndla yelled,

"These flames threaten me. But even more threatening is the sun who will soon be showing on the horizon. I am not within the protective lands of Jötunheim, so the Sun's rays will soon turn me to stone. You leave me no choice but to give you this cup. But before I do, I curse it and curse Ottr the Simple who will profit unfairly from my knowledge."

The flames lowered and Freyja took the cup. She set it before Ottr. While he drank she stroked his bristly back.

"You give Ottr a curse, I give him my blessing and assurance he will prosper. Time will tell whose words are more potent."

Hyndla did not reply. Instead, she jumped onto her wolf and hurried back to Jötunheim, lest the rays of the sun catch her and turn her into a new mountain in Asgardr.

6. The Taming of Brisingamen

Freyja, the Shining One, often wandered through the endless heather moors on nights similar to this. She very much enjoyed walking alone in the night, hoping to discover new secrets. Tonight, there was a glorious blue Moon hanging in the heavens like a shining pearl, with tufts of thunderous looking clouds hovering around a great illuminated circle more than five times the Moon's own circumference. The shining circle acting almost like a great barrier, protecting the Moon.

As Freyja wondered to herself.

'What is wrong with me, I am always exhausted.' and a feeling of great emptiness fluid through her.

The nights cutting wind brought a chill as well as a vague autumn scent of rot and dying leaves from the forest and the moist heather moors.

She wrapped her silken fur cloak around closer to the nude shivering flesh lying directly beneath.

Freyja hears what appears to be grumbling voices in the distance. Excitedly walking in the direction of the voices carrying along the wind. As she grows nearer, she spots the vague shape of what looks like a cave through the wisping fog.

She listens, curiously but ever cautiously. It seems to be several mail voices arguing over something. Stealthily creeping along deeper and deeper into a path leading down from the opening of the cave. It is dark and damp, water dripping from the moss that covers the walls, little slithering things moving about in the shadows. Eventually the cave starts to illuminate more and more with each step. It is definitely men's voices arguing in low grumbling, harsh curses.

Amidst the space surrounding a fire, an anvil, and four hideous looking Dwarfs! Uglier than she has ever seen! A small, startled shriek escapes her.

Immediately the Dwarfs stop their fight and four pair of eyes stare at her in greedy surprise. Slowly they feign recognition that it is Freyja! Her heavenly blue silk cloak edged with cat fur hardly hides her feminine curves or the effect the chill of the night has on her ample breasts. Fiery golden-red hair flows over her shoulders and her sky blue eyes glow like the heavens in the fire light. She is the most beautiful thing they have ever laid eyes upon. Before the dwarves can close their gaping mouths Freyja starts to speak in a soft lovely voice, a voice as beautiful as she is.

'Dear Sirs, I heard your voices from the moors and was concerned that maybe something might be awry. It seems that something quite serious must be going on that has caused you to make such a racket on an evening quite like this?'

The four Dwarfs stared un-moving at Freyja with concern and suspicion in their beady glaring eyes. It was Freyja after all, but that still was no reason to change their inherent distrust.

'My lady, it is nothing, just a small difference of opinions',

Said Dwalin, the eldest of the dwarves, while stroking his long greasy beard and poking at the fire with a tool made of an odd looking metal.

'We are working the forge as you can see, we have just come to a misunderstanding of our direction.'

All the while trying to signal his brothers as inconspicuously as he can, while trying to hold Freyja's attention elsewhere.

'Oh, beautiful Freyja may we offer you one of our priceless pieces of jewelry?'

Berling and Alfrigg, the twin brothers rush clumsily to offer Freyja one of their most beautiful pieces of treasure. While Grerr, the bony, pimple faced and youngest of the dwarves tried to hide something in a shoddy built wooden box.

'What is it you little men are trying to hide from me in that horrible little box?'

'Everyone knows that your treasures are the beautiful creations on this Earth. And as you can see I have quite the collection already.'

The horrible little men let their eyes wander over her neck, breasts, arms, hips and ankles where artistically expensively crafted pieces where already accentuating her womanly figure.

'The quarrel I walked in on was definitely of no small dispute. I have never before heard such havoc in these parts, and I visit the moors quite regularly. So, do inform me of what it is you are trying to hide from me, the Beautiful Goddess Freyja?'

Alfrigg slowly twisting sharp points on his black mustache whilst giving his twin brother the look of death.

'My lady, it is Brisingamen, the fire jewel. It should have become our master piece. But that fat gnarled fool ruined it.' continuing his rant at Alfrigg.

'Why couldn't you have just kept your damn hands off of it?'

'You blew it yourself you retarded hothead. This process does not require more fire, but calm and precision, brother.'

The twins commence to pounding each other viscously.

'Dwalin, Dwalin, do something. Anything! They will kill each other!'

But Dwalin just stares into space with glazed over eyes.

'We would make the Brisingamen together. A perfect piece, more glorious than any of us could have imagined on our own.'

He drops to the ground like stone, impossible to move.

During all of the confusion Freyja walks over to the box. From the corner of his eye Grerr sees Freyja put her hand on the lid. He tries to move in her direction to stop her, but Freyja has already opened the box.

The fight halts dead at a standstill as all four Dwarfs look in horror as Freyja picks up Brisingamen. Freyja lets the piece slide back and forth through her hands. She is infatuated as it glows with power the dwarves had not seen.

'Is this the subject of your little scuffle?'

A shiver runs through the Dwarfs like lightning striking a tree. Fire swells from Berling's eyes. Alfrigg throws her an ice glare, while Grerr tries to keep it light.

'Uh... uh... did you have a nice walk? Uh... what is the weather like outside? It is getting colder, isn't it? I'm not sure, but you hear like.... '

'Oh, just quiet already' Dwalin interrupts him,

'We are stuck ... hopelessly stuck.'

They fall completely silent, lost in their own thoughts. Freyja contemplatively strokes the Brisingamen,

'Could this be the answer to all of my questions?'

'What possibilities are hidden in this jewel and how do I find out?'

A question that has already arose in the Dwarfs on minds. They know the powers hidden in the Brisingamen: the might of their own elements. Fire, Water, Earth and Air. But what power is strong enough to bind them? What power is strong enough to bring the Brisingamen to life?

A strange thickness fills the atmosphere of the cave. Magick thrashes about and a sexual energy leaves Freyja piercing the souls of the four dwarves.

Not knowing what to do the dwarves stare at each other and start to blush. The sexual current runs through all in the cave, a rush of power fills their blood, coursing through their veins. Freyja feels it as well and it makes her feel uncomfortable and hot.

She places Brisingamen onto the anvil.

The dwarves look at each other and chuckle.

'Is it possible that the key to Brisingamen's power is the melding of of our four elements within Brisingamen and the sexual energy for the Goddess Freyja will be the perfect combination to finish the necklace?'

Freyja stands with a look of fear and contempt in her eyes as she slowly glosses over all four of the dwarves.

'If it is the Brisingamen that you desire then you must mate with us four to properly bring Brisingamen to life in all its glory.' Stated Dwalin.

Excitement grew amongst the Dwarfs.

'Yes, yes, this is how it must be.'

And they all stared at Freyja with much lust and greed in their eyes. Like a lion about to devour its prey, there is no line they wouldn't cross now.

'I cannot commit to this, nothing is worth all of this not even the most beautiful of treasures, but I lust for it so.'

'Lady, let me be the first'. Says Berling with the look of hunger lust in his eyes, almost drooling on himself.

The ferociously looking red-haired Dwarf pokes the fire high and rips the silken fur cloak from around her, her splendid nakedness standing alone in the brilliant heat.

'Lady, I am Berling.'

Immediately Freyja is surrounded by flames. They lick sweat from her firm breasts, then from her ample behind and then between her legs making her quiver. His fiery hands are everywhere.

'Ho, ho my little sweet.'

Freyja pushes him firmly away in disgust. Panting and snorting, Berling stands erect. His bloodshot eyes rape across her body challenging her morals and her strength.

'You said yes, didn't you?'

Freyja looks ever more disgusted at the brute standing steamily in front of her, his scorching heat, his devouring fire.

She gasps heavily then slowly breathes out. The fire overwhelms her taking control still trying to fight, there is no use. She pulls him towards her and kisses him hungry on his drool covered mouth. Again, Freyja hesitates, but the following moment Freyja is curled back growling.

'Give me hell, fire starter.'

In the heat she feels his passion, his creative power, his lust and his purification. Thrashing about in a ring of spark spitting fire, thrusting on one another harder and harder until they come to an outburst. The fire flares up, time and again until they both collapse exhausted with the rising Sun.

Dawn rises as the fire now burns quietly. On the anvil sharp flashes run through the Brisingamen. Berling grins.

'My lady, my fire and your fire have melded within Brisingamen, from now forth we are bound in passion and courage. This power is awoken within Brisingamen forever more.'

The others enter the room silently as they look at the Brisingamen and smile.

'It works!'

Magic is felt intensely between all of them. They stir up the fire again and the day transcends into the night. Freyja looks at Alfrigg. There is no going back at this point, so Freyja says without hesitation...

'You're next Dwarf.'

Immediately the temperature drops to a frightening cold, like an ice storm has suddenly struck, all the water in the air and cave freezes solid as the others loom into the shadows.

His icy blue eyes and impenetrable glance frightens her, and the blood gently pulls away from her fingertips. Cold takes over her chest, the sweat clinging to her erect eraser like nipples turn to tiny glistening ice cycles in the heat of the fire, almost reaching her belly as she goes numb. She gasps again as if she was just dropped into arctic waters, then slowly breathes out, shivering. Then all of a sudden her belly starts to glow, and she touches his freezing skin. Her hand almost freezes, but her warmth is stronger than his cold. And that warmth spreads over Alfrigg's body and slowly begins to thaw him. He grasps her hips with all of his strength, but once again Freyja initiates full contact.

Freyja tears Alfriggs clothes off, skin on skin, sweat in sweat they enter into a swirling pool of lust and desire. She is mirrored in his translucent reflection and together they are sucked down deeper and deeper, with the destructive force of a tsunami, over and over again until they both drop from exhaustion.

Once again dawn rises and the waters of the cave return to normal. On the anvil Brisingamen shines like reflections of the Moon off of still waters of a black lake. Alfrigg sighs contently.

'My lady, my water and your water have leveled. From this day on we are mirrored in healing powers. And in Brisingamen these powers have awoken.'

Once more they gather around the anvil and silently they look at the Brisingamen and smile. They stir up the fire and the day transcends into the night. Dwalin stands still in the middle of the room, solidly petrified. Freyja observes him intensely, smaller and uglier than the rest, a fat crooked nose, long hairs growing from his ears, warts, pussy bumps all over his face and somewhere in there two small squinting eyes.

What to do with him? Intuitively Freyja reaches out. Immediately the floor begins to quake, Iron chains rattle and an enormous heap of coal starts to roil. Soon the anvil shakes, jerking and tilting, then splits the floor. A gaping crevasse opens in the Earth and Freyja is swallowed up. She falls for what seems like eternity until there is nothing but emptiness. In the distance, far above her from the darkness she sees Dwalin hurtling towards her as an impenetrable meteorite with deathly glowing eyes.

She gasps heavily and then slowly breathing out she opens her arms and catches hold of Dwalin as he almost lightnings by. A flickering in Dwalin's eyes, his life force is returning to his veins, and he sees her, and he surrenders fully to receive her nakedness. Their common heartbeat propels them into a hallucinating rhythm. Times slows down. She sees his primal power, everything just is. Their bodies seamlessly fit together. Groaning they become one like churning mud, over and over until they re-solidify as flesh, exhausted, crumpled on the floor.

Dawn rises and order is returned. On the anvil the Brisingamen shines with a deep, full glow. Dwalin states simply.

'My lady, my Earth and your Earth are forged together like iron in a raging hearth. From now on we are bound on the ground of solid trust. This power is awoken in the Brisingamen.'

Again, they all return from the shadows, silently they look at the Brisingamen and smile. It worked. They stir up the fire and the day transcends into the night. Grerr is jumping up and down ecstatically. He cannot wait to get his brothers out of the room. But as soon as he is alone with Freyja, he starts shaking like a leaf and shuffles back and forth nervously. Freyja laughs.

'Do you still want me or not little man?'

She turns around and approaches Grerr fully nude and suddenly Freyja feels a gentle cool breeze stroking her back, her buttocks, and her thighs, then again between her legs like her volva was being caressed by the fingers of a ghost, a sigh escapes her, and she briefly orgasms. Her eyes open to reveal his weedy nakedness, so tiny she could almost blow him away, with translucent skin, veins clearly visible underneath, messy flaxen hair, pale blue eyes...

This grotesque site does not invite her to further action. She sighs again breathing in, then slowly out. She takes his hand and puts it on her heaving breast. He strokes her nipple with his thumb. Wind howls through the hollows of the cave. He grips her hair in his fist and bites her neck passionately. A flash of lightning brightens the cave and Freyja begs him to continue. Freyja groans and slowly mounts the tiny Dwarf. Her breasts stroke his body. She puts her hand on his neck and slowly chokes him, a whirlwind torrent takes them outside of this space and time. She sees as they shatter other dimensions, an elongated scream of ecstasy then silence. They scatter between the star and universes, sparkling in millions of finite pieces. Floating in the universe Freyja feels one with everything. And they lay engulfed in sheer pleasure upon the cave floor.

Dawn arises and complete silence fills the cave. On the anvil Brisingamen shines like the Milky Way. Grerr is delighted.

'My lady, my air and your air breathe together now. From now on we are infinitely bound in inspiration and sound. This power is awoken in the Brisingamen.'

They all stood around the anvil staring in amazement, what beauty, flawlessness and perfection. Dwalin picks up the Brisingamen and walks towards Freyja. The others nod. Freyja bows her head and Dwalin slides the jewel around her neck.

'This belongs to you now, Goddess Freyja. The most beautiful of all beauty.'

'It is your heart and soul now; you are as one.'

At the very moment that Brisingamen contacts her heart, the whole jewel comes to life in Freyja. Energy tingles up and down her spine. Flows to her pelvis. Lines of light find their way to the Earth via her legs. Simultaneously a gleam pushes its way up, to her third eye where a small flame arises and spreads across her skull, like a lotus opening. The palms of her hands start to glow. Sparks spit from her finger tips. A golden red aura of light surrounds her like a cloak of stars. There stands Freyja, the Shining One. She is the Shining One.

'Come,' Freyja reaches out to the Dwarfs.

'We have experienced something other worldly together. Each of you I will cherish in my heart and body and now I shall bring Brisingamen out into the world.'

She felt certain that all was well within her now, all was not well, but very miserable indeed. When Freyja was returned to Ásgarðr once more, and to her palace of Fólkvangr, she sought out her husband Óðr to make him admire her necklace Brisingamen. But Óðr was no longer there.

Loki; the Iron Wood

Freyja's precious felines chomped at their bits as her chariot tore off into the Heavens skimming over Earth and Air with swift, clinging steps, eager and noiseless. The chariot rolled on, and Freyja was carried away up and down into all the parts of the worlds, weeping amber tears wherever she went; falling down from her pale cheeks, and rippled away behind her in little golden red rivers that carried beauty and weeping to every land. She came to the greatest city in the world and drove down its wide streets.

'None of the houses are good enough for my dear Óðr,' said Freyja to herself.

'I will not ask for him at such doors as these.'

So, she went straight on to the palace of the king.

'Is Óðr in this palace?' she demanded of the gatekeeper.

'Is Óðr, the Immortal, living with the king?'

'No, my lady, I have never heard such a name in these halls.' Said the guard as a matter of factly.

Then Freyja turned away, and knocked at many other stately doors, asking for Óðr; but no one in all that great city so much as knew her husband's name. Then Freyja went into the long, narrow lanes and shabby streets, where the poor people lived, but there it was all the same; everyone said only,

'No—not here,' and stared at her.

In the night-time Freyja went quite away from the city, and the lanes, and the cottages, far off to the side of a lake, where she lay down and looked over into the water. By-and-bye the Moon came and looked there too, and the Queen of Night saw a calm face in the water, serene and high; but the Queen of Beauty saw a troubled face, frail and fair. Brisingamen was reflected in the water too, and its rare colours flashed from the little waves. Freyja was pleased at the sight of her favourite ornament and smiled even amid her tears; but as for the Moon, instead of Brisingamen, the deep sky and the stars

were around her. At last Freyja slept by the side of
the lake, and then a dark shape crept up the bank on
which she was lying, sat down beside her, and took
her fair head between its hands. It was Loki, and he
began to whisper into Freyja's ear as she slept.

'You were quite right, Freyja,' he said,

'To go out and try to get something for
yourself in Svartalfheimr, something beautiful
instead of staying at home with your husband. It was
incredibly wise of you to care more for your dress
and your beauty than for Óðr. You went down into
Svartalfheimr and found Brisingamen. Then the
Immortal went away; but is not Brisingamen far better
than he?'

Tears of amber ran down her cheeks
into Loki's hands.

'Why do you cry, Freyja? Why do you start so?'

Freyja turned, moaning, and tried to lift her head from between his hands; but she could not, and it seemed in her dream as if a terrible nightmare brooded over her.

'Brisingamen is dragging me down, dragging all the way to Helheim' she cried in her sleep,

And laid her little hand upon the clasp without knowing what she was doing. Then a great laugh burst forth in Svartalfheimr and came shuddering up through the vaulted caverns until it shook the ground upon which she lay. Loki started up and was gone before Freyja had time to open her eyes. It was morning, and the young Vanir prepared to set out on her journey.

'Brisingamen is fair,' she said, as she bade farewell to her image in the lake.

'Brisingamen is fair; but I find it heavy sometimes.'

After this, Freyja went to many cities, and towns, and villages, asking everywhere for Óðr; but there was not one in all the world who could tell her where he was gone, and at last her chariot rolled eastward and northward to the very borders of Jötunheimr. There Freyja stopped; for before her lay Jarnvid, the Iron Wood, which was one passage from Miðgarðr to the abode of the jötuns, and whose tall trees, black and hard, were trying to pull down the sky with their iron claws, like the skeletonized fingers of the dead. In the entrance sat an Iron Völva, with her back to the dark forest and her face towards the Vanir. Jarnvid was full of the sons and daughters of this Iron Völva; they were wolves, and bears, and crows and many-headed ravenous birds.

'Eastward,' croaked a raven as Freyja drew near—

'Eastward in the Iron Wood The old one sitteth;'

And there she did sit, talking in quarrelsome tones to her wolf-sons and raven-daughters, who answered from the wood behind her, howling, screeching, and screaming all at the same time. There was a horrible din, and Freyja began to fear that her low voice would never be heard. She was obliged to get out of her chariot, and walk close up to the old withered Völva, so that she might whisper in her ear.

'Can you tell me, old mother,' she said,

'Where Óðr is? Have you seen him pass this way?'

'I understand not a single word of what you speak,' answered the iron woman in a dry crackly voice.

'And if I did, I have no time to waste in answering foolish questions for a spoiled little girl.'

Now, the Völva's words struck like daggers into Freyja's heart, and she was not strong enough to pull them out again; so, she stood there for a long while, not knowing what she should do.

'You had better go,' said the crone to her at last.

'There is no use in standing there crying, although your tears might be worth something.'

For this was the grandmother of strong-minded women, and she hated tears, no matter their worth. Then Freyja got into her chariot again, and went westward a long way to the wide, boundless land where impenetrable forests were growing, and undying nature reigned in silence. She knew that the silent Víðarr was living there; for, not finding any pleasure in the gay society of Ásgarðr, he had obtained permission from Father Óðinn to retire to this place.

'He is one of the Æsir, and perhaps he will be able to help me,' said the beautiful sad-hearted young Freyja,

As her chariot rolled on through empty moorlands and forests, seemingly always in the twilight. Her ears hearing no sound, her eye seeing no living thing; but still she went on with a trembling hope till she came to the spot.

'Begrown with branches and high grass, which was Víðarr's dwelling.' She thought.

Viðarr was sitting their firm as an oak, and as silent as night. Long grass grew up through his long hair, and the branches of trees crossed each other over his eyes; his ears were covered with moss, and dewdrops glistened upon his beard.

'It is almost impossible to get to him,' sighed Freyja,

'Through all these wet leaves, and I am afraid his moss-covered ears are very deaf.'

But she threw herself down on the ground before him and spoke.

'Tell me, Viðarr, does Óðr hide among thick trees? Or is he wandering over the broad west lands?'

Viðarr did not answer her—only a pale gleam shot over his face, as if reflected from that of Freyja, like Sunshine breaking through a wood.

'He does not hear me,' said Freyja to herself, and she crunched nearer to him through the branches.

'Only tell me, Viðarr,' she said,

'Is Óðr here?' But Viðarr said nothing, for he had no voice.

Then Freyja hid her face in her lap and wept bitterly for a long time.

'An Asa,' she said, at last, looking up,

'Is no better to one than an Iron Völva when one is really in need;'

And then she gathered her disordered dress about her, threw back her long fiery hair, and springing into her chariot, once again rushed wearily on her way.

The King of the Sea and His Daughters

At last, she came to the wide Sea-coast, and there everything was gloriously beautiful. It was evening, and the western sky looked like a broad crimson flower. No wind stirred the ocean, but the small waves rippled in rose-coloured froth on the shore, like the smiles of a jötun at play. Ægir, the old Sea-king, supported himself on the sand, whilst the cool waters were caressing his breasts and neck, and his ears drank their sweet murmur; for nine waves were his beautiful daughters, and they and their father were talking together. Now, though Ægir, looked stormy and old, he was as gentle as a child, and no mischief would ever have happened in his kingdom if he had been left to himself. But he had a cruel wife, called Ran, who was the daughter of a jötun, and so eagerly fond of fishing that, whenever any of the rough winds came to call upon her husband, she used to steal out of the deep Sea-caves where she lived, following ships for miles under the water, dragging a net after her, so that she might catch anyone who fell overboard into the thrashing waters.

Freyja wandered along the shore towards the place where the Sea King was lying, and as she went, she heard him speaking to his daughters.

'What is the history of Freyja?' he asked.

And the first wave answered, —

'Freyja is a fair young Vana, the most beautiful of all the Vana, who once was happy in Ásgarðr.'

Then the second wave said, —

'But she left her fair palace there, and Óðr, her Immortal Love to seek out more.'

The third wave spake, —

'She went down to the cavern of Dwarfs, paying the greatest of prices for the fire jewel.'

And the fourth wave, —

'She found Brisingamen there, performed acts of lust in payment and carried it away with her.'

Next the fifth wave, —

'But when she got back to Fólkvangr she found that Óðr

was gone.'

Sixth, —

'Because the Vana had loved herself and the beautiful Brisingamen more than Immortal Love.'

The seventh, —

'Freyja will never be happy again, for Óðr will never come back. He has abandoned her forever.'

The eighth wave then chimed in, –

'Óðr will never come back as long as the
world shall last, far beyond Ragnarök.'

Finally, the ninth daughter spake, –

'Óðr will never return, nor Freyja ever forget
to weep in sorrow, for vanity rules her heart.'

Freyja stood still, spell-bound, listening, and
when she heard the last words, that Óðr would never
come back, she wrung her hands, and cried, –

'O, Father Ægir! Trouble comes surging
up from a wide Sea, wave over wave, into my soul.'

And in truth it seemed as if her words had
power to change the whole surface of the ocean—
wave over wave rose higher and spoke louder—Ran
was seen dragging her net in the distance—old Ægir
shouted and dashed into the deep—Sea and sky
mixed in confusion, and night fell upon the storm.
Then Freyja sank down exhausted on the sand,
where she lay until her kind daughter, the sleepy little
Hnoss, came and carried her home again in her arms.
After this the beautiful Vana lived in her palace of
Fólkvangr, with friends and sisters, Æsir and
Ásynjur, but Óðr did not return, nor Freyja forget
to weep.

7. Freyja and Mjölnir

Þórr was the member of the Æsir most feared by the Jötuns. What they feared most about him was his most prized possession, the hammer Mjölnir, forged by the Dwarves Sindri and Brokkr. Though flawed by the evil machinations of the cunning Loki, even with its shortened handle it struck fear in the hearts of the Jötuns. The threat of its use by Þórr kept the Jötuns within the bounds of Jötunheim and out of the sacred land of Asgardr. But what if somehow it were stolen? Who would protect those in Asgardr and Midgardr then?

One day the worst fears of those in Asgardr happened, and the prayers of those in Jötunheim were answered. Þórr had been dozing beneath a tree in Thrudheimr, his estate. The regular rolling thunder echoed overhead with each of his snores. Gradually he awoke, and as he did so he automatically reached out for Mjölnir. But what he gripped was air, not the familiar thong of leather looped through the end of the short handle. His hand felt about. But his grasping yielded nothing. As his sense gradually returned from sleep and he raised up and looked all about, it sunk in on him his hammer was missing.

"*Where could it be?*" he thundered

As he rushed through his hall overturning tables and looking under beds for Mjölnir. He called for Sif, Thrudr, Hlora, Modi, and Magni to help him search. Sif looked at her husband patiently,

"*Maybe you dropped it? Or, perhaps while you were asleep and dreaming of killing Jötuns you accidentally threw it? You know how you can toss and turn in your sleep?*"

"*No, then it would have returned to me. What am I going to do, Sif?*" Þòrr continued looking up and down, hoping to find Mjölnir. Sif tried to help,

"Just calm down and think. Raging and storming about won't help. It's just making it wet in here. Can you remember where you last had it?" Irritated, Þòrr shook his head no.

"If I knew that, then I'd know where to find it, wouldn't I?"

The six continued looking, but without success. Þòrr called for the warriors in his hall to stop fighting and help him look for Mjölnir. Every portion of his estate was searched, all without success. Þòrr became more and more agitated as the unfruitful search wore on. His red hair tossed about wildly, and his red beard seemed to burn with anger. Then a thought occurred to him, and he spoke of it to Sif,

"There is but one in all of Asgardr whom I consider my enemy. There is only one in this sacred land who could profit from our loss of Mjölnir – Loki!"

The name boomed out from him. Þòrr went to the center of Asgardr and yelled out for Loki to show his miserable, twisted face. Loki was easily found, since this time, oddly enough, he was in no way guilty of the mischief. It took him awhile to convince Þòrr and the other Æsir of his innocence in the matter. But he finally did. He even offered to help look for Mjölnir. Þòrr was suspicious, but so far his own efforts had failed. Loki suggested they go see Freyja,

"She has just returned from a journey to Midgardr searching for Ottr. We shall borrow her falcon-guise, Valsharmr, to aid in our search for Mjölnir. Hopefully we'll have more luck than she has had looking for Ottr."

Fortunately Loki had returned Valsharmr just that morning, before Freyja's return. They found Freyja in Sessrumnir, walking around crying tears of amber. Þòrr spoke first,

"We've come to borrow Valsharmr to use to help us find Mjölnir. Will you let us use it?" Freyja signaled for her servant Fulla to fetch it.

When it was brought into the room she took it from her and without even noticing its disheveled condition, handed it to Þórr and motioned for the two to leave her alone with her sadness,

"Here, I'd give it to you even though it was pure gold or silver. Just leave me alone."

Outside the hall Þórr handed Valsharmr to Loki who put it on and flew off heading towards Jötunheimr. As he flew through Midgardr he could see violent storms below him. There was flashing lightning. Thunder rolled over the land followed by downpours that swelled rivers beyond their banks. Then came blinding snowstorms with hail, all blown about by a fierce wind that bit through even the thickest fur coats. One look at all this told Loki who had stolen Mjölnir and was now playing with the hammer. The Hrymthursar, Thrym could of course cause snowstorms, but he didn't have the power of thunder and lightning. Loki flew towards Thrymheimr in Jötunheimr. For all the trouble which was being caused on Midgardr, he found Thrym sitting on a grave mound leisurely braiding leashes out of fine spun gold for his greyhound dogs, and plaiting the manes of his horses, weaving adornments amongst the hairs in intricate patterns. When he tired of these pursuits he stopped long enough to feather his arrows with eagle's quills. Despite the fact Loki walked up on him from behind, he spoke to him without turning around,

"How are things going in Asgardr? How are the Æsir and their friends the Alfs? Things must be boring there if you're seeking out the company of those in Jötunheimr."

Loki replied,

"You know very well how things are in Asgardr since you stole Mjölnir. I'm here to claim it and take it back to Þórr, its rightful owner. Stop sitting there dishonoring the dead and fetch the hammer."

Thrym turned and spoke,

"What concern is it of yours who has Mjölnir? You're as much an enemy of the Æsir as you are of anyone. You shame yourself helping them. How can I be sure your search for Mjölnir is in the Æsir's behalf? Why would Þórr send you to fetch it? I hardly think you are one of his most trusted friends. If I were to fetch the hammer, assuming I had it, and give it to you, how do I know it would find its way back to Þórr?"

Loki became angrier,

"Don't joke with me. Even if you do have Mjölnir, I'm more powerful than you. The longer I stay in Jötunheimr the more powerful I become. Don't seek to test that power."

The warning made Thrym back down a little,

"It's true, I do have Mjölnir. But it's hidden eight rosts beneath the mountains of Jötunheimr. I'm the only one who knows how to retrieve it. So if you harm me you will lose the hammer forever. However, if you treat me in a fitting manner, perhaps we could talk about what I would bargain for to return Mjölnir."

The conversation was becoming interesting for Loki. There was nothing he liked better than to bargain for something, especially if the price to him was nothing. He was very good at dealing in the worst interests of all concerned.

"What is it you desire?"

Thrym thought a little and then spoke,

"I desire what just about everyone in Asgardr and Midgardr desire. It's very lonely and cold in Thrymheimr. The climate is harsh and unwelcoming. What chance do I have of finding a wife who would like it here? I've tried and tried and I have yet to be able to lure a wife here. So I would like you to arrange a marriage for me. That is the price for Mjölnir."

Loki thought it a simple enough request,

"It should be easy to find someone in Thrymheimr for you. I'll leave now and be back by nightfall. While I'm gone you can fetch the hammer and have it ready by the time I return."

Thrym shouted out after the quickly departing Loki,

"Hold on a moment. Don't leave in such haste. I have not agreed to your deal. Nor will I. I don't want just anyone to be my wife. I've thought about this a long time. And as I said, I desire what just about everyone in Asgardr and Midgardr desire."

Loki had returned and didn't like the sound of what he was hearing. It would be easy enough to find some ugly Jötun with no prospects of marriage who would welcome a future of hearth and home, even with Thrym. But, it seemed Thrym had his eyes and heart set on something higher. Thrym continued,

"Many years ago I once saw Freyja. Since then I've been smitten by her and on long winter evenings have often thought how nice it would be if she were next to me sitting by the fire. So she is my price for Mjölnir. Bring her here and after the wedding ceremony has been successfully completed, and the marriage consummated, then

will I gladly return Mjölnir. I'll also become a
friend to the Æsir, wedded to them as well as
Freyja, since I'll be so grateful for the happiness
they will have brought me. Here is a ring set with
a red ruby to represent my love. Give it to
Freyja as the first of many gifts from me."

Loki agreed to the deal having no idea how
he was going to fulfill it.

"As is the custom, I'll bring your wife to you
within nine nights."

He donned Valsharmr and flew back to
Asgardr where he found Þórr in the courtyard
near the main gates pacing back and forth
waiting for him. He yelled out to Loki before
Loki had landed or changed from Valsharmr.

"I don't see the hammer on you. Have you failed?
Do you know where Mjölnir is? Quick, tell me
what our fate will be."

Loki tried to calm Þòrr's anxieties,

"Don't worry, all has been taken care of. The Hrymthursar Thrym has the hammer buried eight rosts deep in Jötunheimr under a tall mountain. But he's willing to dig it up and return it and be a friend to the Æsir if we'll do a very simple thing."

Loki drew out the telling of the story as long as he could. Þòrr became more and more excited with the anticipation.

"Well, what is it? Speak faster." Loki continued more slowly than ever,

"Thrym is a very lonely person. This has led him to gain our attention by stealing Mjölnir. He'll give us his friendship if we'll give him Freyja as a wife." Þòrr thought a moment,

"That seems reasonable enough. She'll certainly make the sacrifice if she realizes it will get Mjölnir back for me. Perhaps this will take her mind off Ottr, as well. We'll be doing her a favor. Everyone wins."

Thus rationalized the two hurried off to Fólkvangr to return Valsharmr and give Freyja the good news of her upcoming marriage. Þòrr was so excited that he made his way unannounced through Sessrumnir to her private chamber.

"Find the bridal dress you so recently wore. Put it on for I have good news for you. Loki and I are going to take you to Thrymheimr so you can become the blushing bride of Thrym. This will help you forget the sadness brought about by Ottr's disappearance. And in exchange for the favor Thrym is giving us by making you so happy, he'll return Mjölnir to me."

Freyja had only recently managed to stop crying. But the news she heard from Þòrr, along with the mention of Ottr's name set her off again. Soon they had to leave the room for another since it had rapidly filled with red gold from her tears. Þòrr continued completely misinterpreting the situation,

"Stop the tears of joy and begin your preparations. I will take you to Thrym today."

Freyja slowly recovered her composure and became quite angry at the very suggestion that she go live with a Jötun just because Þòrr wanted his hammer back,

"I had nothing to do with the carelessness which allowed your hammer to be stolen. Since it was due to your carelessness, you go live with Thrym, for I will not. Get out you oaf."

As she spoke her final words to Loki and
Þórr molten amber began dripping from her blue
eyes and her breasts heaved with such anger
that she broke loose the Brisingamen necklace.
Her exclamation of a scream that sounded like a
thousand ravens told Loki and Þórr she was not
to be reasoned with and hurriedly scattered to
the winds. They sent messengers to all of the
other Æsir and Vanir telling them to meet at
Urdarbrunnr Well for a Thing to discuss how
Þórr's hammer might be retrieved.

That evening at the Thing many suggestions
were made, none of which seemed workable.
One of the Æsir even suggested Freyja be
forced to wed Thrym. But this was not a very
popular idea. Freyja was much loved in Asgardr,
particularly by the male Æsir, and her presence
would have been sorely missed. Njordr, Freyja's
father spoke up,

"I will not permit my only daughter to leave the protection of Asgardr. Anyone who tries to force her to wed the ugly Thrym will have to battle my son, me and all of the Vanir. I'm certain a few of the Æsir would also join us."

Freyr walked over to his father's side, emphasizing the point. So, that was settled. Freyja would stay in Asgardr. But what was to be done about the hammer? Heimdallr had stood silently gazing off before him during all of the arguments. Finally he spoke,

"I've been looking into the future and there are sad times ahead for us as well as those in Midgardr if we don't retrieve Mjölnir. We have no obligation to give Freyja to Thrym or even to bargain with him since Mjölnir was stolen from us. But part of the blame lies with Þórr who was careless enough to leave such a precious object lying about. Therefore, it should fall to him to retrieve Mjölnir. He should not be hiding behind

Freyja's skirts. Rather he should be wearing them. I suggest that he dress as Freyja and go to Thrymheimr in that guise and retrieve the Mjölnir himself."

There was a great deal of laughter at this solution to their problem. But soon there was silence, since no one had offered a better idea. Heimdallr continued,

"Þórr's red hair could be braided. Brísingamen could be repaired and lent to Þórr to wear, as well as Freyja's household keys which he could wear hanging from his side. With a virginal red dress on and a hood over his head to protect his maidenly modesty, as well as long petticoats to hide his hairy legs, he could easily pass for Freyja."

Everyone yelled their approval of the idea. Everyone, that is, except Þórr. He roared out over all the others,

"I'll not do it. There is no way to force me to go. You wouldn't let Freyja leave Asgardr to marry Thrym. Would you force Þòrr, who is much more powerful and useful to you, to do so instead? My answer is no, absolutely not. Even the mere thought of this charade has brought guffaws of laughter to some of you. What then would be your reaction if I were actually to wear such a costume? Some of our fiercest warriors would laugh themselves to death, which certainly wouldn't help us at the last great battle. No!"

Þòrr stomped off causing the whole land to shake. Forseti yelled out to the others,

"We must restrain ourselves in this matter. It's for our own good that we keep our laughter in, for if we don't we'll have nothing to laugh about. Someone fetch Þòrr back here."

Þórr was brought back and one by one everyone there pledged not to laugh if Þórr would dress up as Freyja. Loki even went one better than everyone else,

"And to show you it can be fun, I'll dress up as your handmaiden and accompany you to see Thrym."

However, this was no great sacrifice on Loki's part since he often changed into a woman and was in fact quite fond of dressing up as one whether he was physically transformed or not. Reluctantly Þórr accepted their assurances they would not laugh at him, and agreed to the ruse. Heimdallr supervised the outfitting. Óðinn gave Freyja permission to remove Brísingamen, which had since been repaired, and lend it to Þórr. Then he went off to make a magic salve from the blood of a bear and wild boar's suet. When rubbed on Þórr, this salve caused all of his battle scars to disappear as well as his chest hair and beard. He refused to have his leg hair removed.

"I'll not do that. Imagine Þòrr with smooth legs? It would be unseemly."

He didn't even consider the impression a hairy-legged Freyja would make. Two of Freyja's red dresses were sewn together to make one for Þòrr. Fortunately, Þòrr's favorite color was red which made wearing the dress a little easier. But he insisted on wearing his hauberk under the dress and no amount of persuasion could get him to remove it. A leather bodice was laced around his chest in such a way as to give him the appropriate bulges. Hoping to take Thrym's gaze from his intended's face, Hermodr fashioned two round shields out of copper which were attached to the front of the bodice to accentuate Þòrr's front. Brisingamen was hung around his neck, and a set of household keys were hung about his waist. Þòrr insisted on also wearing his boots, belt and gloves, as well as his battle helmet.

Fortunately the dress hung long enough to cover his hairy legs and boots. Some of the Ásynjur wrapped material around his helmet to try and disguise its true purpose. Hnoss bound together a bunch of peonies, sunflowers and hollyhocks into a corsage which she attached to the front of Þórr's dress, telling him all the while that it would make him even more beautiful than he already looked. Still something was missing, which Óðinn provided. He took a scarlet rope and wrapped it across his son's shoulders and attached a veil to the helmet so it hung down over Þórr's face.

"Now you're ready, my son, to go and get Mjölnir back. Maybe next time you won't be so careless with it. As a father I can only look at my son in wonder at his wedding preparations."

While Þòrr was being attired Loki had gone to dress himself. His problem was not one of having dresses sewn for him, but rather of choosing which one to wear from his wardrobe. He tried on outfit after outfit, flouncing around in front of his mirror, this way and that, to see how the dresses fell on him. Back and forth he went until finally he settled on the perfect little number. But, he took an assortment of others with him. He certainly didn't intend to be seen in the same gown twice. Thjalfi had seen to the readying of Þòrr's chariot. It was bedecked with flowers and misted over with various fragrances. He had also shod the goats with golden shoes and sprayed them lest their smell offend anyone in Thrymheimr.

Now all was in readiness. Þòrr and Loki boarded the chariot. With reins tightly wrapped around his wrist, Þòrr yelled for the goats to proceed. As they flew off Loki could be heard instructing Þòrr in the ways of women,

"You're going to have to talk in a higher voice, Þórr, if we are to convince Thrym of your femininity."

Thunderbolts shot forth from the chariot. The chariot flew swiftly over Midgardr towards Thrymheimr. Loki's taunting all throughout the journey made Þórr angrier and angrier. By the time they neared Thrym's castle, storms, thunder and lightning bolts had set the sky ablaze. Hardly the genteel arrival Thrym expected. Everything had been in readiness for Freyja's arrival for several days. But when Thrym saw the chariot approaching in the distance he jumped up and started yelling out last minute orders,

"See that the benches are covered with fresh straw so my bride will sit comfortably during dinner. Make certain all of the food is set on the table. She'll be hungry after such a long journey.

Soon I'll have all I want in life. I own precious golden-horned cattle. My jet-black oxen are the envy of all in Jötunheimr. I have treasures of gold and jewels stolen from the Svartalfheimr. The most beautiful of all maidens is that I am lacking."

He was practically jumping up and down as the chariot landed. He sent forth six of his servants to greet Freyja while he went to his throne to await her arrival. One servant was dressed in cloth woven of gold. Another wore shining silver. A third was dressed in black mail forged from lead. A fourth wore a similar outfit made of iron which shone blue in the sun. The fifth emissary wore reddish copper. And finally, walking behind the others was a servant who wore mail made of tin. Although it shone almost as brightly as the silver, if one looked at it closely it could be seen to be a lot cheaper.

The six were surprised at the two images alighting from the chariot. Loki held out his hand to be helped down. When the tin servant tried to help ÞòrrFreyja he was unceremoniously shoved to the ground. The six quickly organized themselves as an honor guard around ÞòrrFreyja and Loki and with great majesty escorted the two to the throneroom where Loki and ÞòrrFreyja were presented to Thrym, whom they found seated on his golden throne and dressed in purple and gold awaiting his bride. Thrym spoke to ÞòrrFreyja,

"Freyja, my love. I have waited with great longing for you. And as anticipation in my thoughts has enlarged you in my mind, so do you seem enlarged in person. I've seen you from afar, but I must have misjudged the distance. Because you seem so much larger than I imagined your height. And you seem so much more powerful and muscular than I recall you being when I've seen you. But, you look wonderful so let us be married right away and retire for the night to our

wedding bed, so we might get to know each other better, much better." ÞòrrFreyja answered,

"I'm hungry. What have you got to eat?" In an almost too manly of a growl.

Thrym was slightly taken aback at this reply to his suggestion, but quickly answered her,

"Anything you wish, my love. But first wouldn't you rather get acquainted with your groom? And my, what a deep voice you have?"

Loki answered in a high falsetto voice,

"She is suffering from a slight cold and her voice is hoarse. However, she wouldn't be dissuaded from this visit with you."

Thrym's eyes shone with love. ÞòrrFreyja turned from the throne and followed a servant through room after room in the castle until they reached the banquet hall. He sat at the head of the table and began eating, not even waiting for the others to seat themselves. Loki whispered into Þòrrfreyja's ear,

"Try to be a little more genteel and ladylike in your eating. The grease is dripping off your veil down the front of your dress."

Then Loki sat down to the right of Þòrrfreyja and asked for a servant to cut her meat for her. Thrym arrived in the hall and headed straight for his intended. He reached for the veil,

"Let me lift this veil that hides my treasure. I want to give you a little kiss."

Þòrrfreyja pulled his head back sharply which surprised Thrym. Loki spoke up with an explanation,

"Freyja is virtuous and shy. She has only just met you. Let her become more comfortable here before you make any further advances."

Thrym was impressed, for he had heard awful stories about Freyja's easy virtue. Her behavior convinced him she was pure and innocent, despite being married to Ottr.

"Such modesty in a woman is almost unknown here in Thrymheimr. What a refreshing change."

He sat down to the left of his bride and took her hand in his. ÞòrrFreyja squirmed in his seat which only endeared him all the more to Thrym,

"My, what a strong grip you have?"

ÞòrrFreyja bent back Thrym's hand. Loki intervened before ÞòrrFreyja broke Thrym's hand, taking ÞòrrFreyja's hand and holding it upturned for Thrym to inspect while explaining the strength of her grip to Thrym,

"Her grip has been made strong from sewing all day long."

Loki noticed just as Thrym noticed that ÞòrrFreyja's hand was covered with battle scars.

"And look at the scars she has suffered from needle and thread. Earlier she could not find a thimble but still insisted she sew her own wedding dress."

Loki pulled ÞòrrFreyja's hand away and instead thrust the sleeve of the wedding dress towards Thrym.

"Just look at the fine stitches."

Thrym smiled at the domesticity of his future wife. He didn't even notice how large and hairy the hand was and how ludicrous a needle would have looked in it. Loki, not to be outdone reached to his side and took the hand of the Jötun next to him and began to enjoy the dinner.

What there was of it, considering how much ÞòrrFreyja was wolfing down? ÞòrrFreyja was quite hungry. By the time Thrym had seated himself ÞòrrFreyja had already eaten an ox. Then she swallowed eight large salmon in one gulp, without even taking a breath. Having finished with the main course she started on desert. Sweetcakes and fruit had been prepared in a beautiful design on a tray which ÞòrrFreyja hoisted to her mouth and tilted so all the delicacies slid down her throat. She washed it all down with three tuns of mead. Thrym turned to the others and proudly said,

"Has there ever been a bride with a greater appetite than that? Just think what her other appetites will be like?"

Loki thought an explanation for ÞòrrFreyja's gluttony was in order.

"Dear Thrym, Freyja was so excited at the prospect of becoming your bride she forgot to eat and has tasted neither food nor drink in eight long days."

Thrym was truly touched. He quickly bent over and raised the veil again, hoping to have better luck stealing a kiss. But what he saw startled him so much he sat back and fell off his chair.

"Her eyes are so burning and piercing. They burned through me like fire. It's almost frightening."

Again Loki came to the rescue with an explanation,

"She has slept for the last week so she would be well-rested when she arrived here. What you've seen is the burning look of love and the expectation of what is to come later."

Thrym picked himself up and sat down in his seat,

"Could there have ever been a happier bridegroom than I at this very moment in time?"

He turned to all those assembled. Everyone looked at him and he took the pity in their eyes for envy. He snuggled up close to his beloved. Thrym's ugly gaunt and drawn sister entered the banquet hall and walked directly to the head of the table and demanded Freyja give her her bridal gifts, as was the custom,

"If you want my love and friendship then honor our customs and give me my presents."

A great quiet filled the room. ÞòrrFreyja just stared at her. Loki spoke up,

"We haven't brought any gifts with us. I fear love has made Freyja absentminded about the bridal gifts. Perhaps we can bring something at a later date?"

Thrym's sister was clearly angry as she spoke to ÞòrrFreyja,

"If you have brought nothing, then give me the gold rings on your fingers and the beautiful necklace you wear about your neck."

ÞòrrFreyja started for the sister, but was pulled back into her seat by Loki who spoke to Thrym, changing the subject.

"Thrym, I see everyone has finished eating. Isn't it about time the wedding ceremony was begun? Why not have Mjölnir sent for so the nuptials can be hallowed and consecrated in the name of the Asynjes Var and Frigg, as well as Óðinn and Þórr as is the usual custom?"

Seeing that what he had waited for was now so close at hand Thrym seized upon the suggestion, pushed his sister out of the way and signaled for several Dvergar to go and fetch the hammer. Soon they returned weighted down by the treasure they carried hoisted on their shoulders. It was brought to the head of the table and placed in front of ÞórrFreyja. The Dvergar swore holy vows to the Asynjur Var which were repeated by Thrym who was now standing behind his bride.

They called for blessings of a good home from Frigg, and success in the marriage from Óðinn and Þórr. Then all eyes turned to ÞórrFreyja whose turn it was to repeat the vows. ÞórrFreyja was reluctant to speak, but did so at Loki's urgings, promising to be faithful and loving to her husband. After she finished the hammer was placed in her lap. ÞòrrFreyja reached for it, closed his hand around the handle and stood up. He ripped the veil from his face and all in front of him immediately recognized Þòrr the Thunder God.

Thrym still didn't know what the commotion was about until Þòrr turned around to face him. Never was there a more surprised bridegroom. Everyone began shrinking back from the table. Some turned and ran for the exits as fast as they could. But it was too late. Þòrr swung Mjölnir overhead and let loose lightning and thunderbolts. The first to die was Thrym, followed by his greedy sister.

Soon the roof was ablaze and the walls were crumbling as Þòrr set about slaying all of the wedding party. Loki had hurried out to Þòrr's chariot and hid under it until Þòrr was finished. When Þòrr's rage finally subsided all that was left was smoking rubble. Þòrr calmly, stepping over fallen walls, walked over to his chariot and spoke to Loki,

"You can come out now, Loki. All has been taken care of. Be certain when we are back in Asgardr and you tell your story of how bravely you fought in the regaining of Mjölnir, that you don't leave out the part about hiding under my chariot in the filth where my goats had relieved themselves."

They started on their trip back to Asgardr. Alviss the Dvergar meanwhile had come walking boldly up Bifrost the day before Þòrr's return. He had heard of Mjölnir's theft and the terms Thrym wanted for its return. He decided he might be able to gain a little something for himself using this knowledge. He was stopped on the bridge by Heimdallr,

"Why do you tread on Bifrost and act as if you have some business in Asgardr?"

Alviss replied,

"I don't deal with underlings. Take me to Óðinn for I have a message meant only for his ears. There's not a moment to be wasted. I have important news about the Jötuns and their plans to attack Asgardr." Heimdallr was not impressed,

"There are many who use that story to try and see Óðinn, pale nose. You'll have to do better than that." Alviss changed his strategy,

"I'm the Dvergar Alviss, which means all wise. I have come to take Freyja away."

Heimdallr laughed and replied,

"I hardly think you are the god of her dreams. She is in love with Ottr who is considerably larger in all ways than you. What makes you think you can fill his shoes? However, I'll take you to Óðinn so that he may share in your humor."

Óðinn sat on his throne looking down on the Dvergar,

"So you want to take Freyja. Why is that little man?"

What the Dvergar said next startled Heimdallr and Óðinn,

"Þórr and Loki have been found out in Thrymheimr and both are now bound and trapped in the cellars of Thrymr's hall. The real Freyja must come with me in order to save not only Mjölnir, but now Þórr and Loki as well. Other Jötuns have heard Þórr and Mjölnir have both been captured and are now preparing to invade Asgardr. Only Freyja can stop them."

His story had the ring of truth to it, and Þòrr and Loki had been away a lot longer than had been expected. However, Óðinn was still a little skeptical,

"Why has such an important mission been entrusted to you? Why hasn't Thrym sent one of his Jötuns servants to impress us with his size?"

Alviss thought for a moment. He hadn't anticipated his story being doubted. But he quickly thought of a reply,

"Because I'm the wisest of my kind, and it was thought intelligence was needed to persuade Freyja to come with me rather than using brute force."

Óðinn thought for a moment and then answered, still suspicious,

"In that case you must prove your intelligence to me before we can believe your story and give Freyja up to you."

Alviss was puffed up with how he had so far fooled them and readily agreed to the quiz.

Óðinn began,

"How are the heavens named in all the worlds?"

Alviss smiled,

"That's an easy one. Those in Midgardr talk of the heavens. The Æsir refer to sky or height, while the Vanir think of it as the wind roof or windweaver. In Jötunheimr it is called Upheimr which means high home, and the alfs call it fair-roof. The dvergar, like myself, call it drip-hall, since we suffer more from its effects than others do without benefiting from its beauty."

Óðinn nodded that that had been the correct answer and continued with another question,

"And what of fire?"

Alviss answered,

"Fire for men, eild or flame by the Æsir, the flickering one or wild-fire by the Vanir, and the consuming or hungry wolfish biter by the Jötuns. It is all-burner by the alfs, furnace to the dvergar, and corpse-slayer or destroyer to those in Niflheimr."

"And what of the earth?"

Alviss replied,

"Earth by men, Midgardr or fields amongst the Æsir, ways by the Vanir and all-green by the Jötuns, burgeoning or growing by the alfs."

Óðinn asked yet another question,

"So far you're doing quite well. The names of the moon, if you know them?"

Alviss grew more and more confident with each question,

"Moon amongst those on Midgardr. The Æsir and Vanir know it as mild light, whirling wheel by those in Niflheimr, speeding or rapid traveler by the Jötuns, and Gleamer or splendor by the dvergar, and teller-of-time by the alfs."

Óðinn nodded that the dvergar was correct,

"What of the clouds?"

Alviss answered,

"They are clouds in Midgardr, rain-carriers in Asgardr, windblown or wind-ships in Vanaheimr, rain-hope in Jötunheimr, weather-might in Alfheimr, and hiding or helmets of darkness in Niflheimr."

Óðinn looked at Heimdallr. Could what this dvergar had said about Þórr and Loki be true?

He continued the questioning,

"The wind?"

Alviss was getting tired of such simple questions, but gave the correct answer,

"Men and women of Midgardr call it wind, the Æsir call it wafter, whiner by the Vanir, roarer amongst the Jötuns, traveling noise by the alfs, and whistler by the doomed in Nilfheimr."

"And the calm that follows the wind?"

"Calm by men, sea quiet or stillness by the
Æsir, wind-lull by the Vanir, sultry or humid by
the Jötuns, day rest by the Alfs, and day's
refuge by the dvergues. There is no calm in
Niflheimr, so they have no name for it."

Óðinn thought he had tricked him with that
one. But the dvergar had answered correctly.

He continued,

"The sea?"

Alviss smiled, realizing he was winning,

"Sea by men, smooth gleaming by the Æsir,
wave by the Vanir, eel home by the Jötuns, drink
stuff by the alfs, the deep by the dvergar."

"Wood?"

"Alright, I'll answer that one, but can you come up with some harder questions? Wood by those in Midgardr, mane of the fields or Midgardr's mane by the Æsir, wand of charms by the Vanir, seaweed that grows on the mountains by those in Niflheimr, fuel or firewood by the Jötuns and fair bough by the alfs."

Óðinn asked another,

"Night?"

Alviss quickly replied,

"Night by those in Midgardr, murk by the Æsir, mask or covering of darkness by the Vanir, lightless by the Jötuns, sleep's joyful rest by the alfs, and weaver-of-dreams by the dvergar."

"The seed sown on Midgardr?" was the next question asked by Óðinn.

"Men who sew it call it barley, you call it corn or breadstuff, the Vanir call it growth, the Jötuns call it edible, the alfs grain or drinking stuff, and those in Niflheimr curse it as the hanging since all they are tempted by are its roots."

"And what of beer?" continued Óðinn.

"Surely that's not an important question?" queried Alviss.

Óðinn answered,

"If you don't know the answer, just say so."

Alviss responded,

"I will answer it. Ale by men, beer by the Æsir, foaming strength or wassail brew by the Vanir, clear mist by the Jötuns, mead by those in Niflheimr for they have none and treasure it greatly, and feast draught by the Jötuns. Have you any better questions for me?"

Óðinn smiled and replied,

"I think the best ones are these last two. First tell me the name Nott the daughter of Narfi is known by in each of the worlds?"

Alviss replied,

"Night by those in Midgardr, Nott or the dark amongst the Æsir, and the hood by the Vanir, unlighted by the Jötuns, sleep-joy by the alfs, and bringer of dreams by the dvergar."

Óðinn asked the final question,

"I'm surprised at your wisdom. So here is the last question whereby you can gain the hand of

Freyja. After Nott comes her son Dagr and the start of the day. And with him comes the sun. How is the sun known in all the worlds?"

"That's certainly easy," replied Alviss, confident that he was assured of Freyja's hand with his answer,

"Sun by men, circle of the sun by the Æsir, all-bright by the Vanir, everglow by the Jötuns, fair wheel by the alfs, and finally Dvalin's Doom by such as myself. Now send for Freyja, that I might take her as my bride."

Odinn stood up and pointed to the east as he spoke,

"We have instead sent for Dvalin's Doom. I've quizzed you all this night and now the sun has come. You may be smart but you're not smart enough to hide from the day or your fate of uppr dagr. You've forgotten to wear your red *tarnkappe that would have protected you from the sun's stiffening rays."*

There was a surprised look upon Alviss's face as he began to speak. But his head had already turned to stone and the rest of him was quickly stiffening. His knowledge and ambitions had been too much for him. He was carried out to the courtyard and set up as a statue for birds to rest upon. Later that day Þòrr and Loki returned from their journey having successfully retrieved Mjölnir and killed a lot of Jötuns in the process. Altogether a successful trip. There was peace once more in Asgardr, but only for a short while.

8. Hyndluljóð

Freyja spake:

Maiden, awake! | wake thee, my friend,
My sister Hyndla, | in thy hollow cave!
Already comes darkness, | and ride must
we To Valhalla to seek | the sacred hall.

The favor of Heerfather | seek we to find,
to his followers gold | he gladly gives; To

Hermoth gave he | helm and mail-coat, and
to Sigmund he gave | a sword as gift.

Triumph to some, | and treasure to others,
to many wisdom | and skill in words, Fair
winds to the sailor, | to the singer his art,
and a manly heart | to many a hero.

Thor shall | honor, | and this shall | ask,
That his favor true | mayst thou ever find;
Though little the brides | of the giants he
loves.

From the stall now | one of thy wolves lead
forth, And along with my boar | shalt thou
let him run; for slow my boar goes | on the
road of the gods, and | would not weary |
my worthy steed.

Hyndla spake:

Falsely thou askest me, | Freyja, to go,
for so in the glance | of thine eyes I see;
On the way of the slain | thy lover goes
with thee. Ottr the young, | the son of
Instein.

Freyja spake:

Wild dreams, methinks, | are thine when
thou sayest my lover is with me | on the way
of the slain; There shines the boar | with
bristles of gold, Hildisvini, | he who was
made By Dain and Nabbi, | the cunning
Dwarfs.

Now let us down | from our saddles leap,
and talk of the race | of the heroes twain;
the men who were born | of the gods
above,

A wager have made | in the foreign metal
Ottr the young | and Angantyr;
We must guard, for the hero | young to
have, His father's wealth, | the fruits of his
race.

For me a shrine | of stones he made,--
And now to glass | the rock has grown;--
Oft with the blood | of beasts was it red;
in the goddesses ever | did Ottr trust.

Tell to me now | the ancient names,
And the races of all | that were born of
old: Who are of the Skjoldungs, | who of
the Skilfings, Who of the Othlings, | who
of the Ylfings, Who are the free-born, |
who are the high-born, The noblest of men
| that in Mithgarth dwell?

Hyndla spake:

Thou art, Ottr, | the son of Instein,
And Instein the son | of Alf the Old,
Alf of Ulf, | Ulf of Sæfari, And
Sæfari's father | was Svan the Red.

Thy mother, bright | with bracelets fair,
Hight, methinks, | the priestess Hledis;
Frothi her father, | and Friaut her mother;
her race of the mightiest | men must seem.

Of old the noblest | of all was Ali,
Before him Halfdan, | foremost of
Skjoldungs; Famed were the battles | the
hero fought, To the corners of heaven |
his deeds were carried.

Strengthened by Eymund, | the
strongest of men, Sigtrygg he slew | with
the ice-cold sword; His bride was Almveig,
| the best of women, and eighteen boys |
did Almveig bear him.

Hence come the Skjoldungs, | hence the
Skilfings, Hence the Othlings, | hence
the Ynglings, Hence come the free-born, |
hence the high-born, the noblest of men |
that in Mithgarth dwell: And all are thy
kinsmen, | Ottr, thou fool!

Hildigun then | her mother hight,
The daughter of Svava | and Sækonung;
And all are thy kinsmen, | Ottr, thou fool!
It is much to know, | wilt thou hear yet
more?

The mate of Dag | was a mother of
heroes, Thora, who bore him | the bravest
of fighters, Frathmar and Gyrth | and the
Frekis twain, Am and Jofurmar, | Alf the
Old; It is much to know, | wilt thou hear yet
more?

Her husband was Ketil, | the heir of
Klypp, He was of thy mother | the

mother's-father; before the days | of Kari
was Frothi, and horn of Hild | was Hoalf
then.

Next was Nanna, | daughter of Nokkvi,
Thy father's kinsman | her son became;
Old is the line, | and longer still,
And all are thy kinsmen, | Ottr, thou fool!

Isolf and Osolf, | the sons of Olmoth,
Whose wife was Skurhild, | the daughter
of Skekkil, Count them among | the
heroes mighty,
And all are thy kinsmen, | Ottr, thou fool!

Gunnar the Bulwark, | Grim the Hardy,
Thorir the Iron-shield, | Ulf the Gaper,
Brodd and Hörvir | both did | know; in the
household they were | of Hrolf the Old.

Hervarth, Hjorvarth, | Hrani, Angantyr,
Bui and Brami, | Barri and Reifnir, Tind

and Tyrfing, | the Haddings twain, and all
are thy kinsmen, | Ottr, thou fool!

Eastward in Bolm | were born of old
The sons of Arngrim | and Eyfura;
With berserk-tumult | and baleful deed
Like fire o'er land | and sea they fared,
And all are thy kinsmen, | Ottr, thou fool!

The sons of Jormunrek | all of yore
to the gods in death | were as offerings
given; He was kinsman of Sigurth, | hear
well what I say, the foe of hosts, | and
Fafnir's slayer.

From Volsung's seed | was the hero
sprung, and Hjordis was born | of
Hrauthung's race, And Eylimi | from the
Othlings came, and all are thy kinsmen, |
Ottr, thou fool!

Gunnar and Hogni, | the heirs of Gjuki,
And Guthrun as well, | who their sister
was; But Gotthorm was not | of Gjuki's
race, although the brother | of both he
was: And all are thy kinsmen, | Ottr, thou
fool!

Of Hvethna's sons | was Haki the best,
And Hjorvarth the father | of Hvethna
was;

Harald Battle-tooth | of Auth was born,
Hrörek the Ring-giver | her husband was;
Auth the Deep-minded | was Ivar's
daughter, But Rathbarth the father | of
Randver was: And all are thy kinsmen, |
Ottr, thou fool!

Fragment of "The Short Voluspo

Eleven in number | the gods were known,
When Baldr o'er the hill | of death was

bowed; and this to avenge | was Vali swift,
When his brother's slayer | soon he slew.

He father of Baldr | was the heir of Bur,

Freyr's wife was Gerth, | the daughter of
Gymir, of the giants' brood, | and
Aurbotha bore her; to these as well | was
Thjazi kin, the dark-loving giant; | his
daughter was Skathi.

Much have | told thee, | and further will
tell; There is much that | know; | wilt thou
hear yet more?

Heith and Hrossthjof, | the children of
Hrimnir.

The sybils arose | from Vitholf's race,
From Vilmeith all | the seers are,
And the workers of charms | are

Svarthofthi's children, And from Ymir
sprang | the giants all.

Much have | told thee, | and further will
tell; There is much that | know;-- | wilt thou
hear yet more?

One there was born | in the bygone days,
of the race of the gods, | and great was his
might; Nine giant women, | at the world's
edge, Once bore the man | so mighty in
arms.

Gjolp there bore him, | Greip there bore
him, Eistla bore him, | and Eyrgjafa,
Ulfrun bore him, | and Angeyja,
Imth and Atla, | and Jarnsaxa.

Strong was he made | with the strength of
earth, with the ice-cold sea, | and the blood
of swine.

One there was born, | the best of all,
And strong was he made | with the
strength of earth; The proudest is called |
the kinsman of men Of the rulers all |
throughout the world.

Much have | told thee, | and further will
tell; There is much that | know; | wilt thou
hear yet more?

The wolf did Loki | with Angrbotha win,
And Sleipnir bore he | to Svathilfari;
The worst of marvels | seemed the one
That sprang from the brother | of Byleist
then.

A heart ate Loki, | in the embers it lay,
And half-cooked found he | the woman's
heart; with child from the woman | Lopt
soon was, and thence among men | came
the monsters all.

The sea, storm-driven, | seeks heaven
itself, o'er the earth it flows, | the air grows
sterile; Then follow the snows | and the
furious winds, for the gods are doomed, |
and the end is death.

Then comes another, | a greater than all,
though never | dare | his name to speak;
Few are they now | that farther can see
than the moment when Othin | shall meet
the wolf.

Freyja spake:

To my boar now bring | the memory-beer,
so that all thy words, | that well thou hast
spoken, the third morn hence | he may hold
in mind, When their races Ottr | and
Angantyr tell.

Hyndla spake:

Hence shalt thou fare, | for fain would |
sleep, from me thou gettest | few favors
good; my noble one, out | in the night thou
leapest. As Heithrun goes | the goats
among.

To Oth didst thou run, | who loved thee
ever, and many under | thy apron have
crawled; my noble one, out | in the night
thou leapest, as Heithrun goes | the goats
among.

Freyja spake:

Around the giantess | flames shall | raise,
So that forth unburned | thou mayst not
fare.

Hyndla spake:

Flames | see burning, | the earth is on fire,

And each for his life | the price must lose;

Bring then to Ottr | the draught of beer,

of venom full | for an evil fate.

Freyja spake:

Thine evil words | shall work no ill,

Though, giantess, bitter | thy baleful threats;

A drink full fair | shall Ottr find,

If of all the gods | the favor | get.

9. Prayers to Freyja

Freyja Sing I of Freyja, chief of the
Disir-- well-watchful women! Chief of the
Valkyr, stern battle-maidens. daughter of
Nerthus, mother of all things; child too of Njordr

who rules all the sea-depths; sister of Freyr, the giver of field-wealth; partner of Óðinn, battle-slain sharer. Wild, will-strong woman; weaver of Wyrd and wealth-wearing lady; lover of love-songs; lover of all love. Strong women only following Freyja!

Freyja Hail to Freyja, far-famed goddess, giver of gold, lover of love-poems, stirrer of strife, taker of war-dead. Tears of gold you weep, fair Freyja, bearer of Brisingamen's might. I praise you now, great Vanadis: grant us knowledge, grant us passion. Freyja All hail fair Freyja, peerless Vanir lady; bright-eyed daughter of Njordr, sea-god and wealth-bringer; beloved sister of Freyr, lord of field and folk. Your beauty is far-famed, O radiant Vanadis: many have longed for you, sought you as bride or lover, but only to few have you given of yourself.

Glorious Freyja, shining lady of all love, to you may we turn when our hearts are pierced or worn. Yours are the arts of love, the pleasure of bodies, the sweet and bitter passions that compel us all. Golden-teared Freyja, bearer of Brisingamen; Freyja, mistress of magic and stirrer of strife; Freyja, incomparable goddess, I hail you!

Freyja Hail to Freyja, bright-haired goddess, fire-eyed lady of power and passion. gold and amber tears you shed for love lost; brilliant Brisingamen you bear for might gained. Bold-hearted Freyja, beautiful one, your loved desired by countless men, sought by many, given for your own reasons, at your will alone. Flawless goddess, your gifts abundant and vital enrich and sustain our lives; we thank you for them.

Freyja Hail to Freyja, bright treasure of
Asgardr, fair one, skilled one, sister of Ingvi-
Freyr, beloved daughter of sea-loving Njordr,
lover of Ottr, mate of wandering Ottr, driver of
cats, holder of Brisingamen, strife-stirring
woman, mistress of magics. Radiant Freyja, many
have sought you, sought to claim your hand, your
heart, you might. Many have sought your
wisdom, your lessons, by your will alone may all
these be given. Freyja, glittering goddess, we

thank you for needing that burns through us like white-hot flame, for life-driven passion, precious as gold. In warm skin and quickened breath we know you, in a night of love and a lifetime's desire we seize your gifts.

Hail to Freyja! Freyja Hail to Freyja, fair holder of Brisingamen, mistress of cats, lover of Ottr, wife of Od, child of noble Njordr, sister of deep-hearted Freyr. Wielder of great magics, taker of battle-slain, great Vanadis, your might is known throughout the worlds and is felt throughout the lives of men and women. We know you in love and need, in the heart's sharp edge, in the depth of passion, in the clarity of pain, each tender moment a gift, each agony a lesson, each fall into passion a prayer to Freyja, whose tears of gold fall for love long lost, who knows her children like no other. Hail Freyja!

Freyja, Vanadis, winner of Brisingamen, mistress of Folkvang, hostess of battle-slain, beloved of Ottr, bride of Od, free-hearted goddess, friend of all lovers, granter of our darkest wishes, for your blessings, countless, ceaseless, I thank you. You inspire us to love, you kindle desire in every heart, you persuade and provoke us toward passions tender and savage, sublime and destructive, transcendent and debased. You set us into motion, pushing us toward will and resolve, you move us to action, you show us the vanity of indecision, the folly of hesitation, the sorrow of the missed chance.

Freyja, glorious goddess, you reach into our small sharp hidden places, discovering our most secret fears, making them real, exposing love's fragility, uncertainty, necessity, its substance and its rarity. You tear at wisps of ego, driving us to seek within for what is firmly rooted. Golden-teared one, destroyer of illusion, holder of hearts, you goad us to take the next step, the first step, you soothe us with love's treasures, you inflame us with love's unreason, you hold us steady, Freyja, as we walk between the paths of head and heart.

Freyja Hail to shining Freyja, driver of cats, lover of Óðinn, bride of wandering Ottr, holder of peerless Brisingamen, holder of the hearts of lovers, holder of the souls of warriors, mistress of sturdy, high-walled Folkvang, goddess on whom we all call for aid when love and lust have sent us to madness.

Glorious Freyja, fair one, free one, mighty one, desirable one, peerless beauty whose glance could shake the foundation of any certainty, clear-sighted goddess whose sharp eyes pierce any veil of feeling, whose keen wit perceives what others may hide, who knows the worth of pain in truth, who knows the price of joy in falsehood, who portions each as deserved, as proper. Freyja, kind yet brutal, tender yet severe, player at games of love and of war, of all life's trials, you give to us the sharpest, of all life's treasures, you give to us the sweetest. Hail Freyja!

Hail the Lady of the Vans! Freyja Hail to Freyja, warm breath of life, child of earth and sea, amber-teared goddess, strong-willed driver of cats, watchful wife of wandering Od, holder of Brisingamen's might, chooser of the best of warriors. With eyes soft or steely, your gaze melts the strongest of us, bends us to your will, persuasive Freyja. With touch firm or gentle, your hand guides those you favor to victory. A tongue sharp yet sweet, a keen wit ready for any challenge, a depth of soul unmatched by any-- all these we know in you, fair one. Bright-haired Freyja, we honor you.

Freyja Hail to Freyja, noble mistress of
Folkvang, daughter of sea-faring, wealth-giving
Njordr, sister of mighty Freyr, granter of good,
holder of peerless Brisingamen, driver of cats,
skillful stirrer of strife, desired by many, taken by
none, given only to few, only by your will. Freyja,
we know you in the spark of lust in lovers' eyes, in
each quick step toward self, in the first heart-
lightening signs of spring, in all the needs that
drive us together and in all the needs that turn us
away. Gold-teared Freyja, beautiful goddess,
we thank you for your many gifts.

Freyja Hail to shining Freyja, light of fair Asgardr, amber-teared goddess who holds the hearts of men. Knowing one, canny one, you share with us your might and your insight. Freyja, we feel your hand guiding us through uncertain times; we see your face in sea and sky, we know your touch in wind and rain. Freyja, Vanadis, battle-wise woman, hostess of war-dead, wielder of magics both subtle and plain, granter of boons to those you favor, your courage and your wit inspire us. Golden Freyja, fast friend of lovers, yours is the first spark of any passion, the ember kept warm through long winters, fanned to flame anew each year in spring. Freyja, we thank you for gifts granted, for hearts filled and broken, for warm beds and warm bodies, for the pleasures that bind us together, that bring us to life. Hail to bright Freyja!

Freyja Hail to Freyja, glory of fair Asgardr! We welcome you, we ask your blessing.

Bearer of peerless Brisingamen, embodiment of unknowable might; you know of those things that drive us most, the desires that compel our survival. Wise and willful Freyja, driver of cats, mistress of far-famed Folkvang, granter of our most heartfelt wishes. Hail to Freyja! Freyja

Hail to Freyja, glorious goddess, fair one, wise one, courageous and clever, mighty bearer of incomparable Brisingamen. From the lands of the Vanir you came, Freyja, with knowledge dear and beauty unforeseen. To the Aesir you brought these precious gifts, Freyja, but all things of worth have their price, and all things in the worlds have their time and their end. Freyja, whose tears of red gold flow freely, you measure loss by gain and gain by loss, each taken in turn, a sorrow but not a regret. Freyja, who bears the weight of sacrifice; Freyja, who knows the strength of desire; Freyja, mistress of might both devious and direct, I praise you for all you are, I thank you for gifts granted unasked, for fires that rage within us, for thirsts unquenched. Hail Freyja.

Hail Freyja, peerless goddess, honey-tongued one whose persuasion and guile can charm all the world, fair one whose soft voice hides an iron will and a resolute heart. Freyja, whose hold on the souls of men is firm, whose might and wit are unrivaled in all of Asgardr, who knows the heat of desire and the chill of love lost, we thank you for the sweetest moments of life, for the passions that bring us out of ourselves and into the divine.

Freyja Hail to Freyja, brightest bloom of Asgardr, great and mighty goddess, essence of passion. Freyja, driver of cats, whose steady hand guides us with subtlety and certainty; Freyja, seeker of might and wisdom, who teaches us to understand the cost of what we desire; Freyja, granter of joy and pleasure, who inspires us to relish the gifts of the earth. Freyja, shining one, who holds us in her arms, who sharpens our wits, who for a precious moment lets us see through her eyes the wonders of the worlds. Freyja, daughter of the worthy Vans, holder of mysteries, holder of wisdom, holder of the brilliant Brisingamen, we praise and honor you this day. Hail Freyja!

Freyja Hail to bright Freyja, hail the Vanadis, hail, goddess whose wisdom, might and agile wit work wonders in the worlds. Hail Freyja, whose steady hand makes sure the most headstrong of beasts, whose radiance and grace make silent the most eloquent of men. Hail Freyja, whose voice we hear in the words of lovers, whose heartbeat we feel in the throes of desire. Freyja, shining Freyja, amber-teared goddess who of love and pain knows all. Hail Freyja!

Hailsa, Goddess Freyja...
Hail Freyja...

Printed in Great Britain
by Amazon

little make-up, revealed a number of fine lines and creases, and her greying hair hung limply from a centre parting. She wore a plain, dark blue, two-piece suit over a white linen blouse. The blandness of her attire only served to emphasise the seemingly invisible nature of her presence. As Baz took in her features and tried to remember where she knew this woman from, the subject of her attention looked up suddenly into Baz's quizzical gaze. Baz was immediately startled and taken aback by the piercing intensity of the woman's sharp blue eyes.

Of course, thought Baz to herself with a burst of recognition, *Dr Jennifer Ashfordly, how could I have forgotten?*

In truth Baz had never actually met nor been formally introduced to Jennifer Ashfordly, but she had been pointed out to Baz in the hospital previously. Jennifer Ashfordly, Baz recalled, was often discussed in revered tones around the campus. She was reported to be a legend in scientific circles and was often held up, though allegedly against her will, as a feminist icon. Her battles with the scientific hierarchy were noteworthy. In a male-dominated sphere, she had forced her way to the top, and by all accounts intended to remain there.

'Would you care to explain the nature of your research to the panel?' continued Professor Blackwell-Jones.

'You will have my grant application in front of you, Professor Blackwell-Jones,' stated Baz, trying to appear as professional as possible. 'In it I have presented a working protocol, outlining the background aims and purpose of my work.'

'Indeed so, Miss Clifford,' returned the chairman, flicking absentmindedly through the application. 'However I am quite sure the panel would appreciate hearing about the project from the horse's mouth, so to speak.'

Baz bit hard on her lip. 'Of course, Professor.' But then Baz turned to face Dr Ashfordly as she spoke, deciding in her own mind to seek an ally in her, rather than the elderly professor.

'My thesis involves the investigation of a number of neurotransmitter substances.' She glanced back to Professor Blackwell-Jones, but then continued to address Jennifer Ashfordly. 'Chemicals found naturally within the brain and that are responsible for the transmission of messages from one neurone to another. I am especially interested in the role of these substances in the generation of particular emotions.'

'And how do you propose to explore this?' asked the professor.

'Well,' continued Baz, her confidence growing, 'firstly, I had to obtain samples of brain tissue, given that, at least in the first instance, this is where I might detect changes in the levels of these substances, and secondly, I had to obtain samples from some subjects with documented emotional change and samples from others who did not demonstrate that particular emotion, in other words, a control group.'

'Presumably, then, the samples that you have tested have been from post-mortem material?' asked Dr Morton helpfully.

'Well, I can't see many live brain donors around, can you?' the professor butted in, clearly irritated by the question.

Ignoring the chair's interruption, she went on to explain. 'I have had access to a number of post-mortem samples already, through the department of neuropathology, who, as you know, routinely screen the brain and central nervous system of all unexplained deaths.'

'What good can that be to your research? What sort of emotional upset do you expect to find? People don't die of their moods, you know. Also I suspect that everybody finds death a trifle upsetting, especially if it's their own.'

'I don't think you've quite grasped the issue, Professor. The emotion that I am interested in is fear.'

'Fear? What do you mean, fear?'

'I mean, Professor, the sense of impending doom and destruction. No, actually, I mean much more than that, I mean all those somatic changes that accompany it: the dry mouth, the parched voiceless throat, the pounding heart, the bursting chest and more; essentially I mean all of those sensations that add up to that tiny word... fear.'

'But how does your work on neurotransmitters help our understanding of fear?'

'When you think about it, it's obvious. Where does fear come from?'

'If you think you're going to die or be hurt in some way, then—'

'Exactly!' interrupted Baz.

'What?'

'If you *think*... The point is that if you *think* that you are going to die, then you feel fear. The emotion and sensation of fear originates from the brain itself.'

'Now, I see what you are getting at,' added Dr Ashfordly thinking aloud . 'If the brain is the seat of the feeling of fear, the question must be, what changes within the brain produce the diversity of symptoms associated with it?'

'Precisely.'

'And how are you going about investigating this?'

'Well,' continued Baz, her confidence growing, 'there is some evidence to support the view that the emotion of fear originates from the right temporal lobe—'

'What evidence?' asked Professor Blackwell-Jones.

'Well, for example, there are well-documented reports of certain epileptic patients whose aura before their seizure is one of intense fear. Recent MRI scanning work has revealed many of these patients to have scarring, or more correctly, sclerosis, in their right temporal lobe. EEG work has confirmed that their epilepsy originates from that area. The theory is, therefore, that the increased activity of the seizure in the right temporal lobe enhances the normal activity surrounding it. As the unfortunate afflicted person experiences an intense feeling of fear, it follows that this area, the right temporal lobe, must be the usual site that initiates this sensation.'

'But epilepsy is usually thought of as an electrical disorder?'

'Certainly what we measure on an EEG recording is the normal – or in the case of an epileptic discharge, abnormal – electrical activity, but modern research has lead us to better understanding of the pathophysiological basis for this activity, and that basis is chemical. In recent years a number of the chemicals, the neurotransmitter substances, involved have been identified. Some of these neurotransmitters have been shown to be excitatory and others inhibitory. What I am trying to do is to identify the excitatory neurotransmitter substances involved in the propagation of the feeling of intense fear.'

'So just how do you propose to do that?' questioned Dr Morton.

Baz knew that Dr Morton was already was acquainted with her project and guessed that he was asking the question in order to guide her through the interview.

'Having secured a number of specimens of tissue, I have been analysing cell samples from them with respect to a number of known neurotransmitter substances—'

'This all strikes me as a bit farfetched,' interrupted the Professor. 'What possible benefit can accrue from this sort of work? It's hardly likely that we are going to go around taking brain biopsies from people just to measure their emotional state.'

'With respect, Professor,' Baz lifted herself up in her seat, 'the benefits that this could ultimately result in more than justify the work.'

'How so?'

'Firstly, as you quite rightly say, it seems unlikely that we can obtain brain samples from people just in order to measure their level of fear, or anxiety, or depression or whatever emotional disturbance we can usefully identify, but it might be possible to take a blood sample. If the chemicals involved are secreted to excess, then they may well leak across the blood-brain barrier into the circulation, where we could measure them and hence provide the first truly objective and scientific measure of emotional state.'

'Well, why not do the work on blood samples from the outset then?'

'The chemicals in the blood are too numerous and their concentrations are too small to embark on a fishing expedition. The search has to be more focused. We need to accurately identify the chemical imbalance, if one exists, and quantify it before we can start looking to see if a similar imbalance is present and measurable in the bloodstream.'

'Good point,' rejoined Jennifer Ashfordly.

'Secondly, if we were able to prove that a certain chemical imbalance was present and that this imbalance was the major aetiological factor in the production of the many somatic manifestations of a particular emotional instability, then, given the identification of the neurochemicals involved, it should be possible to manufacture drugs which could increase or decrease, or even block the effects of that substance. This would result in a much more tailored approach to therapeutics than has existed previously. As I understand it, most of the drugs that we use simply alter the body's responses to some of the effects of the condition rather than address the more fundamental issue of the condition itself.'

'Have you investigated any particular neurotransmitters to date?'

Baz glanced round at Dr Morton who had asked the question. She realised that he was now probably trying to move her onto the specifics of her work and away from its more theoretical side, as she was acutely aware that therapeutics was Professor Blackwell-Jones's domain and not one that she was overly qualified to expound on.

'Yes. In fact, I've been able to carry out a number of preliminary analyses. I've been able to detect and estimate the concentrations within neurons of a number of neurochemicals, including the neurotransmitters substances such as dopamine, acetylcholine, glutamate, GABA, that's gamma aminobutyric acid and aspartate.'

'Are there any results that you would like to share with this committee?'

'If you would care to look at appendix A of the grant application, I have included there some preliminary results from our GABA estimations.'

The committee members gathered up and opened the files that lay in front of each of them.

Baz continued, 'I have estimated brain GABA concentrations, in particular the amygdaloid subgroup, from a number of effected cases and from controls. The amygdala, as you know, is in close proximity to the hippocampus, which itself is situated in the temporal lobes. This area has previously been shown to influence cortisol and adrenaline responses from the adrenal gland. So this subgroup does seem the most likely candidate. Obviously, so far the numbers are quite small, only five in each group, but I would hope to enlarge upon these soon—'

'How do you define who is affected and who is a control?' asked Dr Ashfordly.

'In the context of the emotion of fear that we are examining, I have obtained some rudimentary pre-morbid details from the pathologists. They have helped me to classify the samples into those who had demonstrated a propensity to fear before death from those who should not have experienced the emotion.'

'Who would not be afraid before they died?' asked the professor quizzically.

'I take your point, Professor, but those people who died suddenly without warning—'

'As from a sudden cardiac arrest,' interjected Dr Morton helpfully, 'where death is so instantaneous and unheralded the person would not have anticipated it.'

'Exactly,' replied Baz, 'or in people known to have died in their sleep or already in a state of unconsciousness. These people we would not expect to have experienced the sensation nor emotion of fear.'

'That seems a reasonable assumption, does it not?' Dr Morton asked of his fellow panellists. They nodded in agreement.

'The other group, which, if I may, I'll call the "Fear" group, are samples again from the temporal cortex taken post-mortem from people who were known to have died in frightening circumstances, often in road traffic accidents, but in circumstances where it was known that the person had lived and was conscious, if even only temporarily following the event. In these circumstances I made the assumption that these people had been afraid.'

'I don't think that is an unreasonable assumption, given what Professor Blackwell-Jones has already said,' added Dr Morton.

'So turning to my early results, which are presented in table 1.2, you can see that there is a clear separation of the levels of GABA found in the "Fear" group and the control group. The average GABA concentration in the "Fear" group is 120 micromoles per litre compared to less than forty micromoles per litre in the controls. These are, of course, the results of a preliminary analysis only, but it does seem to support my hypothesis that the production and release of the neurotransmitter GABA in the temporal lobe is intimately involved in the sensation of fear. It is this hypothesis that we wish to develop and explore.'

Baz sat back, content that she had presented her case well and having done so, feeling confident of a successful outcome to the interview. At that moment Dr Ashfordly, who had been silent during most of Baz's dissertation, looked up from the file which she had been studying intently. Then, apparently absentmindedly, she asked, 'How specific and sensitive do you think your test is?'

'I think that my method certainly is sensitive enough to detect the GABA that is present,' replied Baz, her confidence now complete.

Dr Ashfordly fixed Baz in a withering stare. 'That is not quite what I meant, Miss Clifford. Do you fully understand the meaning of the terms "specific" and "sensitive" in the scientific sense?'

Baz momentarily taken aback, quickly regathered her thoughts. 'Umm, yes. I think I do.'

'Would you then tell the committee what you understand by those terms?'

'Well, basically, the sensitivity of a test is its ability to detect all the abnormal members. The specificity is the test's ability not to pick out those values that are normal. The specificity and sensitivity of any test taken together, therefore, document the test's abilities in differentiating normal results from abnormal ones.'

'That is indeed, broadly correct. Now, Miss Clifford, so I repeat my original question. How specific and sensitive is your

particular investigation, in other words just how useful, do you think it is in differentiating the abnormal from the normal levels of a particular substance.'

'The work is still in its early days,' Baz realised she was on the defensive now, 'but the initial results, as I have said, do look encouraging. I think you will agree that if the abnormal group average three times the value of the normal group, it does suggest that this test is going to prove both sensitive and specific enough to justify its usage.'

'As you say, the numbers are quite small but, looking at the results in a little more detail, perhaps you would care to go through them with me… Page nine, I think.'

Baz opened her own copy of the grant application.

'Note sample two of the "control" group.'

'Ehh… yes.'

'What is the concentration of GABA from this sample?'

'Umm. It's 134 millimoles per litre.'

'From what you have previously said, that does seem quite high, Miss Clifford, does it not?'

'Well, yes, but when you average across the samples it reduces the impact of one anomalous result.'

'Quite so, but do you see what I'm getting at? This result in your control group is as high, if not higher than many of the results in your study group.'

'Yes…' Baz was struggling and knew she was.

'If that is so, and given the relatively small numbers in each group, it does suggest to me the potential for a very large overlap in results between "normal" and "abnormal". Hence this suggests to me that ultimately this test might prove to be neither sensitive nor specific in the scientific sense. What do you say?'

There was nothing Baz could say. Jennifer Ashfordly's analysis was correct. Baz remained silent just looking from one member of the panel to another as if for guidance.

'I think, if there are no further points or questions for Miss Clifford,' the chairman looked across at his fellow panellists, who shook their heads in turn; he turned again to Baz, 'then perhaps we could let you go. The committee will inform you of its decision in due course. Thank you for attending.'

Baz rose to her feet, a little shakily. 'Thank you,' she replied, if somewhat hesitatingly.

chapter three

Outside the interview room, Baz struggled to regain her composure. Her humiliation was now turning to anger. She wasn't angry at Professor Blackwell-Jones's patronising attitude; that was his way. She wasn't angry with Jennifer Ashfordly for questioning her results; that, after all, was her intellectual grasp of the work in front of her. She wasn't even angry with Dr Morton for not coming to her aid, even when she needed it most; she knew that would have compromised his position on the panel. Mostly she was angry with herself. She had not paid sufficient attention to the anomalous result that had now been highlighted to her and had not been prepared for the questions that followed. She had allowed herself to be ambushed by Jennifer bloody Ashfordly. She was annoyed because she had consciously set out to sway the panel in her favour. Dr Morton was on her side, she knew that, but she had deliberately baited Professor Blackwell-Jones and tried to make an ally instead of Jennifer Ashfordly.

Only for Dr Ashfordly to be the one to rubbish her work.

She felt more like that drink now.

Josh was already in the bar when she arrived. He rose from his seat at the table when he spotted her coming towards him. He smiled broadly. However, his smile faded a little when he saw that Baz did not return the greeting. He opened his mouth to speak as she slumped down in the chair opposite his.

'Don't ask,' she said, raising the palm of her hand in Josh's face. 'Just don't ask. Okay? Mine's a gin and tonic if you are buying… and make it a large one.'

Baz's mood hadn't improved by the time Josh returned with the drinks. She remained slumped in her seat, scowling at the beer mat that she slowly and methodically was ripping to pieces with her hands. Placing Baz's gin in front of her, Josh sat down meekly across the table. Several silent minutes passed before he plucked up the courage to speak.

'Did the interview not go as well as you had hoped?' he asked, somewhat unnecessarily.

Baz shifted her scowling gaze from the unfortunate beer mat and fixed it on Josh instead. Several more minutes passed in silence as Baz sipped at her gin and tonic.

As the effects of the alcohol started to perfuse her system and to make inroads into her melancholia, Baz finally spoke. 'I'm sorry. I didn't mean to take it out on you, but no, the interview did not go well. In fact, I think that I completely blew it. Firstly, I managed to piss off Professor Blackwell-Jones—'

'Blackwell-Jones is a past-it old fart anyway, don't worry about him.' Josh lifted an undamaged beer mat and placed it carefully under Baz's glass.

'That's as may be, but then I made a complete ass of myself in front of Dr Morton and Jennifer bloody Ashfordly.'

'Jennifer Ashfordly. Geeeez.' Josh whistled through his teeth. 'Jennifer Ashfordly, now she is a force to be reckoned with.'

Baz stared blankly into her glass as he spoke.

'I wouldn't have wanted to get on the wrong side of Jennifer Ashfordly. I guess you're right, Baz, you've blown it. Still, it might have been a short career, but I hope you feel it was worthwhile nevertheless.'

Baz looked at Josh quizzically.

'Well, you do know that she is the current Vice-Chairperson on the National Research Evaluation Committee as well as probably one of the country's most respected female medical scientists?'

'Yes, yes… well, no… actually, I didn't know all that, but I have heard of her before, you know.'

'Also,' Josh continued, 'it is rumoured that she has been put forward as a Grand Master in the local branch of the Masons.'

'I don't believe it, surely the Masons is a men-only organisation?'

'New EU rules state that private clubs can no longer discriminate on the grounds of sex. Look what's happening in golf clubs. Besides, if you were a Mason and were being forced to admit women into your society, what sort of female would you choose? Surely Jennifer Ashfordly would represent a reasonable compromise?' Josh leant forward and beckoned Baz to do likewise, then whispered in her ear, 'Rumour has it that she's got balls, you know.'

Baz leant back and laughed. 'You're having me on, aren't you?'

'Just trying to cheer you up. Everybody knows that your project's got potential. There isn't a cat's chance in hell that that committee would turn you down. Besides, Dr Morton is on your side, he won't let them.'

'You weren't there, you don't know how stupid I was.' Baz banged the table with her fist and then glanced around the bar, embarrassed by the noise.

'I can believe that you could get flustered and maybe said the wrong thing in an important interview, but I can't believe that those on the panel wouldn't make allowances for that.'

'Oh, anyway, let's not talk about it anymore. It's my round, what do you want?'

'I haven't finished this one yet, but alright, if we agree not to talk about your interview anymore. Mine's a pint of bitter.'

chapter four

It was apparent that Baz was still feeling the effects of the night before when she arrived at the laboratory building the next morning. The tell-tale signs were there for all to see. For a start, she was twenty minutes late, and Baz was renowned for her punctuality. She lacked her accustomed glow, replaced as it was with a sallow pallor, and she only mumbled a reply to the cheery greetings of her colleagues. Josh had noted her arrival and made his way down to her workbench, at which she now sat, head in her hands, bowed over a collection of papers scattered in front of her.

'Good morning.'

'What's good about it?' She groaned and squinted through her fingers.

'Hungover, eh?'

'You should know, you were there.'

'I did tell you to slow down.'

'I know, I'm sorry. It wasn't your fault.'

'And I did say that those mojitos weren't a good idea, especially on top of the gin and tonics.'

'Okay, okay. No nagging. They seemed a good idea at the time. Anyway, if you've just come over here to gloat, you can clear off. I've work to do.'

'No, the gloating is just an added extra. I have a message for you.'

'A message? From who?'

'Dr Morton.'

Baz slumped in her seat and buried her head further in her hands.

'He wants to see you. As soon as you came in, he said. That was about half an hour ago.'

'That's just what I need right now. An interview with the boss.' She slumped further on her seat. 'He's going to take me apart over yesterday's interview.' She rose from her work stool. 'It's been nice knowing you.'

Baz made her way dejectedly down through the laboratory and up the stairs at the far end. The top of the staircase opened onto a small corridor along the sides of which, interspersed at intervals, were the doors to a number of offices. Dr Morton's office was at the far end of the corridor. Reaching it, she knocked. A shrill voice bade her entry. As she pushed her way through the door, the owner of the shrill voice looked up from her desk.

'Yes?'

Baz recognised her as one of a group of secretaries that she often saw lunching together in the hospital canteen. She hadn't realised that she was Dr Morton's personal secretary, as he himself had usually visited Baz in the laboratories unaccompanied. On the rare occasion previously when she had been to his office, it had been an older lady in attendance.

Presumably, Baz concluded, she had now retired to be replaced by the younger – if, in truth, only slightly younger – woman, now in front of her.

'I'm here to see Dr Morton.'

'Is he expecting you?' the secretary asked somewhat suspiciously.

'I got a message he wanted to see me.'

'And you are?' The secretary assumed an air of superiority.

'Baz Clifford.'

The secretary pressed a button on the intercom machine on her desk, paused for a few seconds and then spoke into it. 'Dr Morton, there is a Miss Clifford here to see you,' and then added, somewhat superciliously, 'She doesn't have an appointment.'

'Thank you, Mrs Stoker, sorry, Cathy,' came the reply from Dr Morton, clearly not yet sure how to address his new employee. 'I'll come and get her.'

The door at the side of the outer office opened and Dr Morton appeared. 'Baz, thanks for coming. Please come on in.'

The friendliness of the greeting surprised Baz. Nevertheless, she was pleased by it, especially so as when she turned to join him, she witnessed from the corner of her gaze the displeasure it appeared to cause his secretary.

'Have a seat. You can probably guess why I wanted to see you.'

'Yesterday's interview?'

'Exactly so. Anything you want to say about it?'

'Well, it wasn't exactly my best performance and Dr Ashfordly caught me out on the analysis of the results, but I realise where I went wrong and I will do better the next time, I promise.'

'There won't be a next time, Baz.'

The colour drained from Baz's face. She knew herself that she had messed up the interview, but she had presumed that there would be other opportunities, other grants and other interviews. After all, her PhD project had already consumed so much of her time that she was determined to get it finished and she was, after all, nearing the home straight. She was not going to be thwarted now... or was she? Was she to lose her place at the Brightman Institute after all?

Dr Morton had noted Baz's change of complexion and added quickly, 'What I meant to say, Baz, was that there is no *need* for a next time...'

Baz regarded him quizzically.

'You got your grant.'

'What?' Baz felt suddenly elated. 'You mean they supported my project after all?'

'Of course they did. It's a very worthwhile exercise, you know that, I know that, and the panel recognised it as such.'

'That... That's fantastic.'

'But listen, Baz, you were right when you said that your performance yesterday was not your best. I have to say, I am a little disappointed in you. Professor Blackwell-Jones is one of the most respected academics this institute has and to bait him the way you did did you absolutely no favours. Also Jennifer Ashfordly was quite right in her criticism of the way that you had not appreciated the significance of that anomalous result. I would have hoped that you would have been a lot better prepared for such questions.'

Baz's elation was immediately tempered by the validity of Dr Morton's criticism.

'Perhaps you could, as a start, go back and re-examine that apparently abnormal control sample and then present me with a possible and feasible explanation for the result it produced.'

'I'll get on it right away.' Baz started to get up to leave the office.

'See you do.' He fixed her with a stern stare. But as she turned to bid him farewell, Baz noted that Dr Morton had also permitted himself the inkling of a small smile. Returning to the laboratory, Baz went straight down to see Josh. She could tell by the look on his face that he had probably already guessed how the meeting had gone. She supposed that the smile which now lit up her former pale complexion had told him all he needed to know before she even had had a chance to speak.

'Good news?' Josh flashed a white smile.

'I got the funding after all.' Baz tried in vain to contain her excitement. She gripped Josh in the tightest of hugs and burled him vigorously around.

'I told you that you were worrying over nothing.' Josh blushed as he struggled to free himself.

'I've still got a problem to sort out, though.'

'What's that?'

'I have to produce some sort of explanation as to why the GABA level was so raised in that control specimen.'

'Okay, perhaps I can help,' offered Josh hopefully.

chapter five

Baz turned right as she left the laboratory to fetch some books from her locker; as she did so, she spied Dr Jennifer Ashfordly approaching from the far end of the corridor.

'Damn,' she whispered under her breath. She did not relish another confrontation with the venerable doctor.

Looking around for a means to escape, she was about to push open the door to a neighbouring laboratory when Dr Ashfordly, spotting her, shouted in her direction.

'Miss Clifford. Can I have a word?' It sounded more like command than a question.

Baz stopped in her tracks and turned to face the approaching Dr Ashfordly; she forced a smile. 'Of course.'

As she neared Baz, she put out her arm and gently steered her down the corridor in the opposite direction to that which Baz had intended to go.

'Come along to my office. We can talk there.'

Baz did as she was bid, though in truth a 'talk' with Jennifer Ashfordly was the last thing she really wanted.

Opening the door of the office and ushering her in, Dr Ashfordly asked the secretary to fetch two cups of coffee.

'Coffee okay for you?' she asked. 'How do you like it?'

'Just black, no sugar,' Baz replied politely.

The secretary got up from behind her desk and left to fetch the required drinks. She clearly already knew her boss's own preference with regard to coffee.

'Come in, come in.' She guided Baz further into her inner sanctum.

The office was exactly as she would have imagined Jennifer Ashfordly's office to be. It was a little bland; anything and everything within the office appeared ordered and organised. Probably, Baz thought, a reflection of the senior doctor's life in general. Across from the door stood a desk, with a chair front and back. Of the two, the chair on the far side of the desk, where presumably Dr Ashfordly would have sat, was by far the more impressive. Leather-covered, high-backed and dark wooden arms. Behind the desk and resting against the back wall, there were neat bundles of files and research papers, but again they appeared to have been methodically organised into related categories. A few other individual files lay on top of the large wooden desk, again neatly arranged.

Jennifer Ashfordly made her way around the desk to sit herself behind it; she gestured for Baz to take the other seat. As Baz pulled the chair towards her to allow her room to sit, she noticed around the walls a series of watercolour paintings depicting a variety of landscapes. They looked out of place and contrasted with the starkness of the rest of the room's interior.

Seeing Baz's confusion, Dr Ashfordly leant across the desk towards her. 'They're mine,' she said.

'Of course they are.' Baz regained her composure. 'I didn't think they came with the office.' She laughed softly.

'No, I mean, they are mine. I painted them.'

'Oh...'

'Not what you were expecting?'

'Errr... Not really... I mean...' She tried to explain what she did mean but couldn't find the words.

'My reputation, I suppose.' She looked at Baz as she sat opposite her, looking around the walls once more. 'I'm supposed to be a hard-nosed bitch. Isn't that what they say about me?'

'Yes... I mean no, I mean...' Baz was floundering.

'Look, Barbara, I may call you Barbara?'

'I'd prefer Baz... If that's alright.'

'That's fine, Baz it is.' Though she didn't look entirely comfortable with it. 'I know exactly what they think of me... Baz,' she continued. 'It's not easy being a woman in a man's world. I'm sure you realise that.'

Baz nodded.

'But it was even harder when I started out, you had to develop a shell, a hard exterior, if you were going to survive. That's what I did, and you will probably have to. But it's hard to shake off once it's established. The art side of things, that's my way to relax.'

'They're very good,' offered Baz, though she actually found them a little old-fashioned and she was still struggling to imagine Jennifer Ashfordly standing at an easel and having a softer creative side.

'They're not. But I enjoy the effort they take and the way they can take my mind off work.' She paused, then continued, 'But I didn't invite you in to discuss the merits or otherwise of my art.'

'What did you ask me in for then, Dr Ashfordly?'

'Call me Jennifer. Please.'

Baz nodded. 'Okay.' But in reality, she didn't feel comfortable calling her senior by her first name.

'Well, Baz, tell me about yourself, what you want to do after you finish here?'

'I need to get my PhD first.'

'That's a given, but afterwards?'

Baz shifted in the chair and wrung her hands; she was embarrassed to express her wishes in front of somebody who had just rubbished her current project.

'I suppose I would like to utilise the skills I've picked up here and maybe become a forensic scientist.'

'That's a good ambition.'

The coffees arrived, breaking up the conversation. Having offered each their cup, the secretary shuffled back out of the room, but not before giving Baz a look that suggested she was not in the habit of supplying research students with drinks.

'I hope we weren't too hard on you today, Miss Clifford.'

Baz noted the reversion to the more formal address.

'But it is important that you appreciate the significance of abnormal results. That is what I wanted to have a chat about.'

'Okay.'

Dr Ashfordly put her cup down and, leaning on her elbows, clasped her hands and leant even further forward towards Baz, as if to emphasise the importance of her words. 'Abnormal results,' she continued, 'are often the most important results. It is often the unexpected that sheds the most light on a theory or experiment. In the interview, I must say, I was a little disappointed that you hadn't appreciated the potential of that anomalous result.'

'I gathered that.' Baz felt more uncomfortable now.

'So, what would a qualified forensic scientist do?'

Baz struggled to find the answer.

'They, or indeed she, would go back and start again, I suggest. Do you not think so, Miss Clifford?'

'Dr Morton said the same thing,' she replied.

'Well, I suggest you get on with it then.'

Baz hadn't quite finished her coffee, but she realised that the interview was over.

As she rose to leave, she once again scanned Jennifer Ashfordly's pictures hanging around the office. *Hidden depths,* she said to herself. *So deep I've yet to see them.*

Baz and Josh spent the remainder of the day trying to locate any residual tissue from the troublesome control sample. They were fortunate enough to track down one remaining small piece of brain tissue dating from the original post-mortem. It was still in its frozen state preserved for possible future investigation and therefore was essentially untainted in terms of their own neurotransmitter estimations.

Baz first carefully thawed the sample, as she had done in her initial experiment, and then started to process the remaining cells. Firstly, she broke down the cell walls using chemical degradation. Then, having freed the intracellular contents into a soup of their own organelles, mitochondria, DNA and cytoplasm, she centrifuged the lot in order to separate out and remove the more solid structures. This left a clear supernatant which should, as her thesis surmised, contain a solution containing the neurochemical substances, which, of course, were the target of her research and which had previously suffused the by now-emulsified cells.

Josh carefully transferred the supernatant for analysis by spectroscopy, then he and Baz waited as the diffusion gradients appeared slowly on the paper read out in front of them. They tested, repeated, retested and conferred, but no matter what, there were small differences in the results; there was little doubt that the GABA levels were consistently elevated above the generally accepted norm.

'Okay,' exclaimed Josh, throwing his arms in the air, 'the result was right. We've redone it over and over again and it always comes out high. So the fault's not in your estimation of the level. It must be high for some other reason.'

'What other reason can there be?' Baz hung her head and sighed in exasperation.

'What do you know about where the sample came from?'

Baz lifted her head and looked thoughtfully at Josh. 'Hang on, I've got a PM summary from the pathologist somewhere.' She rose quickly and walked towards the filing cabinets on the back wall of the laboratory. She felt Josh watching her as she weaved her way deftly between the desks and discarded stools.

'What's the reference number on that bottle?' she called over her shoulder as she pulled open one of the heavy drawers and started to flick through a bunch of files.

'Mmm... BA-1247-99.'

'Yes, I've got it. Here it is...' came back the triumphant cry a few moments later.

Baz brought the small 7x5-inch piece of card back to the table where Josh had remained seated. It contained only the briefest of summaries from the pathologist, Dr Brian Milligan MD FRCPath:

BA-1247-99
Caucasian female, 31 years of age.
No previous medical history.
Death due to hypoxia, whilst in a state of unconsciousness.

Across the bottom of the card somebody had written in blue ink freehand: 'Control'.

Baz presumed the writing to be that of her boss Dr Morton who had obtained the samples, classified them when he had initiated Baz's project.

'What does hypoxia mean?' asked Josh.

'It simply means that the brain was starved of oxygen,' explained Baz thoughtfully. 'But nothing here explains our abnormal result. If, as it says here, she was unconscious at the time that the hypoxia occurred, then she wouldn't have known about it and therefore couldn't have been afraid, could she?' It was a rhetorical question and asked more in anger and frustration than anything else. 'It looks as if my hypothesis is flawed after all.' Her despair increased.

'But,' Josh cut into her self-pity, 'there are so few details in this summary, there may be more to this than meets the eye. For example, was she really unconscious? If so, why was she unconscious? And for how long? Those are things that could have altered your findings, aren't they?' He said the last sentence sheepishly, as if he was acutely aware of saying something stupid.

'You're right! Of course, Josh, you're a genius. Of course there could be other confounding factors.'

'So why don't you ask Professor Wilson, he might know what other things might cause a rise in GABA.'

'Who's Professor Wilson?'

'How long have you been here? And you don't know the eminent Professor Wilson?'

'Okay, okay. Just tell me.

'Professor Wilson is a senior physician at the hospital. He had been heavily involved in research in his younger days, but he's largely given that side of his work up, that's probably why you haven't come across him. But he is a recognised expert in the field of neurochemistry.'

'What are we waiting for?' Baz was already halfway out of the door.

Professor Wilson, stooped, grey-haired and heavily lined, ushered them into his small office without undue ceremony.

'What can I do for you two?' He smiled benignly despite the uninvited intrusion. 'I don't get many young researchers beating a trail to my door these days.'

Baz explained the problem.

The older man stroked his chin and considered things carefully for a number of minutes and then, looking up, replied, 'Neurotransmitter substances can be very volatile and their levels may be affected by a variety of extraneous conditions or substances. Do you know, for example, how the subject died?'

'Hypoxia is all I know.'

'Hypoxia, as in lack of oxygen to the brain. I'm afraid hypoxia can occur in a variety of modes and circumstances. You will need more details, young lady, before you can be sure that the mode of the death itself didn't influence your finding.'

'I thought as much myself.'

'If you can get details, they should be as complete as possible. You would need to know not only the circumstances of death but also whether, for example, the subject had been taking any medications or drugs. Ecstasy, for example, could push neurotransmitters like GABA through the roof; even some prescribed medications I could think of would have the potential to produce similar effects. Did the deceased have any other pre-existing illness? One might imagine that renal or liver disease would affect the excretion or the metabolism of substances such as GABA, changing its estimable level.'

Baz had to admit that she didn't know the answers to his questions.

'Well then, I suggest you try and get as much detail as you can and then come back to me.'

'You're right, of course.' Baz sighed. 'I hadn't really given full thought to the possibility of so many other compounding factors.'

As Baz and Josh left the office, Baz's despair was obvious.

'Cheer up, Professor Wilson's given you something else to think about, that's all.'

'Oh yeah, except there's no way we can get the information he's suggested that we need. Damn, damn and double damn. If only we could get our hands on some more detailed information about the circumstances surrounding the death.'

'You could, if you could get hold of the full post-mortem file and any available medical records of the subject.'

'I'd have to request them and with all the bureaucracy involved it could take months and months, and even then, they probably wouldn't release them to me, as I'm not medically qualified.'

'Maybe I can help you there,' Josh offered eagerly.

'How?' Baz looked at him inquisitively. 'You've got no access to pathology.'

'I haven't, but I know a man who can, as the saying goes.'

Baz stared at him.

'There's a mate of mine who's a technician in the path labs, he owes me a favour. In theory, at least, all the relevant details should be stored there. The pathologist would have had to have access to all the information in order to come to a conclusion for the PM. I'll see what I can do.'

Baz detected that Josh was keen to help her as much as he could, but she wasn't sure that she should ask him to get involved. Especially as it could cause trouble for him. She was acutely aware, but uncertain if Josh himself knew, that access to pathology files and medical records was very strictly controlled. Any unauthorised exposure of such information could result in instant dismissal.

'He won't be allowed to read the files, they're strictly confidential.'

'Look, I'll just persuade him to let you into the path lab after everybody else has gone home and then you can have a quick peek at the relevant file to see if it reveals any important new details of the case. If there are, you could then request the files formally, but at least you'll have a head start. Whose confidentiality are you encroaching on anyway? She's dead, for Christ's sake. A corpse is unlikely to complain.' Josh shrugged.

Baz remained concerned. She knew that hospitals have strict rules and regulations, ones that in many ways appear antiquated; nevertheless, rules and regulations which are in place and are strictly adhered to. Those rules and regulations that protect and respect the individual's right to privacy are considered paramount and are jealously guarded. Baz was only too aware that although the individual was dead, nonetheless those rules still applied and what Josh proposed could jeopardise the hospital's integrity. Despite her misgivings, Baz felt the excitement in what he proposed, and she couldn't suppress that excitement nor indeed her growing curiosity to find out the exact origins of sample two.

The next day, as Baz returned to the laboratory, she was met by an excited Josh, who rushed out of his office to greet her. 'It's on,' he gushed.

'What's on?'

'You know.' He leant closer and whispered, 'What we talked about yesterday.'

Josh ushered Baz into his office and closed the door behind her.

For the rest of the day Baz found herself distracted, unable to concentrate on her work. Her mind continually drifted back to the risk she was taking. But she rationalised that she had been charged with explaining her results and that is what she had to do.

She jumped involuntarily at the soft touch on her shoulder. She whirled round. It was Josh.

'Come on, let's go,' he hissed through his teeth.

Baz looked at her watch: 11.30 am. 'Won't there be people around the department at this time?'

'Bob phoned, apparently they've all gone to a clinico-pathological case conference and they'll be away for the next hour or so. So if we're quick, we can be in and out before they get back.'

Bob, Josh's friend, met them as they turned the corner from the underground walkway that connected the hospital to the department of pathology. It was a dank and dismal tunnel well suited to the passage of corpses which constituted its main traffic. Bob, it turned out, appeared to be well-suited to his role of mortuary attendant. He was about six foot tall, but stooped so he appeared shorter, painfully thin with greasy dark hair, plastered down on his head above a pasty complexion. Bob did not speak much, rather he intimated his wishes by a series of grunts or nods of his head. He grunted and motioned in the direction of a door at the end of the corridor.

After entering the small office beyond, Bob continued to hover by the door, shifting rapidly from foot to foot, his gaze fixed firmly on the floor between his feet. Josh rushed forward and started eagerly pulling open the drawers of a filing cabinet which stood against the back wall. He asked Baz to help him.

'What was that reference number?' as he flicked through a large bundle of files.

'BA-1247-99.'

'Got it,' exclaimed Josh, triumphantly pulling out a plain manila A4 file.

Baz snatched the file from him and started to thumb expertly through the pages. Head down, she engrossed herself in the facts contained in the bundle of typewritten pages. She made the occasional note in a small pad she had brought with her for the task. She was so absorbed by the file that she didn't hear the office door being opened.

'What's going on here?'

Baz looked up hurriedly. A heavyset, middle-aged man in a white coat glared at her from the doorway; Bob had retreated to the far wall of the office, where he now stood and shuffled even more rapidly from foot to foot. Baz recognised the newcomer instantly as Professor Clayton, Head of Pathology and the owner of the office.

Professor Clayton strode purposefully towards Baz and snatched the opened file angrily from her grasp.

'Just what do you think you are doing with this?' His face contorted, red with anger.

'Umm, err. I was just doing a bit of background research, Professor.'

'This...' He waved the file widely around above his head. 'This, young lady, is a confidential medical record. You have no right to open it.' He glanced down at her identity badge, relieved, Baz thought, to find that at least she was on the hospital payroll. 'Just who are you, anyway?'

Baz caught sight of Josh edging his way gingerly towards the office door.

'I'm a PhD student with Dr Morton.' Baz blushed.

'So what exactly were you doing with this file?' continued the professor, unimpressed.

'I have just been doing some studies on a sample we'd received from this patient, Professor,' Baz thought it wise to try to be deferential, 'and the sample kept throwing up some strange results. Dr Morton had asked me to get to the bottom of it, and so I was simply trying to get a bit more background information on the patient, that's all.'

'You still have no right to look at these files without permission.' He replaced the file into its original position in the open drawer of the filing cabinet and then slid the drawer firmly shut, locking it with a key he pulled from his pocket. Then he swung around to face Baz once more. 'And Dr Morton should know better than to tell you otherwise. I'll have to speak to him about this.'

'Um, I don't think it's exactly Dr Morton's fault, Professor,' stumbled out Baz.

'That's as may be, but I don't want to hear anymore. Just get out.'

The three made their way sheepishly towards the door.

'Not you, Bob. You stay here.'

Bob stared hard at the floor and fidgeted wildly, wringing his hands and shifting his weight from one leg to the other.

'Sorry, mate,' whispered Josh over his shoulder as they filed out.

Back in the lab, Baz hoped that Bob wouldn't lose his job. Though in truth, she had found it hard to warm to him.

'Don't worry about him,' Josh smiled benignly. 'Sure, he'll get a bollocking, but he organises that whole department. Without him they'd be lost and they know it.'

Baz couldn't imagine Bob organising anything, let alone the department of pathology, but she let it drop.

'So was it useful?' asked Josh excitedly.

'A definite maybe,' she replied.

chapter six

Baz fluffed up the bulky pillows and propped herself up on them. She started to flick through the pages of her notebook, squinting as she did so, the small bedside light affording only the minimum of illumination. She added to the hastily made scribbles as she remembered other details from the file. Her notes had been of necessity sketchy but, she was gratified to find, contained nonetheless some of the more salient features of the case. There were other aspects, more in the detail rather than specifics, that she now recalled and busily wrote down in longhand, before her memories faded.

Mrs Catherine Marsden
Brook Cottage, 43 Woolmart Lane
East Brookfield
Date of birth: 10/03/1984
Date of death: 14/10/2016

The words seemed to leap out of the page towards her. Previously it had only been about a piece of amorphous tissue in a laboratory bottle; now, all of a sudden, it concerned a human being, albeit one no longer alive.

It had been a coroner's post-mortem. It had to be, because Catherine Marsden had died suddenly and unexpectedly, and she had died outside the confines of a hospital, therefore with no immediate medical attendant. All such deaths would, as a matter of course, Baz knew, be referred to the coroner, who has a statutory duty to establish the cause of death. Even more so when, as in this case, the cause has been due to outside influences. In Catherine Marsden's case, a house fire. Nothing, therefore, unusual in that. According to the pre-morbid history, Catherine Marsden had been perfectly fit and healthy; indeed, the last recorded attendance to her general practitioner had been with a sprained ankle two years previously. She had no other known illnesses and was not taking any form of prescribed medication. *Nothing, therefore, to account for the raised GABA in the tissue sample*, thought Baz, recalling the conversation with Professor Wilson. There had followed four A4 sheets of closely typed pages containing the anatomical findings from the post-mortem itself. Baz had made a short précis of these but again, not unexpectedly, most of the findings had been entirely within normal limits. A toxicology screen alone had revealed one positive finding and that was only a blood alcohol level in the moderate to high range, but there were no traces of illicit or other drugs.

However, microscopic inspection of brain and body samples had confirmed changes typical of oxygen starvation before death. In addition, there was evidence of charring to the face and other areas of the skin due to close proximity of a fire. There had been no obvious trauma or bruising apart from evidence of an earlier minor head injury, but not one of sufficient severity to cause death or prolonged unconsciousness, and really little else to find to suggest an alternative cause of death. The only anomaly, if it was an anomaly, were the findings in the lungs, or rather the lack of findings, i.e. the lack of smoke damage.

The pathologist's, a Dr Brian Milligan, conclusions had been that Catherine Marsden's death had been due to hypoxia. She had been starved of oxygen due to a house fire in which she had been trapped. The post-mortem results did not suggest anything different nor indeed unusual.

The file had also included the proceedings of the coroner's court held a couple of weeks later.

The police had not regarded Catherine Marsden's death as suspicious, but they had carried routine enquires. Baz had noted down the investigating officer's name:

Detective Inspector Denis Warlow,
Bridgetown Police station.

Under the name, she now scribbled some further details. According to the investigation, Catherine Marsden had been alone in the house, asleep upstairs in her bedroom, sleeping soundly, perhaps due to the effects of the alcohol that she had consumed earlier in the evening. A fire had broken out. From the forensic evidence, the seat of the fire appeared to be a wastepaper basket in her bedroom. It was presumed that Catherine Marsden, a known smoker, had discarded a cigarette. This had set alight a newspaper paper and then the flames had quickly spread to the curtains, causing the room to fill with smoke. Altogether a tragic but common enough scenario.

The alarm had been raised by neighbours, who had seen the flames at the bedroom window. They had been unable to enter the house as the front door had been locked. The fire brigade had arrived, forced an entry and found Catherine Marsden in the bedroom unconscious. Despite their efforts at CPR and the frantic efforts of Catherine's husband, a GP who had arrived home just after the fire brigade had arrived, Catherine Marsden died at the scene.

The police had been satisfied that there were no signs of foul play and that the death had been simply due to a terrible accident.

'Death by misadventure' was the recorded verdict of the court.

Baz set the small notebook down on the bedside table and flicked off the light. She fluffed up her pillows once more and snuggled down deep into her duvet. However, despite her best efforts to make herself comfortable, she knew that sleep was still a long way off.

Baz had not chosen her career as a medical scientist through some higher altruistic ambition 'of helping others less fortunate than herself', rather she had drifted into it simply because she had, from an early age, shown an aptitude for that sort of work. Scientific research, it is often said, is one per cent inspiration and ninety-nine per cent perspiration. Above all else, the work requires an ambition borne out of a single-mindedness bordering on obsession. More often than not it is a series of usually mind numbingly boring experiments in order to move one tiny step closer to proving (or indeed disproving) the hypothesis under examination.

Baz's character and personality, she had realised from an early age, was well-suited to this form of single-mindedness; once she had set her mind on a task she could not, nor would not, be deflected from it until that task was finally completed. This characteristic of dogged determination was in her genes and it wasn't going to desert her now. Baz had been stung by

Dr Ashfordly's criticism and had been charged with the task of explanation by Dr Morton, and so it was that she tossed and turned, unable to get over to sleep, her mind racing from one question to another. The contents of the file had not, as she had hoped, provided her with the immediate explanation that she had sought. The only 'drug' involved had been alcohol and she knew from basic neurophysiology that alcohol, despite the most people's perception of it, is in fact a central nervous system depressant, not a stimulant, and therefore would not have raised the levels of GABA in the brain tissue sample. Logically, in fact, alcohol should actually have depressed, not elevated the reading. No, that wasn't the answer. Unfortunately nor did the facts surrounding Cathy Marsden's death shed any light on Baz's anomalous test result.

Baz flicked the light back on. She opened her notebook once more and tried to remember more of the detail. She couldn't be absolutely sure, but she was convinced that the file did not provide sufficient detail to prove that Catherine Marsden did not wake up, did not become aware of her plight and was not acutely frightened by the blaze. *Why*, she thought, *did the police assume as much?* The more she thought, the more she realised that she needed more information, more detail surrounding the events of that night. With that she turned over in the bed and allowed her thoughts to freewheel around in her head.

The next morning, still groggy from her poor night's sleep, Baz downed a lukewarm cup of coffee and reached for the phone to ring work and call in sick. At least she had managed to come to some sort of decision. It wasn't a very wise decision, in fact, it was, she realised, a very foolish decision, but at least it was a decision.

As she pulled up outside the police station, Baz, who up till then had been consumed by feelings of guilt because she had feigned illness, suddenly found this emotion replaced by a weird and tremulous excitement.

At the front desk she was greeted by a fresh-faced but somewhat bored-looking young constable. Confidently, she asked for Detective Inspector Warlow. The young constable looked at her inquisitively but did as he was bid and lifted the telephone receiver. Baz's confidence deserted her and she shuffled uncomfortably behind the desk.

Looking up, the young constable asked, 'Who should I say wants him?'

'Umm, he doesn't actually know me. Tell him I work in the hospital and it's about information on the death of a Mrs Catherine Marsden. I believe he was involved in the case.'

The constable muttered something into the telephone that Baz couldn't quite catch and then, replacing the receiver, he ushered her through the security door behind the reception desk and pointed out her route to the far end of the corridor beyond.

Before Baz could reach the door indicated by the constable, it was opened by a large doughy mountain of a man.

'Hello, I'm Inspector Warlow,' he said extending his hand, which Baz noted was warm and moist. The top button of his shirt was undone and his tie hung limply below, exposing a roll of fat below his chin. Beads of sweat glistened across his forehead below his balding pate.

'You said that you've got some information on Catherine Marsden?'

Before Baz could correct him, he led her through the maze of desks that cluttered the detectives' room.

'Actually,' said Baz, sitting down and crossing her legs, 'I think we've got our wires crossed.'

'How so?' questioned the fat policeman, carefully lowering himself into his own chair on the other side of the desk and then reached for a pen to make notes on a sheet of paper that he had previously pulled from a drawer.

'Because it's not me that has the information, it's you.'

'Sorry, I'm not with you.'

Baz went on to explain about her research, although she wasn't completely sure that the detective inspector completely understood all that she was trying to convey, but at least he did seem to nod in the right places.

'So basically, what you're saying is that you want me to release to you the details surrounding the death of Catherine Marsden.'

'Basically, yes, but...' Baz looked uncomfortably at her feet, 'not formally release... as such...'

'So just what do you want?'

Baz looked up into the policeman's heavily padded face. 'I thought, maybe just a sort of informal chat, a sharing of ideas, if you like.'

'Off the record, you mean?'

'Well... yes... sort of.'

'Now just why should I do that?'

'Because I think that there is something funny about Catherine Marsden's death and I don't understand why the police inquiry and everybody else just dismisses everything.' Baz bit her lip; she realised she was going out on a limb.

Detective Inspector Warlow's expression darkened. He leant forward across the desk and thrust his face close to Baz's. 'Now, just you look here, young lady. I've been a detective for longer than you've been out of nappies. How dare you come in here and try and tell me my business. That case has been thoroughly investigated by my team and is *closed*.' He emphasised the word closed. 'I have absolutely *no* intention,' again he seemed to dwell on the word no, 'of going back and reopening those files just because of some little whim of yours. In any case, this all happened a long time ago. Do. you understand what I'm saying?'

'But… but…' Baz retreated in her seat.

'Do you understand what I'm saying?' the policeman hissed.

'Okay, okay.' Baz recovered a little. 'Just tell me one thing.'

'What?'

'Why does nobody think that Catherine Marsden woke up during the fire?'

'Very simple.'

'Why?'

'Because, young lady, Mrs Marsden's bed was only three feet from the bedroom door. The door was unlocked. The fire started at the opposite side of the bedroom under the window and it was largely confined to the bedroom. If she'd woken up, all she had to do was slide out of bed and get out of there through the bedroom door. It would have taken her less than a minute to make good her escape. But no, she was discovered still tucked up in her bed. So I don't think she woke up. Do you?'

The detective leant back in his seat and flashed a self-satisfied grin at her.

Having nowhere else to go, Baz decided to return to the laboratory and report a miraculous recovery.

When she got there, she wished she hadn't bothered.

'The boss is looking for you,' said Josh on her arrival, 'and he's not in a good mood.'

Before Baz could decide whether she was in the mood for further dressing down, her decision was made for her, as

Dr Morton appeared at the door to the laboratory, effectively blocking any hope of escape.

'Baz. My office. Now.'

Josh was right; he was not in a good mood.

Baz closed the office door quietly behind her as she slunk in behind her boss. Before she had a chance to speak, Dr Morton growled angrily at her, 'Okay, so just what have you been up to?'

'I'm not quite sure what you mean.' Baz decided to play innocent.

'I've had a call from Professor Clayton in pathology.'

'Oh…' Innocent wasn't going to work. 'I was only doing what you told me to do.' Baz tried confrontation instead.

'I don't understand. I don't recall telling you to break into the path lab and steal confidential notes.'

'I didn't steal anything.' Now Baz felt aggrieved and angry; it suppressed the guilt. 'You told me to investigate the causes behind the abnormal test result and not finding any lab error, I suspected a wrong classification. That was why I sneaked a look at the records. I knew I shouldn't have, but it was the quickest way to try and sort things out.'

Dr Morton calmed down a bit. Baz suspected that he wasn't particularly fond of Professor Clayton; she knew he had always found him to be supercilious to the point of annoyance. She guessed that he was just upset that a member of his staff had given the little weasel the opportunity to complain about his department.

'So did you find out anything useful?'

'Not exactly.' Baz detected the change in her boss's tone. 'Enquires are continuing, as they say.' It was out before Baz realised that she'd said it. She stopped. Dr Morton, only a moment before previously calming down, was now flushed with anger and glared at her again.

'Oh no. No you don't. I do not want any more complaints about members of this department from other members of staff. Just drop it. Drop it now. And I mean right now. Do you understand?'

'But... but...'

'Drop it!' he shouted.

Baz turned on her heel and left the office, slamming the door behind her.

Josh intercepted her as she dashed through the lab. She was aware that tears were streaming down her face. Worse still, her mascara ran like a dark, inky river down her cheeks. Josh directed her into his small office and proffered a handkerchief.

'Don't let him get to you, his bark's worse than his bite. Professor Clayton was round here earlier, shouting the odds and threatening all kinds of things. The boss had no alternative but to make sure he covered his own back by ticking you off.'

'You as well...?' Baz sobbed.

'Naturally.'

'I'm sorry, it's all my fault. I got you in trouble, I didn't mean to.'

'Don't worry about it, I just wanted to help.'

Baz thought that he meant it. 'I'm not giving up, you know, Josh. I'm not.'

'Don't you think you should just drop it? What's the big issue, anyway? It's just one stupid result. Forget it.'

'I can't. I know it was just one test, but that was then, things have moved on.'

'What's the big deal?'

'It's the fly and the tree question.'

Josh looked at her. 'What?'

'The fly and the tree, what do they have in common?'

Josh thought for a moment. 'I've absolutely no idea.'

'They are both alive. That is all the two share.'

'What's that got to do with anything?' asked Josh, now even more confused.

'Don't you get it? The fly and the tree and us, life, that's all we have in common. Now Catherine Marsden hasn't even got that. That sample's trying to tell me something and I owe it to her to find out what.'

chapter seven

'Yo, it's Wanker Walker!'
He heard them before he saw them. He had been slowly making his way home and as was his habit, he was staring down at the paving stones rather than looking where he was going. He lifted his gaze and saw them. Some were standing around, others leaning up against the gable wall of the house at the end of the short street that he'd just turned into.

'Shit,' he hissed under his breath.

There were six of them. All of them wore the same school uniform as he. His was smart, pressed and pristine. Their trousers were creased up at the bottom dragging along the ground, their shirt-tails hung below their scruffy navy blazers and their ties were either missing altogether or tied up impossibly short.

Tommy Hardcastle and his gang, Frankie did not need right now. He spotted Tommy squashing a cigarette under his Dr Martens and pointing directly at him.

Frankie turned on his heel and headed off in the opposite direction. He broke into a run when he glanced over his shoulder and spotted them starting to jog towards him. The pile of books, which he clutched tightly to his chest, as well as the heavy rucksack, thrown loosely over his shoulder, ensured that it was a contest he was never going to win.

He had only run a few yards when he felt his trailing foot being kicked up behind his other leg and he plummeted forward. His arms went out in an attempt to cushion the fall. His books scattered on the ground in front of him. He hit the pavement with a thud and there he lay, curled up in the dust and the dirt. He tasted blood in his mouth and felt pain from the palms of his hands, which had been skinned in trying to save himself.

Frankie sensed rather than saw them gather around above him.

'Steek, you dropped your books,' Tommy Hardcastle sneered.

Frankie started to try to get up. He got onto all fours and then tried to regather the fallen books. Darren Whiteside kicked *GCSE Mathematics* beyond his reach; it skidded off the pavement and onto the road.

'Fuck off.' Frankie glared at him. Darren was a coward, that was probably why he hung round with Tommy and the rest of them. But there were six of them and Frankie wasn't going to push it.

'Don't swear, Wanky. Did your mummy not tell that it's rude to swear?' said Tommy Hardcastle, propelling *A Textbook of Biology* beyond his reach.

'Leave my mother out of this.'

'Okay. Just hand it over and we're gone.'

Frankie knew that it was useless to argue. He bit his lip and fumbled deep in his trouser pocket. Pulling out the crumpled five-pound note, he handed it up to Tommy. Tommy

Hardcastle snatched it eagerly and then regarded Frankie with a look of disdain. 'Is that it?'

'It's all I've got.'

It was the five pounds that he had been saving to buy a new novel and it was all he had. He turned his trouser pockets inside out to show Tommy. He felt a tear well up in the corner of his eye, but he wasn't going to give them the satisfaction of seeing him cry. He wiped it away quickly with his sleeve.

'What's wrong, Wanky? Need a hanky?' Tommy dissolved in fits of laughter at his own joke.

'Wanky needs a hanky, Wanky needs a hanky,' they started to chorus.

Amused at their own cleverness and seeing no extra benefit from taunting him further, they started to amble back to their street corner. Frankie was left to struggle to his feet, gather up his books and head home.

'Francis, look at the state of your uniform! Go upstairs and get cleaned...' Mary Walker's sense of order had been immediately offended by her son's dishevelled appearance as he stood in front of her in the small hallway of their house, but her voice tailed off as she noticed the small steak of blood at the angle of his mouth.

'Francis. What's been going on?' She looked at him sternly.

Frankie just shrugged his shoulders.

'Francis. Have those boys been bullying you again?'

Frankie just shrugged his shoulders a second time. Frankie didn't want his mother getting involved. Not again.

'Francis, tell me.'

'Mum, just drop it, please. It's nothing. I tripped, that's all.'

'Francis. Don't lie to me.'

'I'm not lying.'

'If you are going to lie to me, you can go to your room.'

Frankie just looked at her dumbly.

'Go to your room, now! And don't come down until you're prepared to tell me the truth.'

Frankie, head slumped, trudged slowly across the kitchen. As he neared the door, he heard his mother call after him, 'In the meantime, I'm going to ring that headmaster of yours. He's supposed to have stopped this bullying.'

Frankie whirled around. 'Please, Mum, don't do that. Don't ring the school. It only makes things worse. Please, Mum.' Frankie started to cry. This time the tears streamed freely down his cheeks.

'Go to your room, Francis. I will not have hooligans taking it out on you just because you are cleverer than they are. Mother knows best.'

But that was the whole problem as Frankie saw it. His mother did not know best. When he was younger, he had really believed that she did. He hadn't had a father as such, or at least Frankie couldn't remember him. So his mother had been his only source of reference. Looking back, Frankie was aware that she had been kind, loving and protective of him, but now that he was fifteen, nearly sixteen, he had become increasingly aware of her inability to let go. He thought that she needed to allow him a little more slack, a little more freedom. She was stifling him with her love, with her overprotection. The fact that Frankie was of diminutive build, had busy movements and a voice that hadn't broken fully made him appear more childlike than he felt and certainly didn't help his cause.

'Chriiisst!' he hissed as he pushed open his bedroom door.

He dropped his rucksack to the floor and then laid out his schoolbooks in two neat piles on the small table that served as his desk. He collapsed onto the bed and, laying back, staring at the ceiling, he wiped away any remaining tears with the back of his hand.

'Chriiissst, how I hate her,' he whispered to himself.

His mother wasn't entirely to blame for his recent humiliation, he knew that, but she was a big part of it. She'd said he was being picked on because he was clever. Yeah, he was smart, smarter than Tommy fuckin' Hardcastle, that was true. But half the world was smarter than Tommy fuckin' Hardcastle. Jeez, even Tommy Hardcastle's dog was smarter than Tommy Hardcastle. No, it wasn't just that he was smart, loads of others at their school were smart and Frankie wasn't even top of the class, okay, in some subjects he had to admit was, but not all, and anyway, Aaron Blackstaff generally won all the prizes. So why didn't they pick on him?

Even though Frankie was a bit smaller than his classmates, that wasn't the reason either. No, Frankie knew, and he resented her for it. When he was younger, he hadn't minded. He didn't know any different then. But since he had been going to the comprehensive, it had become completely bleeding obvious.

It was okay in primary school when he had mates he could play football in the breaks with, share comics with and even have round for tea. But even then, some of his friends had found it a bit strange. He remembered his best mate from those days, Simon Fellows. Frankie recalled visiting his house once; all he could remember now was the bustle, the noise of Simon and his two brothers as they rampaged about, not at all like his own house.

Frankie was an only child. But it wasn't just that either. When he'd first arrived at Dale Comprehensive, he had become increasingly aware of his differences from the others there. He didn't share their interests, he couldn't follow their conversations, he didn't understand how they could get so animated about things about which he had no knowledge.

There was little he had to talk to them about. So at first he had remained silent, keeping 'wise counsel', his mother had said. *So much for that piece of fuckin' advice*, Frankie thought. The other pupils had interpreted his silence as aloofness and snobbery. So at first they had shunned him. Then they thought of him as weird, more interested in himself than others. They had coined the terms 'Wanker Walker' or 'Wankie Frankie' to goad him. The nicknames had stuck and now most of the school called him Wankie. Things weren't getting any better and Frankie was miserable. And yes, his mother was definitely to blame.

Perhaps if his father had stuck around things might have been different. But he had left when Frankie was only three. His mother never talked about him; she actively avoided or changed the subject at the mention of him. Frankie reckoned she'd driven him off with her stupid ideas. He rolled over on the bed. *Perhaps if he'd stuck around, he could have talked some sense into her. That's what dads do, isn't it? Talk sense into their spouses? Stop them turning their offspring into little swots and mummy's boys? Yes, she bought me a pay-as-you-go phone, but that was only so she could get hold of me more easily. He'd have made her buy me a proper phone and even a computer. Told her to stop being so bloody stupid. So pig-headed. It's only a bloody computer, he'd have said. Chriissst, it is the twenty-first century after all. God, maybe, just maybe he might even have persuaded her to get a satellite dish. No*, he reflected, *that would be a step too far for my mother! Fuck. Fuck. Fuck.*

Frankie sat up on the edge of the bed for a few moments. Then, remembering his secret salvation, he quietly slid open the drawer of his small desk that sat under the solitary window of his room. He lifted out the books and the pencil case and then eased the drawer out and off its runners. He deftly turned it over to reveal the envelope stuck to its underside by several lengths of clear sticky tape. Carefully, so as not to damage the envelope, he removed the tape until he held the package in his hand. As he looked down at it, he tried to remember what had first drawn his attention to it. It was a simple pale blue envelope, handwritten, very normal-looking. Was it the fact that she had thrown it away without even opening it? Nothing unusual in that; his mother often tossed mail in the bin after only a cursory glance. But this was different; this obviously wasn't a circular or an advert. So maybe that was it? He had seen her flicking through the pile of letters, stopping at this one, opening the cupboard under the sink and throwing it quickly into the wastepaper bin. His curiosity had got the better of him, and as soon as she had stepped out into the hall to fetch her coat, he had retrieved it and hidden it in the pocket of his blazer.

As he opened the envelope, his hand trembled slightly. Gently he withdrew the letter, unfolded it and placed it on the tabletop. Then he sat down and, pulling some schoolbooks closer around him in case she came in, he studied its contents for the umpteenth time.

2 February 2016

Dear Mrs Walker,

I'm sorry to write to you again, John said that I shouldn't, not after you didn't reply to the last letter. He said that we should take your lack of response as a refusal, drop it and not to interfere in your life anymore. But I felt that it was just too important.

I would reassure you that we do not wish to usurp your position in any way and we have no idea if Francis is aware of the truth regarding his birth. But, just to say, that we would go along with any compromise you suggested. It is just that after all this time we feel that we, as a couple, would like to be involved in some way, no matter how small, in his future.

You may well say that we have given up any right to him years ago, that it is too late, that you have loved and cared for him for fifteen years and that you are his true mother. I could not and nor would I dispute that.

As you probably know, long before John and I ever met, Francis was the result of a silly childhood romance and that he was given up as a result of parental pressure.

His existence has been essentially a secret within the family ever since. If it hadn't been for recent events I might never have become aware of Francis's life with you.

In all sincerity I hope that you will allow John and I some role, no matter how small, in his future.

With kind regards,
Cathy Marsden

Then Frankie recalled what it was that had grabbed his attention in the first place. It had been the look on his mother's face when she had come across that envelope in among the pile of others. That look as her mouth fell open, as the colour drained from her features and then the tremble of her hand when she had clearly recognised the writing on the envelope. Quickly she had tossed the envelope unopened into the bin. Frankie had never seen his mother look so afraid before… and it was then that he'd found out that she wasn't even his real mother after all.

chapter eight

Frankie was awoken by his alarm at 7.30am; it was the usual time he got up during the week, at weekends she allowed him to lie on until nine o'clock. He climbed slowly out of bed and trudged to the bathroom. He splashed a little water under his armpits and over his face, then dried himself begrudgingly and wandered back to the bedroom to get dressed. As usual his school uniform hung neatly from the back of the door and a freshly laundered shirt lay folded where she'd placed it on his chair.

As he was sitting on the edge of the bed tying his tie, his mother barged in.

'Can't you knock?' he snapped.

'Don't be ridiculous dear,' giving him a patronising glance. 'What would I possibly need to knock for?'

'Just respecting an individual's right to privacy, that's all.'

'Now you're being silly. I'm your mother. You're my child. There's no secrets between us.'

'I'm nearly sixteen, for Christ's sake.'

'Frankie, dear, don't swear. You know I won't have it. Now, hurry up and finish dressing, your breakfast's getting cold downstairs.' She licked her fingers and then flattened down a clump of hair that had been protruding from the crown of his head.

'Gerroff,' he mumbled as he jerked his head away.

After she'd left the room, he sat on the edge of the bed, just staring at the far wall. As he did so, he thought about the evening before. Although he'd found the letter only a few months ago, that must've been the thousandth time he'd read it. Of course, the first hundred times had been in the early days after its discovery. At first he had carried it around with him, hidden deep in his jacket pocket. Once, he recalled, when he had found himself unable to resist the temptation, he had retrieved it and was secretly reading it at the back of the classroom when old 'Jug-ears' Johnson the geography teacher had noticed his inattention and nearly confiscated it. That had frightened him, as did the thought of his mother finding it, so he had compromised on the idea of concealing it in his bedroom, even though there was still a risk that his mother might discover it there. But his hiding place had been a good one and she had never found it.

Since its arrival, the contents of the letter played on his mind continuously. He had kept a lookout for any more envelopes from a similar source. He was sure he'd seen some, but his mother had whipped them away before he could get near them and he certainly never again got to read one again. That his mother had become cautious he recognised was his own stupid fault. For once, in the throes of an argument, just one of their routine set-tos, he had blurted it out. At first, she'd ignored him. Then, becoming irate, he shouted it out at her.

'Stop telling me what to do. You're not even my mother!'

'Don't be silly, Francis, of course I'm your mother. Who do you think I am, the queen?'

'You're not my mother, not my real mother. I know,' he had said triumphantly.

She had stopped immediately, as if hit by a sledgehammer. 'What do you mean by that?' she had asked, ashen-faced.

He had just stood and looked at her, his triumph draining rapidly.

He knew then that it was true.

'Francis, what do you mean?'

'I… I… saw… a letter,' he had stammered, less sure of himself now.

She regarded him through narrowed eyes. 'What letter?'

Frankie realised he'd gone too far, but he never could lie to his mother. 'It… it said I wasn't your son. It said that I was adopted and my mother wanted me back.'

'That's a lie!'

'No, honest, that's what it said.'

'Yes, yes. I know. I know what it said, and I know you're not lying, but the letter is a lie. Come and sit down, over here beside me.' She'd led him over to the sofa. Tears were now streaming down Frankie's cheeks and she'd tried to dab them away with his handkerchief. Sitting side by side, she had held his hands in hers and looked him straight in the eyes. Then she'd explained it all to him.

She'd told him that it was true. That he was adopted.

The shock that Frankie expected to feel from such a revelation didn't come, he presumed because he'd fantasised and convinced himself of the fact anyway over the last few weeks.

He just looked at her wide-eyed. Tears had gathered now at the corners of her eyes too, as she told him that she'd never meant to deceive him, had always meant to confide in him. But she had wanted to wait until he was a bit older, a bit more mature, and better able to deal with it. She'd promised him, over and over again, as the tears rolled down her cheeks and dripped into her lap, that that was the truth.

'What about my real parents?' he asked, though now, seeing her distress, he felt a little ashamed to do so.

'They're dead.' She held onto his hands more tightly as she replied matter-of-factly.

'But… but… the letter said—'

'Never mind what that letter had said.' She transferred her grip to his upper arms and, turning him towards her, she stared directly into his face. 'It's a lie. It's a lie. That letter you saw. It was not from your mother. She is not your mother. Do you understand me?'

'But… but…'

'Look,' she gripped him even more firmly now as she spoke, 'your mother died when you were just a baby. Harry and I adopted you. You became our son. You are still my son and you'll always be my son. No-one will ever change that. I love you now as much as when I first saw you lying in that cot in the hospital. With the same strong emotion as when I first held you in my arms and cuddled you. Nothing, Francis, nothing, can ever change the way I feel about you. You are my son.'

'But the letter said—'

Her face darkened. His arms hurt where she held on to him. 'That letter's from a deluded, obsessive woman who can't have any children of her own. She's just wants you to be her son. She just knows about your adoption and wants to steal you away from me. Whatever you read in that letter it's a lie. She is *not*,' she emphasised the word not, 'your mother. Do you understand what I'm saying, Francis?'

The last few words had been said with a ferocity Frankie had never witnessed from his mother before. He just sat and nodded dumbly at her.

His mother had been in a black mood for days after that conversation. So much so that she'd sent him to stay with her sister in Essex. That was unusual; normally she didn't like him out of her sight. Nevertheless, it had seemed to work, because on his return she had seemed in much better form. They never again talked about the letter or his adoption. His mother went to great lengths to avoid the subject. Frankie, for his part, didn't divulge that he had kept the letter hidden away from her prying eyes.

Ever since then, however, he had still repeatedly returned to the letter, carefully examining every word.

He stood at the corner of the school playground, leaning back against a brick wall, well away from those playing on the tarmac square. Once again he mulled things over in his mind. Just last night, he recalled, after going through the letter one more time, digesting the contents and then analysing every word, over and over again in his mind. Afterwards, he had replaced it in its hiding place and then, lying back on the bed, he tried to imagine what his real mother and father had been like. He wasn't sure that he had believed his mother when she'd told him that his real mother was dead. He certainly preferred to think of her as still alive and the letter seemed to imply that she was.

He enjoyed fantasising about her and the lives they might lead. Lately this had become his favourite pastime and he could while away many idle hours in its pursuit. Sometimes he thought of his real parents as rich, often successful, occasionally famous, but mostly he just imagined them as loving and caring. Sometimes they were together, sometimes they were living separate lives, but they were always happy and content. He imagined that they might still be good friends even if they were apart. He tried to picture what they looked like. He got up and looked in the mirror, taking in his own somewhat bony, angular face, punctuated here and there by purple spots of acne, and tried to imagine which features he had inherited from his mother and which from his father. His chin was a little prominent, he thought, that must be his father's; his eyes were liquid blue, his mother's, presumably; his forehead, again, father's; but his hair? Dark, lanky and at present, he had to admit as he held up a few stands, a bit greasy; he couldn't attribute it. He usually imagined his mother's hair to be a bright and fluffy blonde, smelling of jasmine. His father's coarse and short. But sometimes his father was blond with Aryan looks; his mother dark and sultry.

He'd been in the midst of these deliberations when she'd come to fetch him. He had looked at her critically, hoping she wouldn't notice. She certainly fell well short of the pictures that he'd conjured up of his real parents. She was older to start with. He'd always known that she was older than most of his classmates' parents. She was, after all, in her mid-fifties. Worse still, she dressed older than her years: silk blouses, knee-length shirts usually of a tweedy material, thick beige tights and sensible flat-heeled leather shoes. His friends at school used to think she was his grandmother, not his mother, and they ribbed him about it.

Once, just once, he recalled, she'd made an effort. It was for a cousin's wedding, he thought; her sister had come to stay and help her get ready. It was she who had persuaded her to dress more attractively.

'Come on, Mary, there's a party afterwards, you never might meet. You've been on your own for far eard her say.

That day she'd put on a dress, one that she'd borrowed from her sister; it was blue and patterned. She'd tied her hair up and even bought a stick of red lipstick. Frankie had thought she was beautiful and had told her so. She'd blushed at that. She'd gone to the wedding but dragged him home only a couple hours later. Later, she'd told him that she'd felt so self-conscious that she couldn't stay any longer.

Now she didn't try any more. Her hair was greyer and was tied back simply in a ponytail. She rarely wore any make-up.

Last night she'd sat on the edge of his bed, arm around his shoulders and talked to him for a while. *At least*, he had thought, *she didn't ring the headmaster this time.*

Then they'd gone downstairs and had tea together. Beef stew, broccoli and boiled potatoes, one of his favourites, eaten off trays which they'd balanced on their laps as they watched *Emmerdale* and *Coronation Street*. He'd had to admit his mother was a pretty good cook, even though she had a tendency to overcook the vegetables, which always seemed to end up limp and faded with yellow edges.

Frankie had lifted both trays, washed and cleared the dishes away. Then he had sat down beside her on the sofa; she had smiled. The opening titles a new murder mystery series were just starting.

Then the screen had gone black.

'Aw, come on, Mum, just this once.'

Mary Walker had gripped the remote control firmly. 'Now, Francis. You know the rules.'

Frankie had known the rules alright. He resented the rules, but he knew the rules, her rules, right enough.

'Go and get your book, I've been waiting all day for the next chapter.'

Frankie had known that it was pointless to argue. She'd just get angry and send him off to bed. So, reluctantly, he'd gone to fetch the book from his rucksack. When he came back, he had sat on the other chair, away from her, and had stared hard at the blank TV screen. Most people were aware of the 9pm watershed; what he had was the 8pm curfew. Occasionally, and it was only occasionally, if there was a wildlife programme or something of an educational nature on later, she might allow him to watch it with her. Every other night, like tonight, he had to read to her. This week it was *Hard Times* by Charles Dickens. *'The book' was always a Penguin classic,* he had thought, *never a Nick Hornby or even a crime novel. No, way 'too frivolous' for her.* Those, he had chuckled to himself, he kept well hidden in his desk at school and only read during break when his classmates were engrossed in discussions of new girlfriends or how to download new games onto their phones.

To oblige her, he had read a single chapter of the novel. He had read it slowly and deliberately, enunciating every word as he did so. The way she had told him to. When he'd finished, he'd looked at her and asked if the television could be switched on again. But he already knew the answer to that question.

She had started to try to engage him in a conversation, something to do with the Victorian utilitarian work ethic as portrayed by Mr Gradgrind in the novel. He really wasn't in the mood and had had about as much as he could take, so he'd made his excuses and simply went to bed.

The next morning, he joined her in the kitchen for breakfast. His mood was immediately lifted by the delicious smell of grilled bacon. He looked in under the grill and was pleased to find that the edges were already curled up and crispy.

'Ow, out of the way or it'll burn. What kept you, anyway? I told you to get down here ages ago.'

He moved aside but didn't reply.

As he sat down at the table she pushed the plate containing the bacon, now wrapped in two slices of buttery toast, towards him, closely followed by a cup of steaming tea. She sat down opposite him and sipped at her own tea.

'What's on at school today?' she asked, trying to make conversation.

He glanced up and looked into her heavily lined face. Her pink cotton dressing gown was buttoned tightly to the neck. 'Nothing much.'

'Why do I bother sending you to that school if you don't do anything there?'

'Good question.'

'Come on Francis, it's not that bad, surely? You're getting good marks and with the O Levels around the corner, things can only get better—'

'They're GCSEs.'

'What?'

'They're called GCSEs. They haven't been "O Levels" for centuries.'

'Whatever. But my point is, I bet those bullies won't be back to school after their exams. Will they?'

'Who cares?'

'Francis, I do. I care. I hate to see you so miserable. If that headmaster of yours doesn't do something to stop those thugs picking on you then I'll have to do something myself.'

'Oh! Just drop it, Mum. Please.'

As Frankie opened the front door to leave, he felt her hand on his shoulder. He half-turned and she kissed him lightly on the cheek.

'Mum! Get off!'

'You used to like being kissed.'

Frankie glanced up and down the street to ensure that nobody had seen her. 'That was then, when I was a little kid. I'm nearly sixteen.'

'You're still my little boy.'

The day hadn't gone too badly. Two periods of science and technology, one each of biology, maths and English. Best of all, no PE. Frankie detested PE. Being a bit smaller, slighter and more awkward than his classmates, he was always last to be picked for any sporting team. Even if it was a mixed team, it seemed to him that some of the girls would be chosen before him. Usually, when there was nobody else left, the captain, whose turn it was next to pick, would look at him disappointedly, as if he would have preferred just to leave him standing there. Mr Flowers, the PE teacher, understood and usually came to the rescue.

'Okay, Frankie, join Andrew's team.'

'Oh. Does he have to, Sir?' accompanied by groans from the rest of Andrew's team.

'Stop that, you lot.'

'Right. You're in nets, Wanker.'

He always ended up as the goalie. Everybody else got to run around the field while he stood freezing between the posts. Nobody else wanted to be there, so he had to do it, even though he was useless at it. It wouldn't be long before he'd let a goal in. Then they'd all stop and stare at him, as if it was all his fault, even though they knew all along that he was no good at keeping goals. But still they wouldn't let him join them on the outfield.

Today was definitely going to be a better day. By lunchtime Frankie was actually in quite good form. He stuffed a novel into his rucksack and slipped unnoticed out the school gates for a short walk to a nearby park to have a read and eat his sandwich.

Even though it was sunny it was quite cold in the clear autumn air and the park was deserted. Frankie kicked a stone ahead of him as he ambled along the leafy path. He looked around for somewhere to sit down. Suddenly, the silence was broken by the shrill roar of a scooter engine somewhere up ahead and coming in his direction. *Shouldn't be in here,* thought Frankie to himself, *it's against the rules.* But Frankie also realised that although he tended to live life by the rules, others didn't, and he for one wasn't going to interfere.

Before reaching him, the engine noise died and Frankie heard voices just around the corner ahead of him. He seemed to recognise the tone of one voice even though he couldn't make out any words.

'Shit,' he whispered to himself as he dived in behind a tree. 'Tommy Hardcastle.'

From his hiding place, he risked a quick look. There were just the two of them. The scooter rider sat astride his machine. One foot on the ground on either side. He was tall and lanky with dirty jeans and a denim jacket. He kept his brightly coloured crash helmet on; Frankie had never seen him before. Tommy was standing close to the scooter, one hand resting on the handlebar. The other he waved about as he conversed with the scooter man. Frankie couldn't hear their conversation. In truth, he'd didn't much care. He just wanted to avoid another thumping from Tommy Hardcastle.

'Aw, go on, please fuck off, why don't you?' he mouthed as he leant back against the tree. He heard his stomach rumble; he wanted his sandwich.

He peered around the tree once more to make sure that Tommy hadn't heard his abdominal protestations. Scooter man and Tommy were still deep in discussions. Then, suddenly, scooter man pulled out a wad of banknotes, peeled off a couple of twenty-pound notes and handed them over to Tommy. *What's the cash for?* thought Frankie. But before he could answer his own question, he saw Tommy reach inside his denim jacket, pull out two clear plastic envelopes and press them into scooter man's outstretched hand.

'Shit,' hissed Frankie, jerking back behind the tree again. 'I wish I hadn't seen that.' He'd been around long enough to know exactly what Tommy Hardcastle had been selling. If he hadn't known, then there were plenty of rumours circulating about Tommy's habits, in any case. But what Frankie did not want to do was get involved. He decided to make a break for it.

Easing himself away from the tree, he tiptoed back to the path. He glanced over his shoulder to make sure that they hadn't seen him. But that was his mistake. By looking back he hadn't noticed the tree root protruding through the flattened earth; his toe snagged it and over he went, crashing to the ground.

'What the…?' he heard from behind him.

As he struggled to his feet, he started to run as fast as his legs would carry him back towards the school; he heard Tommy's voice calling after him: 'Wanker Walker. You're dead! Do you hear me? You're dead!'

Frankie congratulated himself on having managed to avoid Tommy and his gang for the rest of the day. He surveyed the playground through the small pane in the door. It was time to go home and he still didn't relish the idea of bumping into Tommy or any of his mates, so he was being careful, ultra-careful.

No sign of any of them, he thought as he pushed the door open and eased himself out silently through the gap. He headed off in the direction of the school gates, manoeuvring past the small groups of pupils that were still milling around the playground. He looked from side to side as he skipped quickly across the tarmac. He was just outside the gates and thought himself safe when he heard them.

'There's the little bastard... there!'

Then there was the clatter of feet as the three of them gave chase. He didn't get far; only ten yards from the gate they caught him, pulled him to a halt and stood around him.

'Okay, Wankie,' growled Tommy, putting his face right in Frankie's. 'What did you see this lunchtime?'

'Nothing, Tommy. Nothing. I didn't see anything... honest,' simpered Frankie.

'Right answer, Wankie. Right answer.'

'I didn't see anything, I promise.'

'See you keep it that way, Wankie, or you'll get more than this.' He lifted his knee, sharply catching Frankie hard in the testicles. Frankie groaned, screwed up his face in agony and sank to his knees. He closed his eyes and brought his arms up to shield himself from further blows.

Then it happened.

No more punches or kicks. Instead he heard Tommy yelp in surprise.

'What the...?'

'Get away from him, you monsters!'

Frankie opened his eyes to see Tommy and his mates backing off, staring hard, over Frankie's crumpled form. Everyone in the playground seemed to have stopped what they were doing too and were looking in the same direction.

Frankie swivelled round. 'Oh no! Please no!' He sunk lower to the ground.

His mother ran right past him and straight up to his three attackers. She hit Tommy hard in the face with her handbag and then, as he tried to stem the blood pouring from his nose, she proceeded to prod at him with her forefinger, at the same time telling him exactly what she thought of him.

Tommy's mates just stood there, staring at her. But they didn't do anything. Finally, her anger assuaged, Mary Walker turned and lifted Frankie to his feet and led him further down the road towards home; as she did so, Frankie glanced back. The whole school, or at least it looked like the whole school, had stopped and now stood staring at Frankie and his mother. Then someone started to laugh, a raucous belly laugh that echoed around the playground. Then they were all laughing. All, that was, except Tommy Hardcastle and his two friends, who just stood and stared hard in his direction. Tommy made a gesture as if cutting his throat with his hand.

Frankie knew exactly what he meant by that.

Frankie didn't speak to his mother all the way home. When they arrived at the house, he continued to ignore her and headed for his bedroom. Once inside, he emptied out the schoolbooks from his rucksack and then tossed a few essentials in in their place.

'Fuck, fuck, fuck,' he repeated over and over to himself. 'She's really done it this time. I'm a bloody laughing stock. And Tommy's gonna kill me for sure now.'

He raided his savings, counting out the money carefully as he did so: '£38.25p.'

He had only one option left. He realised that. He was getting out and he knew exactly where he was headed.

chapter nine

'Excuse me, everybody. Could I have your attention for a moment?'

It was mid-afternoon and Baz was busy with her paperwork. At the announcement everyone turned and looked in the direction of the voice. Dr Morton stood at the far end of the laboratory; behind him were two men that Baz didn't recognise. One was in his late fifties, the other some twenty years younger. Both men wore suits, which immediately set them apart from the more casually dressed laboratory staff. However, the older man's baggy grey suit had seen better days. The younger man's outfit appeared sharper, altogether more fashionable. Both men, though, wore a similar expression of serious intent.

'This is Mr Kennedy and Mr Sheppard,' continued Dr Morton, indicating his two companions. 'They are from the Department of Health and will be carrying out an inspection of the lab. Your fullest co-operation with this inspection would be appreciated. They have assured me that the disruption to normal working will be kept to a minimum. Nevertheless, Mr Kennedy,' he turned to the older of the two, 'has asked that we suspend all activity for the time being to allow them to carry out an initial survey.'

Everyone looked at one another. An audible groan filled the room.

'If you could just pack up your things with the minimum of fuss.'

'How long is this going to take?' somebody asked.

The older man in the grey suit stepped forward and assumed control. 'At the moment, we're not sure. It depends on how many samples there are and how good the documentation is. Probably a few days, a week at most.'

Another groan.

'Josh Hewitt will keep you informed,' shouted Dr Morton, now largely addressing the backs of his flock who were readying themselves to leave.

Baz pulled on her coat, retrieved her bag and turned to follow the crowd. As she passed, Josh was standing in the doorway of his office.

'Josh, what's all this about?'

'Don't you know…? Oh yeah, I forgot, you were late in yesterday. You missed the announcement.'

'What announcement?'

'They don't need me here right now, so let's go and have a cup of coffee and I'll tell you all about it.'

Josh ambled along a few feet ahead of Baz as they left the building. They turned right and he led her through the maze of corridors to the hospital cafeteria.

The cafeteria was busy. Most of the tables were already taken. Cliques of uniformed nurses huddled around, swapping stories and sharing the occasional joke. On other tables sat groups of young, fresh-faced junior doctors, some still with stethoscopes hanging loosely around their necks. Most were informally dressed, with open collars and short-sleeved shirts, the days of the formal collar and tie under a white coat long since gone. They seemed to be quietly comparing notes or sorting out rotas.

Baz and Josh picked up a couple of cardboard cups, filled them with coffee from the machine and joined the queue for the cashier.

The strong black coffee helped to lift Baz's spirits.

'Well?'

Josh scratched his head. 'Well, what?'

'Come on, tell me what's going on.'

'Okay. You mean those two guys with Dr Morton?'

'Yes.' Baz was getting a little irritated with Josh's hesitancy to explain things.

'They're from the Department of Health.'

'He told us that already.'

'But what he didn't tell you was that they are from the Retention of Organs Enquiry Team.'

'The what…?'

'The Retention of Organs—'

'I heard you, I just don't understand what you mean.' Baz gritted her teeth.

'You remember the Alder Hay scandal?'

'The—'

'That's right,' Josh interrupted before Baz could speak. 'The children's hospital in Liverpool where they discovered that they kept all sorts of bits of kids after they'd died and had never gotten the parent's permission. It was in all the papers a while back. Kiddies' body parts being returned years later to their parents. Second, third and in some cases, even fourth funerals being required to reunite the bodies.'

'That's awful. But what's that got to do with us?'

'It's obvious, isn't it?'

'Duh. No.'

'What do we do for a living?'

Baz thought for a moment. 'Well, I do research on neurochemicals.'

'And…?'

'And, what?'

'And, where do those neurochemicals come from?'

'Oh, shit!'

'Yep, you got it. Those guys from the department are here to trace every single sample of brain, gut, muscle or whatever, to make absolutely sure that we have, in each and every case, full written authority to be hanging on to that material.'

'What if we haven't got consent?'

'Then the tissue will be removed and returned to its rightful owner.'

'But… but, what'll they want it for? They'll just bury it or get rid of it. When we're actually trying to something worthwhile with it.'

'That doesn't matter. Not in this case. There's been a public outcry, it's all about perception and attitude and at present the public perceives the medical profession in a pretty dim and paternalistic, "the doctor knows best", light. What's happening in our lab is no different to what's happening up and down the country at the moment.'

'Christ. If I lose my samples, it could destroy my work.'

'It'll probably not come to that. Our docs are usually pretty sticky at getting consent.'

'I've few enough samples as it is, for Christ's sake, if they take even some of them away I'm sunk.'

'There might be worse to come.'

'I'm not sure I really want to hear this.'

'The word on the street, or more correctly the word from the pathology department, is that the number of post-mortems being carried out has dropped dramatically following all the publicity. People don't trust us anymore. Also the docs are scared of getting themselves sued. So it's going to get more and more difficult, at least in the short term, to get material for research.'

'You really are a Job's comforter, aren't you, Josh?'

Leaving Josh, who sat on sipping slowly at his coffee, Baz headed off to do what she always did when she felt a bit stressed or under pressure: she headed for the gym.

Occasionally Baz would use the weight machines or the treadmills, sometimes she even played a game of tennis, but those, she had found, did not provide the relaxation she craved. So, gracefully she slipped into her turquoise one-piece before making her way to the swimming pool. As she stood over the deep end, looking at the rippled surface, she took a few quick breaths, just enough to blow off the CO_2, then, with an agile leap, she dived in and struck out immediately under the surface for the far end. The cool water invigorated her. On and on she swam, never once breaking the surface. At first she seemed to glide through the water effortlessly. But then, with each new stroke, her arms ached. Next her chest felt as if was going to explode. But she forced herself to go on. Just when she knew that she couldn't hold her breath a moment longer, her hand touched the tiled wall at the end of the pool. She broke the surface, gasping noisily for breath. Greedily she gulped down a great lungful of air.

When she had sufficiently recovered, she noticed that the lifeguard was on his feet and staring in her direction. Obviously he'd seen her dive in; the lifeguards always tended to notice her. She guessed that when she hadn't come up for air, he'd had become alarmed. Baz smiled to herself. She liked to show off. She knew that she was one of the few people at that gym that could swim the full twenty-five metres underwater. She ignored the lifeguard's puzzled looks, turned and headed back down the pool, this time more conventionally. She continued to plough up and down the lengths until the tiredness of her limbs had sufficiently distracted her brain from the trials of the day.

As she pulled herself out of the pool, she sat for a few moments on its edge to regain her breath. A soft touch on her shoulder made her jump. 'I suppose you think that's funny?'

She turned quickly. The lifeguard stood immediately behind her. She hadn't heard him approach. 'What?'

'Making me think you'd drowned.'

The words appeared to be a chastisement, but they were said with a smile. Baz guessed that the lifeguard was attempting to chat her up. 'Sorry about that, it's just a little trick of mine. I didn't mean to upset you.' Baz struggled to her feet. She wasn't really in the mood to be chatted up; besides, she felt cold. 'Gotta go, bye.'

At least the swim had cleared her head of the day's frustrations and, more importantly, she felt she'd managed to come to some sort of decision. Back home, sitting alone after dinner, she flicked on the TV and caught the end of *Have I Got News for You*. Paul Merton was having one of his manic days, or so it seemed to Baz. He interrupted the chairman at the earliest opportunity and seemed to have a quick-fire answer to everything. As most of what he said was completely outrageous, it was accompanied by squeals of laughter from the audience. It wasn't long before Baz caught the mood and her depression started to lift. When the panel got onto a heated debate as to whether one female panellist was wearing FM shoes, Baz couldn't contain herself any longer and started to giggle uncontrollably.

After *Have I Got News for You*, Baz sitting in her favourite armchair, relaxed, to watch *Frasier*. Though, as usual, it was a repeat, it bore repeating. Baz loved the clever exchanges that characterised Frasier and his brother Niles' relationship. When Frasier 'had left the building', Baz yawned involuntarily.

Climbing into bed and easing herself under the duvet, Baz's pyjama top rode up and she felt the coolness of her shorts against her thighs. She reflected moodily on the day just past, but she couldn't remain morose for long as her spirits had been lifted by her swim and her relaxing evening. She lay on her back and let the warmth of her body fill the cavity around her. She reached over, turned off the light and then snuggled down. The bed had warmed up quickly. When she'd gone to bed, she had felt tired, but now she lay there, peering at the ceiling through the darkness, sleep wouldn't come.

Her thoughts moved to the gym and her brief meeting with the lifeguard. She tried to remember what he looked like. It had been a while since anyone had attempted to chat Baz up, she reflected. Mostly her own fault, she realised that, too pre-occupied with her studies and her research. No time for men in her life. Her thoughts flitted back to her last proper boyfriend, Justin Harrison. He had played out-half for the local rugby club. *Great thighs*, mused Baz, *firm, very firm.* It was his thighs that she'd first noticed when she'd gone with friends to watch the match. Poor Justin, she hadn't treated him very fairly, but she had her career and he couldn't accept that. She wondered where he was now and who he was with. *Melissa bloody Ferguson, I bet, she had always fancied him.*

She struggled to remember just how long it had been since she last had gone out with Justin. *God. It must be six months.* Maybe, she mused, she'd been a bit too quick to dismiss that lifeguard today. Now all she could remember clearly about him were his legs too. But they were good legs, long and muscular, still tanned from the summer. *God, she thought, I must be obsessed with muscular thighs!*

As she drifted off to sleep, she imagined the lifeguard was helping her to her feet at the pool's edge. Strong, muscular arms and firm pectorals bulged beneath his T-shirt. He held on to her as she stood facing him. His broad white smile lit up his dark handsome features. His deep brown eyes transfixed her gaze. He drew her body close to his. She felt the water from her swimsuit dampen his T-shirt, sticking it to his chest and defining more perfectly the ripples of his muscular chest beneath. The lifeguard slowly and deliberately inclined his head towards her and then carefully placed his lips on hers.

Maybe she had been a bit quick in dismissing him.

chapter ten

Baz was woken by the ringtone of her mobile phone. Wearily, she eased herself out of bed and fumbled for the phone, which she had placed on her beside cabinet before retiring for the night.

She swiped the screen. 'Uhh… Hello?'

'I was beginning to think that I'd missed you.'

Baz immediately recognised the refined southern accent with its clipped vowels. Rubbing at her eyes, she glanced at her bedside clock. *Eight forty-five.*

'Oh. Hi, Mum. I've got a day off.'

'It's not like you to take a day off. Is something wrong?'

'No, no, it was sort of forced upon us. It's a long story. Don't worry about it. What do you want, anyway?'

'Well, I was talking to your dad last night about the fact that you hadn't rung us for a while—'

'I know, I know, I'm sorry. I've been very busy, my PhD, you know what it's like.'

'You work too hard, Baz. Your father and I were wondering if you'd take the weekend off and come down and visit us. Come down on Friday night and stay till Sunday?'

'Umm… well, I don't know…' Baz struggled to find an excuse. 'I can't make it this weekend anyway, but maybe in a week or two. I'll give you a ring and firm it up. Okay?'

'Your father will be disappointed if you don't come. He's not been too well lately, you know that?'

Baz recognised the emotional blackmail for what it was. 'Is his chest playing up again?'

'Yes, but it's been much worse recently. The doctor thinks he's got a touch of angina on top of everything else. He gets so short of breath when we go for a walk now.'

'He should have given those cigarettes up years ago.'

'You know that I've been on at him for years, but you know him, stubborn old fool. Please say that you'll come down and see us, Baz. It's important to your dad and I am worried about him, really I am.'

'I promise I'll try and get down for a visit as soon as I can, Mum, honest.'

'If that's the best you can do.' The voice was heavy with disappointment.

'It is, Mum. But I will visit.'

'Soon?'

'Yes, soon.'

'Okay, bye.'

'Bye, Mum.'

Baz put down the receiver. 'Shit,' she cursed out of a combination of the frustration and guilt that the call had evoked. It wasn't exactly the start to the day that she wanted or had planned. Baz recognised that her relationship with her mother had always been a little strained. No, not always. That was overstating it, but certainly since her teenage years. Since

Baz had developed her own personality her own independence, she had come to recognise the differences between herself and her parents. Not just in age, but in values, in all sorts of things that seemed to matter to her, but not them. Her dad wasn't too bad, she had to admit that; he just got on with things and let her do her own thing. She did miss her dad. But as the years had passed, Baz had found it more and more difficult even to converse with her mother as the gulf between them had grown in magnitude. At times, like now following the phone call, Baz felt guilty about the breakdown in their relationship. Nevertheless, on a day-to-day basis she had found it easier simply to ignore the situation and in recent years that strategy had worked well, especially now that it was easier to simply to avoid contact, as there was some distance physically between them.

'Shit and bloody shit.' She punched the bed as she realised that she had committed herself to a weekend with her mother once again.

But before that she had work to do. She had made a decision. Probably not a wise one, but a decision nonetheless. She had decided what to do with the unexpected time off that had befallen her. Her mother's unwanted invitation had simply galvanised her resolve.

Baz pulled her red Fiat 500 to the side of the road and stopped briefly to consult Google Maps on her phone. She'd left the city well behind and swapped the congested streets for near-deserted country roads. She marvelled at the freedom the leafy, twisty lanes afforded after the traffic jams of the town. The going hadn't been as quick as she had anticipated and hadn't been helped by the succession of other road users, all of whom, it seemed to Baz, had got ahead of her simply for the purpose of slowing her down. Certainly they had seemed to be in no particular hurry to reach their own destinations. Baz had to admit that although she was not under any time obligation either, the adrenaline had been pumping in her veins as she had neared her goal, and it made her increasingly impatient to get there.

Baz placed the open phone on the passenger seat and angled it towards her. She had intended to fix the guidance to East Brookfield but had foolishly decided to wait till she was closer to her target, relying on road signage instead. Even with the electronic guidance, she still struggled to work out exactly where she was at the moment. She knew that she had just passed through Somerton, a small, tranquil and picturesque village. The sort of village that was the stuff of tourist brochures and picture postcards common to this area of south-west England. Baz imagined that the white-washed pub with the thatched roof, which she had passed en route, boasted local ales served in frothy tankards by a smiling, ruddy-faced publican. The phone seemed to indicate that there were many similar-sized villages in the area and she wondered did they all hold such olde-worlde charm.

Finally working out her location and setting the guidance to East Brookfield, she grumbled over the fact that she hadn't invested in a proper built-in satellite navigation system when she had bought the car.

She estimated that it would take her only another fifteen minutes or thereabouts. She looked at her watch: 12.15pm.

Be there in time for lunch, she thought.

Looking down at the phone to once more check the route, she moved off and started to accelerate away from the roadside.

There was an immediate squeal of brakes as a Land Rover appeared at speed alongside her, its driver frantically hauling at the steering wheel, trying to avoid her. There was a loud bang as the Land Rover's bumper collided with the front wing of Baz's Fiat. Baz was thrown sideways by the impact. Her car came to rest up on the mossy verge. The Land Rover skidded a few metres more before coming to a halt skewed across the roadway, lines of black rubber marking its path.

Baz sat, holding on to the steering wheel tightly with both hands, unmoving, frightened by the suddenness of the crash.

Gradually she became aware that somebody was tapping noisily on the window beside her. She shuddered to regain her composure, and the rolled the window down a little way.

'Are you okay?' the stranger talked through the gap at the top of the glass.

'I… I… think so,' she stammered.

'Didn't you see me?' asked the stranger.

Baz looked round at him. He was standing bent over, his face close to the side window of the car. There didn't appear to be any malevolence in his demeanour, rather, he appeared genuinely concerned. Baz, momentarily uncertain what to say, stared blankly into the man's face. He had a slightly weather-beaten appearance but was clean-shaven with slightly reddened cheeks. The heavily creased waxed jacket and the tweed flat cap that he wore added to the country façade. Despite his rather old-fashioned, agricultural garb, his face appeared young-ish, probably not that much older than Baz herself; early thirties, she thought.

'I said, did you not see me?' he repeated.

'Sorry… Sorry… just a little shocked.'

'You're not hurt?' Again, Baz detected genuine concern in his voice.

Baz reached for the door handle and stepped out of the car. She felt a little shaky on her feet at first but rapidly steadied up.

'I'm okay,' she confirmed.

The stranger stepped back to allow her out of the vehicle, then turned and walked around to the front of the Fiat and bent over the front wing, inspecting the damage.

'It's not too bad. Probably looks a lot worse than it actually is. There's a small dent in your wing and the headlight's broken, but it should be easily fixable.'

Baz looked at the damage herself. 'Shit… Sorry.'

'That's okay.' He smiled at her.

'Look, I'm really sorry about the crash. I was looking at my phone as I pulled out and I just didn't see you coming.'

'You shouldn't say that.'

'What?'

'That it was your fault and that you were looking at your phone.'

'But I was—'

'Yes, I know. But don't the insurance people say never admit liability?'

'Oh well, too late now, I guess.' Baz returned his smile.

'Just as long as nobody got hurt—'

'But what about your car?' Baz interrupted.

'That old lump of a thing? I wouldn't worry about it. It's years old and built like a tank, I bet there's hardly a scratch.'

'We better have a look,' Baz offered and then followed him over to where the Land Rover had stopped.

'See what I mean?' He pointed to the front bumper where there was a small streak of red paint where it had struck her car. But he was right: apart from that, there was no evidence of any damage.

'Should we call the police or something?' Baz was uncertain of the correct procedure.

'I don't really think there's any need, do you? No injuries, my jeep's okay, you admit it was your fault and the only damage is to your car. I don't feel the need to sue you, so let's just call it quits and leave it at that.'

'That… that's very good of you.'

'Where are you headed anyway?'

'I'm visiting a village called East Brookfield. Do you know it?'

'Brookfield. Yeah, I know it well, actually, I live close by. Have you friends there?'

'No. Not exactly. I'm just doing some background research.'

'Background research, eh? Sounds intriguing. Are you writing a book or something?'

'Something like that.' Baz shifted uncomfortably. *Well, a PhD is a bit like a book,* she thought to herself.

'Not much excitement in East Brookfield, not enough to base a novel on. It's quite a sleepy little place.'

'It's not really a novel… as such.'

'Are you planning to stay in the village?'

'Just for a night or two.'

'Well, if you're looking for somewhere to stay, try Freda Turner's on Bridge Street, she does bed and breakfast.'

'I will, thanks.'

'And Billy, her husband, runs the local garage. He could probably knock that dent out for you and replace the headlight.'

'Thanks, that's good to know.'

The last remark was addressed to the benevolent stranger's back, as he was already climbing into the Land Rover.

'Thank you, and sorry!' Baz shouted over the throaty roar of the engine.

In reply he offered only a cursory wave before heading off down the road.

East Brookfield was separated from its smaller sister West Brookfield by a small river. Baz presumed that this was the original 'brook' from which both villages derived their name. East Brookfield was nowhere near as picturesque or attractive as most of the villages Baz had passed through to get here. The four main streets, around which the village was built, met in the centre at a crossroads. A small grass square with a war memorial, which Baz noted was stained with bird excreta, stood in one corner of this junction. In all other directions, parallel lines of flat, square-fronted terraces snaked virtually to the beginnings of the countryside once again. The houses declared the individuality of their owner's tastes by sporting different colours or hues on their façade. Pastel yellows, pinks and blues abounded, giving the village a peculiar dolly mixture appearance. The dwellings were punctuated by the occasional village shop, a grocers here, a butchers there, but none expressing anything more than functionality. Passing through East Brookfield, travellers to West Brookfield were obliged to pass over the ancient stone bridge that carried the roadway and crossed the river that separated the two parts of what would have been otherwise a single habitat. The street that led from the central square to this bridge was, unsurprisingly, called Bridge Street, and it was here that Baz was able to locate Freda Turner's B&B.

'There 'e are, dear. What do 'e think?'

Freda Turner, late sixties, early seventies, wrinkled, but clearly sprightly for her age, was wearing her blue housecoat over a faded skirt and torn cardigan, as she showed Baz the guest accommodation. Baz looked around the small converted attic room. Light streamed in through two streaked Velux windows, highlighting the myriad small particles of dust that had been released upon their entry. It was clear that the room had not been occupied for some considerable time.

'It's £40 a night. Breakfast, full English, is £8.50 extra.'

Baz shook the older woman's hand. 'It's a deal. I would like to stay for two nights anyway, maybe a bit longer. I haven't quite made my mind up yet.'

'Well, when 'e do, 'e can let me know. Not much demand this time of year anyhow. 'E can stay as long as 'e wants.'

'My car had a bit of a bump on the way here. I heard your husband might be able to have a look at it for me.'

'Billy's out back in the garage, I'll tell him you're looking for him.'

Baz unpacked her small overnight bag and then went out to find Freda's husband. She located him bent over inside the bonnet of a dilapidated Transit van. Billy Turner confirmed that he could replace the headlight but that the bodywork might need a little more attention than he could provide.

'If I fix the light, though,' he said in a slow, south-west England accent that perfectly matched that of his wife's, 'there shouldn't be a problem driving around and 'e can get the rest done when 'e gets back to London.'

The necessities done, Baz set off to explore the village. The early afternoon sun blinked through the patchy clouds and a cool breeze made her tighten her coat around her. Her tummy rumbled, reminding her that it was lunchtime. On the corner of the street, Baz was pleased to find a cosy-looking café painted in cream and pale blue colours, which proclaimed to sell coffee, tea, soup and sandwiches. There were two outside tables, but both were stripped of any linen or utensils. An English autumn, even in the south of England, did not lend itself to al fresco dining.

The cardboard 'Open' sign swung wildly on its strings and a bell chimed as Baz pushed open the neat glass-panelled door. The warmth of the interior and the smell of warm bread and coffee immediately made her feel welcome.

A comely, perspiration-laden face thrust itself through the beaded curtain that screened the kitchen from the small dining area.

'Hello there. Take a seat, anywhere at all and I'll be with you in the shake of a lamb's tail.' With that, she disappeared once more behind the screen.

Baz chose a small table beside the window and studied the handwritten menu.

'Sorry about that, my dear. I was just baking some scones and I needed to get them out of the oven.'

She wiped her brow with the back of her forearm as she spoke. Looking up, Baz noted the tousled grey hair, the friendly, heavily lined face and the flour-stained apron, which strained to cover her ample proportions. This was a woman who enjoyed her cooking and clearly also its results.

'I'll just have a black coffee and a piece of your homemade apple pie.' The look on her hostess's face made Baz suspect that her frugality had simply confirmed the older woman's view of what she probably referred to as 'modern girls'. But she smiled, said nothing and wrote down the order before disappearing again.

Baz drank the coffee and finished the apple pie in solitary silence, but she had to admit the pie was the best she'd tasted for some time. No other customers appeared to disrupt the tranquillity and the café owner spent the majority of the time ensconced in the kitchen, from whence came intermittent crashes or clatters as oven doors were firmly closed or plates stacked.

As Baz paid the bill, she asked the owner, 'Do you know where Brook Cottage, Woolmart Lane is?'

The woman fixed Baz in an inquisitive stare. 'Top of Bridge Street, turn left, Woolmart Lane is second on the right; the cottage is at the end of the row. Are you feeling poorly?'

'I'm sorry, I don't understand.'

'Wouldn't make no difference if you did anyhow.'

'Now you've really lost me.' Baz was getting a little irri.
with the older woman's riddles.

'Well, he doesn't practise there.'

'Practise... practise what?'

'His medicinaries or whatever you call it. No, his surgery
is in West Brookfield.'

'Whose surgery is in West Brookfield?'

'The doctor's. Dr Marsden, of course.'

'John Marsden's a doctor?'

'He's our GP. But how come you didn't know that?'

'I've never met him.'

'So why are you asking about his house?'

Baz felt herself flush a little at that question and stumbled
for a reply. 'I... I... work for an insurance company and I hear
there was a fire there about two years ago. Some loose ends to
be tied up, that's all.'

'Terrible thing, that fire.'

'Uh... uh?'

'Yes, that poor girl Cathy... Mrs Marsden, the doctor's
wife. Burnt to death, she was, you know.'

'I heard.'

'Lovely, lovely girl.'

'I heard that too,' Baz agreed, hoping she sounded sincere.

'Yes, there's some folk didn't like her. Said she was too
headstrong, bossed the poor doctor about, they said. But
I always liked her, I did, and poor Dr Marsden, he was
devastated when she died.'

'What happened to her?'

'Not absolutely certain, but most folk say that the doctor
and her had some big argument, don't know about what, but
anyhow, he storms off, she sits and drinks all night, waiting

for him to get back, but she gets so drunk she falls asleep and accidentally sets the house on fire. Terrible, just terrible.'

'That's awful.'

'Yeah, it was. Funny thing, though.'

'What?'

'Well, most of us round here thought that the doctor would give up working here, move away someplace, after something like that.'

'But he stayed?'

'Yep, just buried himself in his work, got the house fixed, continues to live there, just got on with his life as if nothing happened. Don't know how he's done it, but he has. I don't think I could've coped as well as he has. But it was two years ago now and time is a great healer, I suppose.'

'Strong man?' Baz got up to leave.

'Must be, but don't you go upsetting him, you hear, young lady.'

Baz spent the afternoon walking around the village getting her bearings. She'd located Woolmart Lane fairly quickly and walked past the row of four neat Georgian cottages. The cottages were superficially identical, but the owners had clearly gone to great lengths to individualise their homes. Most were white-washed, but one had been painted a vanilla yellow, two were overgrown with an ivy façade, whilst one had a pretty rose bush archway that overhung the garden gate. Brook Cottage was the end of the row. It appeared to Baz that it had received a little less care and attention over the years than its neighbours had. The white walls, though, had clearly been repainted in the last year or so, presumably after the fire. Some of the window frames still looked like they needed a bit more attention, others though were obviously new. As for the garden. *Mmm… the garden*, thought Baz. Well, frankly, it was a mess. In stark contrast to the neatly manicured hedgerows and expertly clipped lawns of the adjoining cottages, the garden of Brook Cottage was overgrown, with tall weeds sprouting from what had been orderly collections of shrubs and bushes. Probably, Baz guessed, now without the care and attention they had received before Mrs Marsden's untimely death.

Baz had walked past the cottage, glancing over the twisted slats of the garden gate, which hung at a precarious angle from its one remaining hinge. The cottage almost gave the appearance of being abandoned. She had then continued up the lane, passing a small copse and the turning the corner at the open countryside. The trees had lost most of their foliage, but the grass remained lush and verdant. Stopping at a wide farm gate, she stopped and observed some cows meandering apparently aimlessly in the field beyond. As she stood, she was aware of her heart beating rapidly and vigorously in her chest. She paused, trying to regain control before tracing her steps back along the narrow roadway. At Brook Cottage, she stopped and stooped down as if examining an interesting plant, all the while trying to take in as many other features of the house as she could. She could see the pretty floral curtains that hung on the upstairs windows, the cracked tiles on the roof and the heavy brass knocker in the centre of the brightly painted wooden front door. The interior of the house was too dark to distinguish any other features. Her heart started to race once more as she tried to pluck up the courage to approach the house and get a better view.

A dirty green Volvo turned into the lane from Bridge Street. Baz straightened up, suddenly startled by the sudden engine noise breaking into the tranquillity of the surrounding countryside. She resumed her walk, moving quickly back down the lane towards the approaching car, afraid its occupant might be the owner of the house she was surveying. She moved aside onto the verge as the Volvo manoeuvred around her and then accelerated away on up the lane, past the copse and disappeared around the bend in the road. Baz felt too afraid now to return to the cottage and she cursed herself for that. She headed back to her digs to organise her thoughts more clearly.

For the remaining few hours of the afternoon, Baz sat in her small room at Mr and Mrs Turner's B&B, rereading her notes over and over again, and trying to decide how she was going to get closer to solving the particular riddle that she had set herself.

Still partially confused as how best to proceed, she climbed off the bed and decided to visit the pub that she had spotted, but previously ignored, in her village tour. There at least she might get to hear some more local gossip about the Marsdens and the disaster that had befallen them.

The Black Bull was nowhere near as appealing as the pretty country pub she had passed en route earlier in the day. Its red-brick façade was more practical than attractive. As Baz approached, she spotted a familiar face seated at an outside trestle table. A pint of bitter, nearly finished, in one hand and a manual of some sort in the other. So engrossed was he in his reading that he didn't hear Baz approach.

'I guess I owe you a drink.'

'Sorry, what?' Taken aback, the friendly stranger with the slightly weather-beaten complexion looked up from his reading material to face Baz.

'I said, I guess I owe you a drink. For the car crash I caused, you remember.'

The stranger smiled, the same warm, friendly smile she had seen earlier. Baz noted with some satisfaction that he still wore the creased waxed jacket, but now the stupid tweed cap was nowhere to be seen, revealing a mat of tousled dark hair.

'There's no need, honestly.'

'I insist. It's the least I can do. What's that? A pint of bitter?'

'Well, if you put it like that, how can I refuse?'

At the bar, Baz ignored the bemused stares of the locals; clearly they were unused to strangers, especially young, single, independently minded and attractive female strangers. Gathering the drinks, she turned and quickly retreated from the interior of bar, her newfound friend's pint of beer in one hand and a gin and tonic for herself in the other.

Then, uninvited, she eased herself onto the bench opposite her fellow car crash victim.

'Look, thanks, but there really was no need.' But he gratefully accepted the pint anyway. Then he extended his hand. 'My name's John, by the way, John Marsden. Pleased to meet you.'

Baz froze.

'What's wrong? You look like you've seen a ghost.'

chapter eleven

Baz stared hard at the wooden beams that stretched from one side of the ceiling of the small bedroom. Dawn was just starting to force its way in, producing dappled streaks of sunlight shining through gaps in the carelessly pulled curtains. She rubbed at her wearisome eyes and flicked her tangled hair back from her face as she struggled to sit up. Sleep had eluded her through most of the night. The unplanned, and certainly unexpected, meeting with John Marsden had played continuously on her mind. Not that, once she had recovered from the initial shock, he had not proven good company. Far from it, in point of fact, he had been a most amiable companion. But maybe that was it; if he had been less friendly, less charming, then perhaps she would not have felt the heavy burden of shame and guilt that her own deceit had inflicted on her.

Not to have suspected his identity was stupid, she conceded, but then he didn't really reflect her preconceptions of a medical doctor, not even a country GP. He was far too down to earth, none of the arrogance she had witnessed and disliked in so many of the hospital-based consultants that she had dealt with previously. His dress sense, she smiled, was more that of a vet than a doctor; he drank beer and she suspected that he smoked. Smoking was generally held as a filthy evil in the hospital medical circles. True, he had not produced a cigarette whilst in her presence, but she had caught a tell-tale whiff of stale nicotine on his breath as he had leant over to pass her the second gin and tonic. But, she reflected, he had come across as a genuinely nice person, nevertheless the sense of relief that she had experienced when he had taken his leave had been tangible. She hoped that he had not picked up on it.

She drew her knees up to her chest, still under the cotton duvet, and enfolded them in her arms. No, she didn't believe that he had noticed. He had even suggested another drink if she stayed in the village for a day or two longer. Whether she should, or indeed could, remain now, was the question that troubled her most. He had told her that he was away all day holding a clinic in the cottage hospital in a neighbouring village. A fact which had provided her with only a small degree of comfort.

Breakfast at Freda Turner's under normal circumstances would have been an enormously pleasurable experience. Orange juice, home cured bacon, two generously proportioned sausages and a fried egg, which, judging from the deep orange of its yolk, was undoubtedly from a free-range hen. It was served with more than sufficient quantities of crusty brown toast dripping in butter. Baz, however, wasn't in the mood; she simply pushed the fry-up around the plate, nibbling occasionally at the corner of a piece of toast whenever Freda Turner started to fuss around her.

Making her excuses early, Baz slipped out into the crisp, frosty morning that shrouded the village, adding to its autumnal feel. Still deep in thought, she wandered along the narrow and still-deserted laneways. Before she had time to really think which way she was headed or the route that she had subconsciously taken, she found herself standing outside the small cottage that had once been Catherine Marsden's home.

There she stopped and stood motionless, staring at its pale façade as if transfixed by the small rustic dwelling. The house, for its part, seemed almost to stare back at her, its windows fixing her in their unblinking gaze. No movement to disturb Baz's pensive mood. It was clear that despite the early hour, the owner had already left to begin his rounds.

Seeing no movement in the neighbouring houses either, Baz plucked up her courage and strode purposefully forward through the lopsided gate and on up to the house itself.

Hesitating only briefly, she reached for the heavy cast iron door knocker and rapped it twice. There was no response. She let out a sigh of relief; if someone had responded, Baz felt she would have become a quivering wreck, unable to explain her presence at this early hour. Her confidence growing, she waited a few moments longer to be sure and then stepped down off the small doorstep and moved quickly to the rectangular-panelled window to the left of the front door. She cupped her hands to her face and peered through the grimy panes. It was dark inside, a small window to the back of the room afforded only a little light to illuminate its contents. Squinting, she could just about make out a fireplace on the gable wall, stone surround and cast iron kettle by its side. A pile of dark ashes resided in the grate and a few logs peeked carelessly above the rim of a nearby wicker basket. Two floral patterned sofas with crumpled throws, a brass standard lamp with opaque glass shade and a small pine table under the window at the far end of the room completed the main furnishings in what was obviously the sitting room.

Struggling to take in more detail, she noted on either side of the fireplace were a series of shelves containing clusters of haphazardly arranged books, a mottled silver trophy and a couple of dead or dying plants in ceramic pots. Baz strove to examine the features in greater detail but failed to gain any further insight into the Marsdens' home.

She stepped away from the window and, still undetected, moved around the side of the house and then picked her way gingerly through the overgrown brambles that hung like a threatening waterfall over the fence between this house and its neighbour. Whatever else John Mardsen was, he was clearly no gardener. The gap between the fence and the gable wall was narrow, and the bramble thorns plucked at her clothes as she tried to force her way through. A branch scrapped across her outstretched hand, drawing blood. Baz cursed softly, wishing she'd had the foresight to bring some gloves.

Finally emerging in the back garden, she scanned the overgrown tangle of weeds and shrubs beyond. A small garden shed at the bottom of the garden was almost completely hidden by the encircling mass of green and brown foliage. The remnants of a previously cared for lawn still existed but was now overgrown and littered with tall weeds. A circular wooden table, its top bleached an off-white with exposure to rain and sun stood near to the back door. There were four equally bleached chairs, one of which reclined at a crazy angle.

Baz rattled the back door. Firmly bolted. She peered through the condensation that filled the lower portions of the kitchen window. A grease-stained Aga, a paper-strewn table and a sink piled with discarded dishes all simply helped to confirm that John Marsden was leading a somewhat disorganised bachelor life.

Unable to gain entry and the house apparently unwilling to yield up any further information, Baz turned to leave, somewhat despondent by her lack of success and feeling stupid or at least annoyed at thinking that she might have hoped for more. As she was about to re-enter the bramble thicket, she had one last thought. She picked her way across the thick grass towards the garden shed. A small wooden structure with a tall door and tiny dirty window. The bushes and nettles had grown up nearly to the roof and were pushing their way in through the wooden slates. As she neared, Baz felt a tremulousness sweep over her. For although the tangle of shrubbery almost engulfed the shed, she noticed that around the door, the weeds had been trampled, their stems broken as if somebody, or something, had forced its way through relatively recently.

Baz hesitated, unsure whether to proceed. Then, summoning up all her courage, she advanced, gripped the door handle and pulled with all her strength.

The door yielded surprisingly easily, throwing Baz backwards and causing her to lose her footing as she did so. Struggling to regain her balance, Baz gasped in horror as she spotted the dark, shadowy human form lurking in the murky depths of the interior, among the turmoil of rusting garden utensils.

Fighting to regain her breath, Baz watched the figure slowly rise to its feet. He, for it seemed to be a he, clutched the torn, dirty, brown blanket which had covered him when she had thrust the door ajar. Unable to move, frozen by a mixture of shock and fear, Baz watched as he advanced towards her. She tried to scream but her throat had become suddenly dry and only a cracked hustle emerged. Summoning up all her reserves, she turned to flee. But before she could do so, the figure had reached for her, grasping her upper arm in its tight, bony grip.

'Hello, Mum.'

chapter twelve

Mary Walker didn't initially notice that Frankie wasn't home. She simply assumed that the unaccustomed silence meant that he was up in his bedroom, probably still sulking or hopefully doing his homework.

She decided to leave him in peace. Give him time to forgive her for interfering in the dispute with those other teenagers. In truth, she did regret it; she realised that she was too possessive, smothering him, but despite herself she just couldn't let go. Not after James.

James, that was what she had named him, even though he had never been officially christened. James Walker, after her own father. She had adored her father, but he had shared her traits, for he too had probably been too overbearing, too controlling. Even though Mary was one of three children, it was she that he seemed to exert most of his restrictions upon. It was probably, Mary reasoned, because she was the eldest, the firstborn, and therefore lacking previous parental experience and, being of a different generation, he had imposed his will more completely on her than her siblings. It was obvious to all in the family circle that her two sisters, Joyce and Emily, enjoyed much more freedom than she ever did.

She now only rarely saw her sisters, as they had married and moved away. An occasional phone call had become the norm in recent years. It wasn't until her father had passed away that Mary had left home and tried to build a life of her own. She had, initially at least, tried to rebuild a relationship with her ever-suffering mother, but she had even failed with this enterprise. There was just too much baggage.

It was at about this time that she had met her future husband; he was a few years older than Mary herself. *A father figure?* she pondered. Had she been unable to shake off the bonds her own father had for so long imposed upon her? If so, it hadn't turned out to be the case. Fred was kind and caring, at least at first. That was before baby James had come along. James had been born two years after Mary and Fred had got married. He was a beautiful baby, warm and cuddly, bright blue eyes, and chubby pink cheeks. That was the way she remembered him; again, was she deluding herself? Babies weren't always easy and she had been a first-time mother, after all, but that was the way she recalled her life with him, an unshakable recollection of happy times. Fred had been over the moon: a son, one he could spoil and indulge. He looked forward to watching him grow up becoming a man, he looked forward to sharing stories and hobbies, guiding James into adulthood until finally he would accompany him to church to pass his care over to a woman who would love him as much as Fred and Mary did.

It was not to be.

Mary sat thinking what could have been, but the reality was so different. A tear ran down her cheek as she remembered the day her world had fallen apart. James had been about six months old, just starting to make attempts to crawl. The evening before, she and Fred had sat and observed him rolling over and making as yet largely ineffective efforts to coordinate his movements, trying to move off the mat on which he lay at their feet. She recalled Fred's smiling face as he looked down upon his son; she was sure she could detect small tears of pleasure, happiness and almost certainly pride, well up in the corner of his eyes as they sat in silence, hand in hand and watched. Eventually she had interrupted his efforts, lifted him, offered him to his father for a goodnight kiss and carried him gently up to bed.

She had lowered him into his cot, wrapped him carefully in his blanket to limit his rolling around and keep him covered throughout the night, then she had leant over the side of the cot and planted an affectionate and loving kiss on his cheek. Again she remembered him gurgling and smiling up at her as she paused before leaving, simply standing content to watch this little miracle as he slowly drifted off to sleep.

James had let them have a full night's sleep that night. There hadn't been the usual midnight cries summoning one of them to get up and change his nappy or just to lift and cuddle him. Perhaps that should have alerted them. That was a thought that they both shared but rarely spoke about.

The next morning Mary had been the one to go and fetch him. Fred was readying himself for work and would join them over breakfast.

James was still asleep. Or at least that is what Mary had thought as she opened the door to his small bedroom and quietly approached his cot. She had leant over to pick him up. Still he hadn't moved. She had lifted him still wrapped in his blanket. Then she had seen his face; his little eyes had been open, but they had stared blankly ahead, unmoving, not, as she had hoped, up at his loving mother. As she had taken in more of his face, she had realised his lips were blue, his features expressionless. Also, there had been none of the usual struggling, rather he lay limply, still, within his blanket.

The truth had hit her. It had been like a sledgehammer. She couldn't get a breath. She had sunk to her knees, still clutching his lifeless body. Regaining her breath, she had let out an animalistic wail.

Within seconds, Fred at her side. He snatched little James from her. He unwrapped him from the blanket, but as he did so James's body hung limply in his father's hand his little arms dangling below him.

Fred slapped his cheeks, he shook him. He implored him to wake up. There was no response.

'Call an ambulance. Quickly.' He had shouted at her as he hugged his son close to his chest.

Mary had run down the stairs two by two and summoned help, but in her heart of hearts she knew it was too late. Her son was dead.

The ambulance crew had been sympathetic. They had prised James's body from Fred despite his reluctance to give him up. Some neighbours had come in and tried to comfort Mary and then Fred as he gave up the struggle and had returned to sit down beside his wife. They sat side by side, Fred's arm around her as she held her head in her hands sobbing loudly as one of her neighbours offered her a cup of steaming tea.

'Cot death.' That was the verdict the coroner had imparted. She remembered sitting in that cold unwelcoming court room as he had delivered the result of his examinations. He had offered his condolences, she recalled as she and then Fred had risen slowly and laboriously from their seats at the front of the court. She had acknowledged the coroner with a nod of the head and then they had left, hand in hand, Fred's, body visibly slumped and both silent and overwhelmed by a feeling loneliness.

Over time the pain lessened, but it never left.

Mary and Fred had no more children, either because they couldn't have bared to have endured another life-changing episode such as they had had to endure with James's death, or because over time Fred and she grew gradually further and further apart.

It was a few years later that, in an attempt to repair her marriage, she had put Fred and herself forward as foster parents. After many months and an endless series of interviews with social workers and others, they were finally approved. It was, however, made clear to them that they were to be the exception rather than the norm, for it was much preferred that children were fostered into existing family groups rather than childless couples. But it was admitted there was at that time a shortage of willing parents. It stressed to them, however, that a further condition was that supervision by experienced social workers would be mandatory, at least for a number of years.

Fred and Mary had waited expectantly. Time had seemed to drag by following their initial acceptance onto the foster parent panel. Despite, or perhaps because of the wait, Fred and Mary's relationship had once again warmed, as together they faced the prospect of a worthwhile and less lonely future.

It was actually three years before their first foster child arrived. He was twelve and had behavioural difficulties. Social work staff were reluctant and apprehensive of allowing him to stay with Fred and Mary, but in fact they had turned out to be exceptional parents and by the time the young man left to return to his own parents, he was a transformed person.

Mary had grieved at his leaving. Despite her realism and the knowledge that it had never been more than a temporary relationship, she couldn't dismiss the sense that once again she had lost a child.

There followed a number of short-term foster children, until one memorable day when there was a knock on the door and two senior social workers had visited and discussed, firstly with Mary and then the next day with both her and her husband, the prospect of a longer term fostering arrangement. A baby born to a teenage girl had been put into care by the girl's parents. They apparently said that the family couldn't cope with a young baby and her parents were reluctant to try.

Mary had jumped at the chance and could barely contain her enthusiasm. Fred was less sure, but he had kept quiet during the meeting, not wishing to upset or overrule his wife in any way. After the meeting was over, he had raised his concerns privately with her, expressing his concerns, especially those of introducing a baby into the household and the subsequent risk of reviving painful memories of James. Mary had been quick to dismiss such concerns and it wasn't long before Frankie, now six months, old had arrived at their home.

Mary and Fred had proven loving and kind parents and as the years rolled by, they raised the subject of adoption. Initially social services had resisted the proposal, but with Frankie settled and no realistic prospect of his natural parents ever claiming him, and by now, the fact that Mary and Fred had been the only parents that he had ever known, they eventually relented and Frankie was formally adopted by the couple.

Fred still harboured doubts; he had found it difficult from the outset to accept Francis as his own child, but he had suppressed these doubts for Mary's sake. As time passed, things had become more and more strained between Fred and his wife. Mary had spent more and more time with Francis now he was hers, officially and legally, if not by birth. Fred had felt marginalised. Mary hadn't seemed to notice Fred's dilemma as her attentions focused on Frankie and his welfare.

She had only taken cognisance of Fred's unhappiness when it was too late. He had packed a suitcase and announced that he was leaving.

At first Mary hadn't believed him. She had thought he was just looking for attention, jealous of the close relationship she had had with Francis, or, as she had reluctantly conceded, Frankie, as he preferred to be called. Anyway, where would he go?

When he hadn't returned that night or the following one, only then did Mary seek him out. After a number of enquires around the neighbourhood and at his place of work, she had found out, only after a reluctant work colleague had spilled the beans, that Fred had moved to Liverpool and was living with a younger female colleague who had herself left her husband and moved there a few months back. It had been widely speculated that the two had been having an affair for some time previously.

Mary had been devastated by this revelation and blamed herself for not seeing the signs: the working late into the evenings, the so-called work-related weekends away, the phone calls that rung off when she answered. It had all made sense. In retrospect she realised that it was, at least in part, her own fault for spending less time with him, less interest in his work, his hobbies; she had been so devoted to Frankie's upbringing.

Fred's departure did not, however, lessen Mary's devotion to Frankie. She could not hold him in any way responsible for the break-up of her marriage. In fact, following it Mary had spent more and more time with Frankie, becoming increasingly dependent on his presence in her life.

Over time, as Mary's focus and attention on Frankie's wellbeing grew, Frankie, now rapidly becoming an adolescent, became himself increasingly resentful of Mary's overwhelming and obsessive nature.

It seemed only a matter of time before Mary would be lonely once more.

She called to him as she mounted the stairs.

No answer.

She called again. Louder this time, presuming he was engrossed in something or that he was huffing and deliberately ignoring her.

Again there was no response.

She knocked on his door.

'Francis, I know you are upset but come downstairs and we can talk about it.'

Still no answer.

She pushed the door open a little way and peered round it.

The room was quiet. Nothing out of place, but she couldn't see Frankie. She opened the door wider and looked around the room.

He wasn't there.

A growing sense of panic gripped her; she tried to suppress it, but it kept rising so she could feel it in her chest, in her throat. She struggled to call his name again, this time to the empty landing in case he was in the bathroom or her bedroom.

Whatever else she was, Mary was a realist. She knew that she was overprotective of Frankie and that Frankie was becoming increasingly resentful of it. Although she had the insight and tried to treat Frankie as an adult, she slipped back time and time again into her old ways. Today's event with those boys had just been the culmination of her anxieties of ultimately losing Frankie as she'd lost James, and she couldn't bear the thought of being lonely again.

She rushed about, looking in every room, becoming increasingly distraught with each empty area.

Finally, she gave up. He wasn't in the house. She went back downstairs and sat silently in the living room, gripping the arms of her chair as tears rolled down her face and she said a silent prayer for his safe return.

chapter thirteen

The gloom of the evening had started to engulf her as she sat lonely and abandoned in her living room, hoping and praying for Frankie's safe return.

That dammed letter. I knew I should have destroyed it, she kept saying over and over to herself. As she did so, she gripped and picked at the fabric of the arms of the chair. She generated such force that the stitching was by now starting to come apart.

Mary Walker had been Frankie's mother since he was a baby. She was his real mother, not the parent who had abandoned him all those years ago. Mary knew the story of Frankie's birth and his rejection, but not once had she ever rejected him. She had nurtured him, she had watched him grow up and above all she loved him.

She thought back to the time when those fateful letters from Cathy Marsden had started to arrive. She recalled the first one. It had looked like any other letter, but when she had torn it open and started to read the contents, her body had frozen. Time had seemed to stand still.

Frankie had obviously found one of the letters and kept it. That was how he knew about Cathy Marsden.

She recalled with remorse and regret the decision that she had come to back then. After the set-to with Frankie over that letter, for reasons she couldn't think of now, she had foolishly decided to go and see Cathy Marsden herself and have it out with her. To put a stop to her demands to see her son.

She had made arrangements for Frankie to go and stay with her sister for a few days, using their fight as an excuse. It would allow her time to figure out exactly what to do and, more importantly, what to say if and when she met with Cathy Marsden.

Of course, it hadn't gone well. Mary had travelled down to Cathy's village and then after arriving she had simply sat in her car opposite the Marsdens' cottage, not having the courage to approach the house.

As she had sat, suddenly the front door opened and a man, Cathy's husband, Mary thought, stepped outside. He had been holding a suitcase; presumably he was staying somewhere overnight. He had turned to kiss a woman, who by now had also appeared at the doorstep. She had been younger and prettier than Mary had imagined, but there had been no doubt in her mind that this was Cathy Marsden.

Mary had slid down her seat as Cathy's husband reversed out of the driveway and then sped off down the road.

Watching his departure had emboldened Mary to leave the car and approach the house. At least Cathy Marsden would be alone in facing her.

Cathy Marsden had been surprised to open the front door and be confronted by an older woman wearing tired and unfashionable clothing, but the most alarming aspect had been the look on the other women's face.

Mary Walker's frustration had increased when, after announcing who she was and why she was there, she had not only found Cathy Marsden unhelpful and unwilling to listen, but that she had doggedly held her ground, barring Mary's entrance and flatly trying to argue her 'rights' regarding Frankie. She had even threatened to call the police and have Mary arrested for harassment.

All the frustration and anger that Mary had felt and had stored up now came rushing to the surface. She recalled, but only vaguely, how she had tried to push past Cathy with a strength and determination she did not know she possessed.

Cathy had put her arm across the doorway, determined once more to prevent Mary's entry to the house.

It was then, Mary remembered, that she had snapped. Mary was not a violent woman, but she had been angry and Cathy Marsden had refused to listen to her.

It was then that she had raised her hands and pushed Cathy hard, so hard in fact that that the younger woman had stumbled backwards, tripped and fallen to the ground. As she fell, Cathy Marsden had struck her head on the corner of a wooden cabinet at the side of the hallway.

Mary had stopped in her tracks and stood, looking dumbly down at the now slumped and motionless figure of her adversary, lying on her back on the ground in front of her.

Regaining her composure, Mary had calmly closed the front door behind her, moved forward and then lifted up the younger and still only semiconscious woman, before carrying her further into the house.

The regret of that fateful meeting now weighed heavily on her conscience.

chapter fourteen

Seated at the same table she'd occupied just the day
before in East Brookfield's small café, Baz struggled to
piece together the day's events. She felt her body give an
unconscious shiver. She couldn't determine if it had been the
cold weather or the shock she'd just had that had made her
do so.

She regarded her new companion with a mixture of
apprehension and curiosity. He cupped the mug of milky,
steaming tea in both hands and drank thirstily from it. He
was about sixteen, she thought, though he looked younger.
The thin, pale and as yet hairless features along with his gaunt,
bony frame added to the appearance of his immaturity. His
clothes were dirty from sleeping rough and his hair was greasy
and matted. He glanced up as he reached for a piece of toast
and caught her staring at him.

Baz averted her gaze, embarrassed.

'What?' The cracked, intermittently lower pitch of his voice betrayed his emerging adulthood.

'Nothing, just curious that's all,' she replied quickly.

'Curious? Curious about what?'

'Well, for a start why you were sleeping in that shed, and secondly, and more importantly, why you thought I was your mother.'

His cheeks flushed, giving him for the first time since Baz had met him, a nearly healthy glow. At the same time, he shifted awkwardly in his seat. 'Oh, that. Just a case of mistaken identity, that's all. I couldn't see you properly, it was dark in there and the light from the door blinded me.' He tried to divert the conversation by demolishing the piece of toast and reaching for another.

'Fair enough, but you still haven't told me what you were doing in there in the first place.'

'It's a long story,' he admitted somewhat reluctantly as he gulped down another mouthful of tea.

'Okay, okay, maybe we haven't got off on the right foot. My name's Baz, by the way.' She extended her right hand towards him.

The young man paused momentarily and regarded the outstretched limb inquisitively, before dropping the remains of the toast onto the tablecloth, rubbing his hand on his trouser leg and then gripping her hand in his. His grasp was light and gentle.

'Pleased to meet you, Baz. Sorry to give you such a shock back there.'

Baz fixed him in a stare.

'What?' he asked quizzically.

'And...'

'And, what?'

'And, your name is?'

'Oh, sorry.' He hesitated; it seemed to Baz that he was uncertain whether to divulge his identity or not. 'Oh, okay, it's Francis, Francis Walker, my friends call me Frankie.'

'That wasn't too difficult now, was it, Frankie? Now, how's about you tell me why you were in that shed in the first place.'

'I'd rather not, if you don't mind.'

'Actually, I do mind.' Baz's blood was up and she wasn't going to let him off the hook so easily. 'You're what, sixteen? You're sleeping in a garden shed and presumably not your own garden shed? You scare me half to death and you want me just to drop it? *Dream on, kid.*' She fixed his eyes in a cold, hard stare and the last few words were uttered slowly and deliberately and with a certain resonance that ensured he understood, implicitly, that she was not going to be fobbed off.

'Look, I am really sorry that I frightened you. I didn't mean to.' Baz noticed a small tear well up in the corner of his eye.

'I know you didn't—'

'But, seriously,' he continued, leaning forward and at the same time dropping his voice, 'if I tell you something, you promise you won't tell the police or anything?'

Baz sensed his unease and made a cross over her heart with her index finger.

'The fact is…' he continued haltingly, 'the fact is… I've run away from home. There's a guy back home, he's into drugs and things—'

'What sort of things?'

'That doesn't matter, anyway, what does matter he's going to kill me and I had to get away.'

'Surely the police should be involved or at least your parents could help…?'

Frankie started to cry. He brushed aside the tears with the back of his grimy sleeve. 'But that's the whole point,' then, almost inaudibly, 'I don't have any parents, or at least, real parents.'

'Sorry, Frankie.' Baz rested her hand reassuringly on his shoulder. 'I don't understand, everybody has parents.'

'Not me, I don't, or at least, I didn't.' His voice quivered with pent-up emotion. 'Well, except for her.'

'Who?'

'Cathy.'

'Cathy?' Baz repeated, almost afraid of the answer.

'Cathy Marsden. She's my mum, my real mum.'

The floodgates were open now and Frankie, uninterrupted, poured out the story of Tommy Hardcastle and his gang, but mostly he talked about his discovery of his adoption and the problems with his adoptive mother. Baz sat silent, staring at the grubby, skinny adolescent and trying to take in what he was saying. In truth, she took in little. After the mention of Cathy Marsden, Baz's blood had frozen in her veins; it no longer seemed capable of supplying her brain with oxygen. She struggled to listen to what he was saying, to make sense of it. But none of it seemed to register, just the fact that she was sitting in a café in Cathy Marsden's home village drinking tea with a kid who claimed to be her son. As she regained her composure, she held up her hand to stop the flow of vilification about his adoptive mother that he had seemingly moved on to.

'Hold on. One minute. Have I got this right? You're telling me that Cathy Marsden is your real mother?'

Frankie looked at her strangely. 'That's what I said. Don't you believe me?'

'Well, actually, come to think of it, no, I don't. Cathy didn't have any children.'

'Look, I've got her letter.' Frankie looked hurt by Baz's rebuttal. He reached into his anorak pocket and produced a crumpled piece of paper which he handed triumphantly to Baz.

Slowly and carefully, Baz unfolded the sheet and read and then reread the contents, watched eagerly all the while by Frankie's unblinking gaze. As she let the letter slip from her now trembling hands, Frankie continued 'See. Now, do you believe me?'

Baz could hardly speak but managed to whisper the words, 'Yes, Frankie, I do believe you.'

'So…' Elated by his success, he continued, 'Do you know her? I've been watching the house since I got here last night, but I didn't see her. It was dark when I got here. I found the shed and I thought if I slept there last night, I'd be able to see her this morning before I actually introduced myself. When you opened the door, I thought you were her. I am really sorry that I scared you.'

Baz now felt tears running down her own cheeks. She reached out and grasped Frankie's hands in hers and squeezed them tight.

'What's wrong? Why are you crying?'

'Frankie, listen to me. I'm sorry, I'm really sorry…'

'Sorry? Sorry about what?'

'Frankie, Cathy Marsden's dead.'

Frankie struggled free of her grip. He slammed his fists hard on the tabletop. 'I don't believe you… My so-called mother has sent you, hasn't she? To lie to me again!' He almost screamed the words at her as he rose to his feet, flinging his chair aside and bolting for the door.

Baz leapt up to pursue him, only slightly aware of the owner's concerned face, startled by the sudden commotion, peering through the curtain from the kitchen.

Baz caught up with Frankie just outside the café door. She tried to restrain him by holding on to the shoulder of his anorak. But he shook his arm out of the jacket sleeve and attempted to escape once again.

'Gerroff!' he growled.

'Frankie… Frankie. Wait a minute, please. Let me explain.'

Frankie paused, half-turned, his anger slowly abating, salty streams of tears pouring down his face. He rested his head against the café wall.

'It's true, isn't it? My mother's sent you down here?'

'Frankie, I don't know your mother.'

'She's not dead. Please tell me that she's not dead.' He clung on to her, shaking uncontrollably. Baz encircled him in her arms and led him gently back into the warmth of the café.

Frankie was quiet throughout the journey back to London. He just sat on his hands and stared blankly at the passing countryside. She'd simply explained to the Turners that something had come up and she'd had to return to London unexpectantly. Reluctantly Frankie had agreed to allow her to bring him home too. His dreams shattered, there appeared to be no further reason for him to remain in East Brookfield.

'Are you going to be okay?' she asked as they reached the outskirts of the city.

'Just have to be. Won't I?' he mumbled in reply.

'What about that Hardcastle guy? You need any help to deal with him?'

'I'll cope.' Frankie stared discontentedly at his knees.

'What about your mum? What do you want me to tell her?'

'Tell her whatever you like. It doesn't matter anymore.'

'Come on, Frankie, I'm trying to help. Really, I am.'

Frankie paused for a minute, seemed to be thinking of something and then, turning to Baz, he asked, 'Okay, then, I told you why I was in Cathy's shed, but tell me, what exactly were you doing looking in there?'

'Oh.' Baz gripped the steering wheel tightly and tried to concentrate on driving through the increasingly congested streets.

'Well…?'

Baz thought for a moment and then pulled the car to the side of the road, turned off the ignition and then swung around to face Frankie. 'Frankie, I'm really not sure that I should tell you this.'

'What?' Frankie leant closer to her, intrigued.

'This is between you and me. Okay?'

'Okay.'

They sat at the roadside, oblivious to the hum of the passing traffic, as Baz tried to explain, in as gentle terms as possible, so as not to upset him further, the nature of her investigations, the manner of Cathy's death and her suspicions surrounding it. When she finished, she looked hard into Frankie's face, trying to detect if she had hurt him with what she'd had to say. Frankie, for his part, seemed only to look harder, more resolute.

Finally he spoke, in hushed tones at first. 'I was told she died shortly after I was born, then I see a letter from her and she wants to see me. So she's alive, and now you tell me that she is dead and you think she might even have been murdered?'

'Frankie, I didn't say that! Oh, God, I shouldn't have brought all this up. Look, it's just me being paranoid, that's all. Just forget I mentioned it. If you do, I will. I'll just drop the whole thing and get back to my lab and get on with my PhD.'

Frankie grabbed her two hands and, squeezing them so hard that it hurt, he pulled her with unexpected strength across the car towards him. The handbrake dug into her ribs.

'No. No,' he pleaded. 'Don't give up. You promise me that you won't give up. Promise me that you'll get to the truth about my mother's death.' Tears cascaded down his face as his head dropped below his shoulders, but still he held her in a vice-like grip. 'Promise me, promise me. Please.'

Baz's heart melted at his obvious distress. 'Okay, Frankie, if that's what you want, I'll go back to East Brookfield and see what I can find out. Are you sure you want me to do that?'

'Yes, yes, absolutely.' He held his face now inches from hers and shook her hands.

'Okay, okay. I'll do it.' Though in truth, Baz was very unsure of the wisdom in what she was saying. 'Now we've got to get you home.'

chapter fifteen

Baz lay in bed, eyes open, staring at the ceiling. She thought through all that had happened since she'd made that promise to Frankie. She had delivered him home safe and sound. When she'd knocked at his front door, she recalled how he had slunk defensively around behind her and remained there even after the door was opened.

Frankie's mother had been older than Baz had expected. It was obvious that she had been crying. She looked Baz up and down suspiciously, but then she shook slightly as she spied Frankie. Her face changed instantly, a smile breaking out across her lined features.

Frankie eased himself around Baz and was instantly engulfed in an all-consuming embrace. Mary Walker then ushered them both inside and fussed about making tea as Baz sat uncomfortably in the living room. Frankie had deserted her and snuck up to his bedroom. Over the tea,

Mary Walker, her reticence now disappeared, thanked Baz profusely for 'rescuing' Frankie and returning him to her safe and sound.

Baz tried to explain how and where she had encountered Frankie and the story of her own interest in Cathy Marsden and her death.

Mary Walker at first appeared disinterested and dismissed many of Baz's concerns about Frankie and his mental wellbeing. But when Baz started to recount the story of her own research and her doubts about the nature of Cathy Marsden's death, Mary Walker suddenly became agitated. She wrung her hands, looked around the room as if for support and then finally got up and stood behind the chair she had been sitting in, gripping its back firmly with both hands.

'I think you should leave,' she announced, staring at the floor.

Baz admitted that she was a little surprised that Mary Walker wasn't interested or didn't seem to care about the loss of Frankie's birth mother. She was certainly being more than evasive regarding any further talk of Cathy Marsden or the manner of her demise. Baz took the hint. It was clear that Mary Walker was not going to tolerate any further discussion on the subject, so she decided to take her leave of the Walker household before things became even more difficult.

As she was leaving, Mary Walker shook her hand but deliberately avoided her gaze.

Opening the front door, Baz thought she could detect a look of relief in Mary's expression.

As she stepped outside, she turned one last time to say her goodbyes; as she did so she spotted Frankie sitting at the top of the stairs, shoulders slumped in a pose of resignation.

Baz waved towards him and shouted, 'I'll see you again soon, Frankie, I promise.'

He lifted his head at the call and mumbled something that Baz couldn't quite make out. She was about to ask him to repeat it when Mary Walker slammed the door in her face, leaving her standing on the doorstep alone.

The welcoming early-morning rays of pale sunlight were just beginning to filter through the chinks in the curtain. She was acutely aware of the soft rhythmic snoring to her left.

At least John Marsden was still asleep.

In truth, she'd been awake for the last few hours unable to sleep. She fixed her gaze on a small fly making its way across the ceiling above her and tried to focus her thoughts. Alternately she felt embarrassed and ashamed. She had deluded him. *Just to sneak a better look around the house? No, no, surely that wasn't it*, she kept telling herself. She did like him, she admitted that, and she was flattered by his attention, there was no doubt about that. At this moment, though, she wished for nothing more than to be somewhere else, somewhere far away from East Brookfield, and that, she conceded, was a bad sign. A sign that she had not been honest with herself or with him. Worse, though, she had discovered things, things she wished she hadn't, things she knew that she had no right to. Why, she asked herself for the hundredth time that morning, had she promised Frankie that she would come back to East Brookfield? Why was she persisting with her fruitless investigations when everybody was telling her, even her own common sense was telling her, just to drop the whole thing and get on with her life?

She had returned to the village and had manufactured an 'accidental' encounter with the doctor.

They had hit it off immediately and had shared some time over coffee and a doughnut in a local café. He had taken her number and the next day had phoned her at work, explaining that he had the day off the following day and would she join him for a picnic in a local beauty spot?

Over the next few weeks, they had managed, despite their individual work commitments, to meet up for short periods of time which they both appeared to enjoy. And both seemed to look forward to their next encounter.

During their time together, Baz, though she always felt guilty about it, tried to glean more information surrounding his wife's death. John Marsden was sullen on the subject; he said as little as he could. It was clear that although her death was now some time ago and he had appeared to be over it, that he was unwilling, or unable, to discuss it with a third party, even one that he was growing close to.

Despite her misgivings, particularly regarding her initial motives in meeting John, as more time passed, their feelings for each other grew. The feelings. Her feelings for him appeared entirely reciprocated. Gradually, therefore, her probing into Cathy's death diminished.

However, back at work and after another interview with her supervisor, the subject of the brain sample result had once again arisen.

Baz had to admit she was no further on in explaining the anomaly.

As luck would have it, shortly after that encounter, John Marsden telephoned and she graciously accepted his invitation to dinner at his place. He offered to cook for her.

Baz felt guilty in accepting the invitation, especially as Dr Morton's criticism of the lack of progress was still stinging in her ears and, reluctantly, she had made the decision that, despite her growing feelings for John Marsden, she had to explain Cathy's death in terms of her awareness and fear. Therefore, she was destined once again to deceive the man she was now essentially dating.

John had, of course, once again been reluctant to discuss Cathy during their evening together. *Fair enough, that was understandable*, Baz thought.

'She died in an accident, a terrible accident,' had been his only comment on the subject before he'd lapsed into a temporary morose silence.

Baz tossed and turned and wished for the sleep that wouldn't come. At the time she had wanted to, he had asked her to, but staying the night and searching his house had, at best, been deceitful.

She felt gentle rubbing at her shoulder. She startled, realising she must have finally fallen into a fitful sleep. She sat up quickly, pulling the sheet around her.

'Sorry, to wake you. But I have to go to work. I've brought you some toast and coffee.'

'What?' Wearily Baz blinked her eyes and looked up into his smiling face. He was already dressed. Checked shirt open at the collar, green corduroys and sensible brown brogues. He still looked more like a vet. She smiled back at him.

'What's that?' she asked, pointing to the CD cover nestling beside the plate of toast.

'Oh, that. That's the Fleetwood Mac CD you so liked last night. Keep it. It's the best of… I've got all the tracks on other CDs, it's yours. Listen, I've got to go. See you tonight, maybe?' He looked at her hopefully.

'I don't know. I think I should go back to London, get back to work.'

He looked crestfallen.

'But do you have to rush off?' she asked. 'Stay for a few minutes. I'll never eat all that toast anyway.'

He glanced at his watch. 'Well, maybe I have a couple of minutes.'

He reached for a piece of toast and bit off a corner. Baz watched him as he did so. 'Tell me something, John.'

He glanced up from the toast, a fragment sticking to the side of his lower lip. 'What?'

Baz reached forward and stoked the errant crumb aside. 'Do you get lonely?' Then, embarrassed by her forthrightness, 'I mean, living out here in the country.'

John Marsden laughed. 'You townies are all the same, aren't you? You just can't cope without the reassuring roar of traffic or the embrace of the inevitable exhaust fumes. You think that it's all peace and tranquillity out here, do you?

'No, but—'

'Listen.'

Baz looked quizzically at him. 'Listen? Listen to what?'

'Just listen.'

Baz screwed up her face and concentrated hard. At first the silence seemed oppressive. Then she heard it.

A bluebottle buzzed around, occasionally bumping into the windowpane in its attempts to escape the confines of the room. Outside a gentle wind was blowing against the few remaining leaves on the trees. In the distance, a tractor chugged across some far-off field. Nearby, a dog barked once, then again, from a neighbour's garden. A flight of crows cawed, wings flapping, as if startled by the sudden noise. Suddenly the cacophony of noises seemed deafening.

She smiled. 'Okay, I get it. It's not quiet and peaceful at all. It's all going on out there, isn't it?'

'Nature.' John Marsden smiled back at her, crunching another piece of toast and then, to be sure, wiped his chin with the back of his hand. 'That's what it's all about. I love it out here. It's never the same, it's always changing, the noises, the countryside, no two days are exactly the same. That's why I live here, why I don't want to move. But you're right, sometimes I do get lonely. Cathy, my wife...' He hesitated. 'Cathy, she died...'

'I know, you said last night.'

'I loved her very much, but I didn't treat her well, always out working.' He hesitated. 'I guess you've probably heard that excuse a hundred times before. But I did love her and I miss her. It's been nearly two years now and I still think of her. You are the first... the first... well, you know.' He seemed almost ashamed and he avoided Baz's attentive stare as he fixed his gaze silently down at the pillows.

'Did you ever live in the city?' asked Baz, trying to change the subject which was clearly painful for him.

'Of course I did. If truth be told, I'm actually a townie myself.'

'You are...?'

'Yes. I was born and bred in Southwark. Then moved to Glasgow to train. After that I hawked my medical skills around a load of inner-city practices before almost on a whim I accepted a locum post out here. Loved it. Stayed and been here ever since.'

'I would never have guessed.'

'No reason you should. There's a lot you don't know about me.'

'Why here? Do you have relations from around here?'

'No...' He hesitated. 'Cathy has... had a brother nearby.'

Baz looked at him questioningly. 'Why did you hesitate?'

'Oh, it's nothing. It's just that we don't see eye to eye, that's all. Bit of a family rift, that sort of thing.'

'Surely he must have been some support when Cathy died?' Baz encouraged him to continue.

'Actually, no. Brian's a bit bitter. Kind of blames me for her death…'

'But why should he do that?' Baz realised she was probing.

'It's a bit personal. Anyway, look, I really have to go. Duty calls.'

Before Baz could apologise, he'd spun around and had disappeared out the door and down the stairs. She heard the front door slam behind him.

Baz punched the pillows angrily, annoyed not with him but rather with herself. She lowered the small breakfast tray down onto the floor and raised herself up in the bed before burying her head between her knees.

After a few moments she glanced down at the CD he'd given her.

'Ugghh. Fleetwood Mac. I don't believe it.'

chapter sixteen

'Well, hello, stranger.'

Baz wheeled around at the words. She had thought that the building was deserted. Certainly there wasn't the hustle and bustle that was usual for this time of the morning. When she had arrived, she had poked her head tentatively around the door of the laboratory; she had been surprised to find that the workbenches still lay idle. The men from the Department of Health were also nowhere to be seen. The silence that now pervaded the large room was almost oppressive. So she was startled by the sudden intrusion as she had moved quietly towards her own workstation. She turned and was not unhappy to find Josh, leaning on his office doorframe, a bottle of Coke in his hand. He was smiling.

Josh took a swig and then straightened up and walked over towards her. 'I've been trying to get hold of you.'

'You have? Why?' Baz tried to regain her composure. She had hoped to get in unnoticed but wasn't entirely displeased that it was Josh who'd blown her cover.

'We're in the clear.'

'What do you mean we're in the clear?' So much had happened in the last few weeks that Baz wasn't quite on his wavelength.

'What I say, I've just heard, we're in the clear. The inspectors have been and gone. It seems everything is above board, the paperwork's done, no errant bits of tissue found. So we're in business again.'

'That's great news.'

'It is and it isn't.'

'Stop talking in riddles, Josh.' A hint of irritation in her voice.

'Well,' he continued, ignoring her tetchiness. 'It's still going to be more difficult than before to obtain new samples. At least till all the fuss dies down.'

'Oh, yeah. I suppose so. How long do you think that's going to take?'

'What with all the media interest and that, probably somewhere in the region of ten years.'

'Ugh. Do you really think so?'

"Fraid so, but anyway, as it stands, at least we can get going again. Dr Morton gave the go ahead just this morning. That's why I was trying to get hold of you. You were the first person I tried to ring but you weren't answering your phone.'

'I was away,' Baz winced.

'So what brings you in?'

'I wanted to review some of the results. They're in my desk.' The tiredness from her sleepless night and the drive back was starting to kick in. She didn't really relish the thought of trying to explain to Josh what she'd really been up to.

'Okay, see you later.' Josh ambled back to his office and resumed his series of calls to inform his colleagues of recent events.

The guilt from her deception of John Marsden and her unwillingness to share it with Josh – even though he had been a co-conspirator, if only a partial one – weighed heavily on Baz as she climbed onto her stool at the workstation. She was genuinely an uncomplicated person. Or at least she had been until all of this had kicked off.

Baz sorted through her papers and then reviewed the data on her laptop but only became more frustrated as the hours passed. When Dr Morton tapped her on the shoulder and suggested a talk in his office, she was actually quite pleased for the interruption.

'So you got the word, then?' he said as he manoeuvred himself behind his desk and indicated for her to sit on the chair opposite.

'Yes, but I gather it's going to be difficult to get fresh samples.'

'Possibly, there are moves to produce new post-mortem consent forms that should cover all eventualities and be more open in explaining exactly what's involved in a PM. That's what the politicians want, anyway, but it could take time and it's likely to hold up our research.'

'So what should I do?'

'Well, that's why I wanted a chat.' He leant forward on his desk with an earnest expression. 'Look, you're not the only one in this predicament. There are probably hundreds of research projects up and down the country that are going to be similarly affected. Human tissue research has been set back years because of this scenario. Most people recognise that, and the examiners of your PhD are certainly going to have to accept that also.'

'So...?'

'So, we aren't going to just give in, are we?'

'No, but—'

'No buts, you're a resourceful and intelligent young lady and more importantly, a very capable and promising young scientist. So you will do what all scientists do when faced with a difficult situation.'

'What do you mean?'

'Do you think that Darwin was ready to throw in the towel when he was threatened with excommunication because his theory clashed with the bible's teachings? Did Alexander Fleming, after a stray penicillin fungus invaded his precious bacterial culture, killing all around it, throw a tantrum, run around the lab swearing, throw his hands up in horror and then toss the petri dish in the bin?'

'No.' Baz laughed at the vision.

'No, they did not and nor will we. No, we will just have to adapt.'

'So, what do you suggest?'

'I suggest, for a start, you recheck the work you've already done, sort it all out and get it written up, perhaps even try to get it published in a journal. Given the small numbers, you'll just have to present it as preliminary results. Then, given that you've still got samples left, try to think of other neurochemicals or other substances that could be detected, what value it would be to identify them, what methods already exist to detect and measure them. Perhaps it might actually then be better to work on and try to develop new methods of detection and analysis, rather than what you've been doing to date, which is simply employing established methods and trying to quantify them in standard ways.'

'But... but that changes the whole emphasis of my thesis...'

'What's all this obsession with fear? What is fear, anyway? It's just a series of automatic responses to a given stimulus, a fight or flight response. It results in increases in heart rate, sweating and adrenaline surges. If truth be told, it's an outdated and outmoded response. Don't you tell me that palpations, and damp, sweaty palms ever got someone a date with the girl or boy of their dreams, or even that the butterflies in your stomach actually helped you in your recent interview.' Dr Morton fixed Baz in his gaze, rose to his feet and continued, 'Look, they're just suggestions, go away and have a think about it. I have no doubt you'll come up with a good idea. I've got every confidence in you.'

Baz sought solace in a chocolate brownie and an espresso coffee in the staff canteen. Dr Morton's pep talk had done little to relieve the sickening feeling of scientific demise. She had skulked out of the laboratory; the weight of his apparent confidence hung heavy on her shoulders.

The buzz in the restaurant helped to distract her thoughts. It was nowhere near full. It was between breakfast and lunch and still a little early for the administrative staff's mid-morning coffee break. Nonetheless, there was still plenty of activity. Catering staff were busying themselves in preparation for the lunchtime rush. An aproned attendant loaded pre-packed sandwiches onto shelves in the display units, while others piled fresh plates and trays into their racks. A couple of ancillaries, both in their late teens, were clearing the tables of discarded cups and plates, sweeping the crumbs from their surface into large plastic bags. Some of the cooks and kitchen orderlies, taking advantage of the slack time between meals, sat around a large table talking quietly or enjoying a hurried cup of coffee.

A door slammed, caught by the wind, at the far end of the canteen, and the seated group was joined by two others, a man in his fifties and a woman in her mid-twenties with bleached blonde hair cut very short. The man was energetically trying to stuff a packet of twenty Marlboro lights into his trouser pocket. The hospital had declared a no smoking policy some years ago, which had only resulted in groups of staff and patients huddled together in many of the outer doorways around the hospital puffing away as if their life depended upon it. Baz guessed that it was from just such an impromptu gathering that they had just returned.

Around the canteen there were smaller groups of customers, mostly nurses, whose breaks were staggered, so they tended to eat and drink at unusual times. In one corner a junior doctor, probably at registrar level as he looked about the same age as Baz, was sharing coffee with a group of medical students, while at the same time holding court on the finer details of some obscure medical diagnosis.

Baz contemplated the remains of her chocolate brownie as she pondered her future.

Later on that day, she found herself in the more sombre surroundings of the Registry of births, deaths and marriages. She had convinced herself that she was simply doing what Dr Morton had suggested, tidying up the loose ends and drawing a line under that part of her project. It hadn't been too difficult to convince the attendant of her bona fides, a glimpse of her medical ID and a winning smile was all that had been required to grant her access to the registry's computer.

As she punched the details into the keyboard, she became more and more frustrated by the results. Firstly, she had successfully located the Marsden's wedding details, the date, the place, but more importantly, Catherine Marsden's Christian name: *McGrath*. Then she texted Frankie, asking him for his date of birth.

Her phone rang almost immediately, disturbing the only other occupant of the record office. He glared across at her, annoyed by the interruption to his studies.

'Why do you want my date of birth?' came Frankie's voice.

'Bit of background research,' she whispered into the phone, trying to keep her voice as low as possible so as not to disturb her fellow researcher. 'I'll explain when I see you.'

'Alright, then, I suppose,' he replied. 'It's 12th February 2003.'

'Thanks Frankie, see you soon.' She rang off before he could protest any further.

She returned to her studies. *Two thousand and three*, she calculated in her head, *Cathy would have only been sixteen years old*. She scrolled through the births section; coming to 12th February 2003, she cross-referenced it with Catherine McGrath. Nothing. She tried Cathy McGrath, again, nothing. She tried dates either side of the 12th, widening the search, in case Frankie, being adopted, hadn't actually been born on the date he thought he had but had only been told that was his birthday.

Still nothing.

Strange, she thought. Why had Frankie's birth not been registered? Was there more to the circumstances of his birth and subsequent adoption than they already knew?

chapter seventeen

Frankie was feeling pretty miserable. It wasn't that his mother had been fairly off-hand with him since he'd returned from East Brookfield. It wasn't even the malevolent stares from Tommy and his gang as he'd arrived at the school gates that morning and climbed out of her ageing Ford Fiesta. He knew that she'd watched him all the way into the building and that Tommy had too. No, it wasn't that that caused him to feel so downcast. He hadn't actually met Cathy Marsden, so he couldn't even grieve properly at the news of her death and that did upset him. But what really got to him was that now he knew he was trapped, there was no escape. For so long, ever since he had discovered that letter, he had clung on to the hope and belief that one day, against all the odds, his real parents would come and claim some part in his life. Things would be better. Now that wasn't to be. There just didn't seem to be any hope any longer. No light at the end of that particular tunnel.

The first lesson was science. Frankie usually enjoyed the subject, the experiments, testing theories. Today, he just took his place at the workbench, dejectedly pulling himself up onto the stool and sat still, resting his head in his hands, staring straight ahead into space. Nobody seemed to notice him and the lesson passed by without him registering anything of its content.

The bell rang and the rest of the class leapt to their feet and headed for the laboratory door. Frankie looked up and slowly followed, heaving his rucksack of books over his shoulder.

'You're very quiet today, Frankie, something up?'

Frankie glanced over his shoulder. Mr Thompson, the science teacher, had paused from wiping the whiteboard with a heavy cloth, noticed Frankie's sullen demeanour and spoken.

'No. Nothing really.'

'Well, cheer up, old son, it may never happen.' Mr Thompson resumed his cleaning, whistling softly as he did so.

'So much you know,' whispered Frankie to himself as he pulled the door behind him.

The rest of the morning's classes dragged by in a similar fashion, Frankie mentally opting out of each in turn. At last, the bell rang for break; he dragged himself wearily outside and propped himself up against a wall at the far end of the playground. He stood quietly staring at the ground in front of him. The day was cold and grey, and soon a light drizzle started causing most of the other pupils to seek refuge indoors. Frankie remained oblivious to the elements; he didn't hear the footsteps approaching but was suddenly aware of a pair of shiny brown brogues stopping directly in front of him. Frankie glanced up. The familiar lined, bespectacled face of 'Beaky' Baker, the headmaster, was frowning down at him. 'Walker, a word in my office, please.'

Frankie struggled to his feet. 'Oh, right, Mr Baker. Err... when?'

'Now, Walker, if you please, follow me.'

Frankie trailed back into the building, trying to keep up with Mr Baker's long, striding pace.

The headmaster sat down behind his cluttered desk, pushed his glasses further back on his large proboscis, the facial feature which had given rise to his nickname, and beckoned for Frankie to sit down on the opposite side. 'Your mother rang me this morning, Walker.'

'Oh?' Frankie visibly slumped into his seat.

'She mentioned that she thought that you were having some trouble.'

'Trouble…?' All of a sudden Frankie didn't want to be here.

'Yes, Francis, trouble.'

Frankie noted the use of his Christian name and reckoned that this was Beaky's way of trying to ingratiate himself.

'Trouble. No, Sir. No trouble.' This was the last thing Frankie wanted. He shifted uncomfortably on his seat.

'Don't be obtuse, boy.'

Frankie didn't quite know what obtuse was, but whatever it was, he agreed that he probably was being it.

'Your mother told me, in no uncertain terms, that she thought you were being bullied here in school,' Beaky fixed Frankie in an unblinking stare, 'and even ran away from home because of it.' Before Frankie could make any kind of response, the headmaster continued, 'You are aware, Francis, that St Gerrard's prides itself on its policy against such behaviour. Bullying at any level cannot and will not be tolerated. So if there is any truth in your mother's allegations, I want to hear about it, directly from the injured party if possible.'

Frankie stared hard at the floor between his feet.

'Well…?'

'I've nothing to say, Sir.'

146

'Nothing to say!' The headmaster was getting agitated. 'That's not good enough, Walker. Serious allegations have been made and they will be investigated, with or without your co-operation.'

Frankie stuck to his ground and remained silent.

'Look, Walker,' the headmaster regained his composure and tried another tack. 'We're on your side in this. If there's a problem, then we can help.'

'I've really nothing to say, Sir.' A tear welled up in the corner of Frankie's eye, but he brushed it aside with the back of his hand before the headmaster noticed.

'Now look, Francis. If you won't tell me exactly what's been going on, I'll have to pursue the matter anyway,' and then added ominously, 'in other directions.'

'Other directions?'

'Yes, Francis, other directions. Your mother mentioned the name of another boy.' He reached for a piece of file paper on the desk, readjusted his glasses and studied the note for a few seconds before adding, 'A certain Thomas Hardcastle.'

That's it, I'm dead, thought Frankie, sinking even further into his seat.

'I really don't know what she meant,' he blurted out.

'Alright, Walker, have it your way. You've put me in a very difficult situation. If you won't co-operate, then I've no alternative but to talk to Hardcastle myself.'

'Do you have to, Sir?'

'Yes, Walker, I do. You can leave now.'

'But… but…' Frankie tried to stand up, but his legs felt like jelly.

'No buts, Walker, and perhaps a bit of detention might help jog your memory. Report to Mr Jones at four o'clock. One hour's detention and then I want to see you again, shall we say break time tomorrow? Now get out.' The headmaster rose to his feet to emphasise the final words.

Frankie beat a hasty retreat, slamming the study door behind him.

The extra hour in school had passed quickly enough. It had at least allowed him to catch up on some of the schoolwork he'd missed when he'd been away. But neither that nor the peace and quiet had lifted his spirits. So it was with a heavy heart that he turned right at the school gates and headed for home. It was already getting dark and a cold wind clawed at his face as he trudged along, pulling his blazer tightly around his skinny frame.

Suddenly from the surrounding gloom, a figure emerged threateningly directly in front of him. Alarmed, he turned to flee, but another larger figure stepped out of a doorway and stood immediately behind him. Before he could take any other evasive action, they grabbed him. He felt a hard blow to his head before he sank unconscious to the ground.

chapter eighteen

Baz sat at her desk and pondered her next step. Despite Dr Morton's insistence on taking a different track in her research, she could not stop herself from mulling over the events of the last few days and the increasing turmoil she felt around the death of Cathy Marsden. Undoubtedly there remained unanswered questions. If for no other reason, she felt that she at least owed it to Frankie Walker to get to the truth surrounding her death.

After turning things over in her mind, oblivious of the surrounding activity in the laboratory, she finally came to a decision. She rose to her feet and removed her white coat, draped it over the stool on which she had been perched and headed for the door. The coat, she hoped, would lead anyone who enquired to the conclusion that she was still in the building if not at her workstation at that particular moment.

She slipped quietly out of the laboratory and made for the main hospital entrance. There she wound her way along myriad corridors until she reached the pathology department. She was cautious, as she knew that if Professor Clayton spotted her there again there would be trouble.

She searched for the office that she needed.

There it was, on the right, halfway down the corridor. It bore the nameplate 'Brian Milligan, Pathologist'.

She knocked tentatively at the door. 'Come in,' came the reply from within.

Baz opened the door cautiously and put her head around it. She immediately saw the occupant who was seated behind a small wooden desk in the centre of the room. He was surrounded by piles of books and files, seemingly haphazardly distributed around the small room.

'Dr Milligan?'

'That's what the sign on the door says. What can I do for you, young lady?'

Baz started to speak but was interrupted by Dr Milligan waving her into the room itself.

When he had moved some of the heaps of files aside and she had seated herself on a chair that he had revealed from under yet another large pile, she continued, 'I'm one of the researchers in Dr Morton's department. Baz Clifford.' She introduced herself and, partially rising, offered her hand to shake.

Dr Milligan returned the handshake.

'Mmm... I think I've heard your name before. I think Professor Clayton might have mentioned you.'

*Uh, Oh,...*thought Baz.

The pathologist, who usually only dealt with dead and hence expressionless people, did, however, detect the immediate concern in Baz's expression.

But she needn't have worried. Dr Milligan's face broke into a wide smile. 'Professor Clayton and I don't often see eye to eye. So tell me what can I do for you?'

Baz went on to, as succinctly as she could, explain the findings from her tissue sample and the anomalies it threw up. She left out the visit to the Marsden's home, her meeting with Frankie Walker and most of all, her brief relationship with John Marsden.

'So what is you want from me?'

'You were the pathologist that carried out Cathy Marsden's post-mortem.'

'I was?'

'Yes.' Baz declined to admit who she had come by this information.

'Okay, I'll take your word for it. I admit my memory of individual post-mortems is sketchy. I carry out a lot, you know.'

'This one was on an unexpected death of a young woman in a fire.'

'Mmm... I do seem to recall something of that nature. It was how long ago, did you say?'

Baz recounted the exact date of death and of the post-mortem. They were, by now, firmly implanted in her brain.

Dr Milligan got up, walked around his desk and started to rummage in some of the piles of files propped up against the back wall of his office.

'It'll be here... somewhere.'

'Can I help?' asked Baz, watching him move a series of files from one pile to another.

'No, no. It will be here somewhere.' Then he somewhat triumphantly, Baz thought, pulled out and held one file above his head.

'Here it is. This place may look like a chaotic mess, but it is organised chaos. I do have a system, you know.'

Baz looked sceptical but had to admit he had located Cathy's file.

'Okay. So what do you want to know?'

chapter nineteen

Baz sat quietly and watched as the pathologist slowly read and reread the file that he had plucked from the piles of other very similar files. He stroked his chin and occasionally nodded his head as he did so, then he looked up.

'I do remember this case.'

He looked hard at Baz, seemingly trying to decide if he should divulge any concerns that he had harboured concerning it. Finally, he appeared to come to a decision.'I remember this case quite well, actually, there were issues at the time, I recall.'

'Issues?' Baz was now all ears.

'Yes. I recall that the police were quite pushy to get it resolved ASAP. I felt that I was being railroaded a bit.'

'Railroaded?'

'Yes, okay, they were under pressure. We were under pressure. Everybody just wanted a nice, clean, quick solution.'

'What do you mean?'

'Superficially, it all looked straightforward. The reports from the scene confirmed a house fire. The police detective who attended the post-mortem explained the circumstances, that is, or was, that she had been found in bed, had made no attempt to escape, there was alcohol in her system and clear signs of charring from the fire. Death by hypoxia was suggested by the appearance of cyanosis, a darkening of the haemoglobin in the red cells which occurs when they are starved of oxygen. There was also evidence of ischaemic lesions within the brain. Ischaemic lesions are a common finding when the brain is starved of blood, or rather, oxygenated blood. So we concluded that cause of death was lack of oxygen, i.e. hypoxia, but...' His voice trailed off.

'But?' Baz sat forward.

'Well. I'm not really sure I should tell you this, it's really only speculation.'

'Tell me.' She gripped his desk and fixed her eyes on his.

The pathologist shifted in his seat, clearly uncomfortable. 'Well,' he continued, 'there were, what shall I say, certain anomalies.'

'Anomalies?'

'For example, we didn't find any charring in the respiratory passages. But that could be explained by the fact that she died from hypoxia due to the smoke before the fire reached her and she had time to inhale heat or flame.'

'Fair enough.'

'Except that we also didn't find any evidence of smoke inhalation either, nor raised levels of carbon monoxide in the blood as we would have expected to.'

'So she might not have died due to the fire.'

'I didn't say that.' He fidgeted more obviously now. 'As I said, the policeman was quite pushy on getting a result. He suggested that the fire might have sucked the oxygen out of the room, so she became hypoxic before she actually inhaled the actual smoke.'

'Is that common?'

'It's a possibility, but no, it is not a common scenario.'

'So,' Baz considered the facts she had been presented with carefully, 'it is possible that Cathy Marsden was dead before the fire started?'

'It's a possibility, actually, come to think of it, I do remember there were signs of a recent head injury.' He reread the notes. 'Yes, there it is, though it didn't seem to be severe and it certainly wasn't the cause of her death, she definitely died of hypoxia and that is the commonest mode of death in house fires, not actually burning, as most people might think.'

'But you didn't raise your concerns with anybody? For example, could the blow to the head have knocked her out and somebody put her in bed, then set fire to the house to cover their tracks?'

'Well, I did try, but as I said, the policeman seemed quite content to accept that she died accidentally due to the house fire.'

'I think I know what you mean. I've already met Detective Inspector Warlow, he can be quite stubborn.'

'Warlow? No, I don't think that was the name.' He consulted his file once more. 'Yes, I'm right, here it is. It was a detective sergeant that was in attendance. According to the file, one Detective Sergeant Brown. I think he might have been one of the inspector's team.'

Mmm, Baz thought, *Inspector Warlow did indeed seem the type to delegate work to others.*

chapter twenty

Armed with the new information, Baz decided to return and confront DI Warlow with it in the hope, however small, that he might reopen the investigation into Cathy's death.

Arriving, if somewhat apprehensively, back at the police station, she asked the desk sergeant if she could see Inspector Warlow. He looked at her with suspicion. It was the same desk sergeant as the last time she had visited and he clearly knew that Warlow had given her short shift on that occasion. Baz suspected that he had her down as a time-waster. But he, albeit somewhat reluctantly, Baz thought, lifted the telephone and got through to his superior to inform him of her presence. Replacing the receiver, the sergeant motioned for her to sit and wait on the bench across the foyer.

It seemed like hours that she sat waiting before DI Warlow finally arrived. During this time the desk sergeant had intermittently glanced up from his desk to reassure himself that she was still there but was probably hoping that she wasn't. But Baz was going nowhere, not until she had a chance to discuss things with Warlow once more.

When he finally did appear, he did not look particularly pleased to see her.

She rose to greet him, feigning a smile as she shook his hand. 'I have some new information for you.'

'You said that the last time,' he replied with clipped tones.

'Actually, I didn't, but let's not get off on the wrong foot—'

'It might be a bit late for that.' He regarded her scornfully.

'Wait, wait, honestly, this time I do have new information. Important information.'

'Let's hear it, then.'

'Can we go somewhere a little more private?' she asked, glancing around the foyer.

Denis Warlow looked about. The desk sergeant was watching them out of the side of his eye and now other people were milling around.

'Alright, we'll go to my office. You better not be wasting my time, though, young lady.'

With that he turned on his heel, proffered his ID card to the electronic sensor at the door to the inner sanctum of the police station, pushed the door open and beckoned Baz to follow him through.

They ascended two flights of stairs and navigated their way through a sea of cluttered desks, the occupants of which barely raised their heads to acknowledge their senior officer, before finally reaching DI Warlow's office. In contrast to the communal office outside, it was neat and tidy. Baz hadn't really noticed last time as that visit had been a little fraught and she hadn't taken in the detail. Whatever paperwork there was had been carefully sorted into neat piles or filed away in one of the many filing cabinets that stretched over one wall of the office. Warlow, despite his overweight and rather unkempt personal appearance, was clearly a meticulous man when it came to official matters.

The inspector puffed his way around his desk and sat down, waving to Baz to sit also on her side of the desk facing him.

'Okay, shoot.' He leant forward and fixed her in a hard stare.

Baz was not, on this occasion at least, going to be intimidated by him. She was on a mission and the fat policeman was going to listen. 'Regarding the Catherine Marsden case, I believe that there are certain facts which you may not be aware of,' she began.

'Certain facts?' He looked sceptical.

Baz was not going to be sidelined, not this time. 'Yes, for example,' she continued. 'Were you aware of the fact that the pathologist harboured doubts about Mrs Marsden being alive at the time of the fire?'

DI Warlow now looked puzzled. 'What do you mean, doubts?'

'I mean the finding, or rather the lack of the finding, of smoke in her lungs.'

'How do you know this?'

'I talked to the pathologist myself. He said the police basically took the whole scenario as a *fait a complet* and so ignored it.'

'Well, maybe so, perhaps I should talk to him myself.'

'Please do.' She went on to give him the pathologist's contact details. 'I think he's expecting a call from you.'

'Alright then, could you sit outside and I'll try and ring him now, just to see what he actually has to say.'

Baz rose and exited the office. She was a bit annoyed at having to do so, as it was apparent that Warlow still didn't believe her. She sat just outside the office on a chair at the back wall of the communal office, observing the buzz of activity that was happening all around her.

After several minutes, the inspector opened his door and ushered in once more. Baz detected a clear change in the atmosphere.

'It appears you are correct. Dr Milligan has confirmed the… what shall we call it… discrepancy, but he also confirmed that the lack of smoke in the lungs is not conclusive evidence that she was dead before the fire happened.'

'I appreciate that, but there's more.'

'More?' The inspector looked aghast.

'Cathy Marsden was having an affair before she died.'

Denis Warlow slumped back in his chair. 'An affair, you say, just how do you know this?'

Baz hesitated; she was reluctant to tell the fat inspector of her deceiving of John Marsden and even more so of how she happened to see the letter that suggested the affair.

'I just know, that's all. You will just have to take my word for it. She was having an affair.'

'When and who with?'

'To be honest, I don't know for sure, but I think not long before she died.'

'It's not much to go on.' He paused as if in thought.

Baz waited patiently for his decision.

Finally he spoke, 'Alright, you may, and I emphasise, may, be onto something. There is reasonable doubt about the mode of death and now you suggest a motive. So I agree we will look at this again, but for your sake I really hope that you are not wasting our time on this.'

With that he got up and moved to the door of the office. Opening it, he looked about and then summoned another man into the office.

'This is Miss Clifford.' He indicated Baz to the younger man that now stood in the doorway. 'She has some new information regarding the unexpected death of a Catherine Marsden. Do you remember the case?'

The younger man pondered for a few seconds and then replied, 'I think I do recall it actually, but it was quite a while ago. Fairly open and shut, if I remember correctly.'

Denis Warlow turned to Baz. 'Miss Clifford, this is DS William Brown, he led the original enquiry.'

Baz remembered the name from her discussions with Dr Milligan in the pathology department and as she had suspected, DI Warlow had now confirmed that he had delegated the task of investigating Cathy Marsden's death to his subordinate.

'So what is this all about?' the detective sergeant asked.

Baz noted the younger man's slim athletic figure, which was in marked contrast to that of his senior colleague.

DI Warlow produced a second chair and sat his sergeant down beside Baz. He then asked her to repeat what she had told him.

When she had finished, DI Warlow turned to his junior colleague and asked, 'Well, what do you think?'

'Not wishing to insult Miss Clifford, I think it's simply supposition. There doesn't really appear to be much new hard evidence in what she says.'

'I hear what you are saying, William, but in my opinion, it does cast some doubt on the verdict of misadventure. I think it is worthy of a second look.'

'I disagree, Sir. But you are the boss.'

Baz looked from man to man. She felt she had been vindicated.

'Your doubts have been noted, DS Brown, but nevertheless, as you were in charge of the original investigation, I'd like you to reopen enquires and consult with Miss Clifford. Is that understood?'

'Loud and clear, Sir.'

As they left the office, DS Brown guided Baz over to his own desk, which was in the centre of the communal area. As they sat down, DS Brown leant forward and said, 'I'm not really happy with this. You know that?'

'I did get that impression.'

'I have a hundred other cases that I'd rather be getting on with rather than reopen this one, but the DI has given me an order. So be it.'

Baz sat across the desk from Detective Sergeant William Brown. He listened politely, if somewhat disinterestedly, to Baz's description of her findings.

Finally, she paused and, addressing him directly, asked, 'Well, what do you think?'

The detective sergeant sat forward in his seat, resting his elbows on the desk, and placed his hands on his chin. He seemed to be considering things at least, Baz thought.

'So what do *you* think?' he asked.

'Surely it changes things? The post-mortem findings are—'

'Inconclusive at best,' he interrupted, sitting back on his seat.

'But taken together with the fact that Cathy Marsden was having an affair?'

'We only have your word for that,' he answered, clearly unable to conceal his irritation.

'Yes, but it must cast some doubt on the case. It must raise the possibility that Cathy Marsden could have been killed, rather than dying simply due to an accident?'

'By killed, you mean murdered?'

'I suppose I do,' though she hesitated to put her thoughts into words.

'Murdered by whom?'

The question took Baz by surprise even though it was an obvious one and that Baz had spent many hours mulling over Cathy Marsden's demise. 'I suppose,.' she hesitated, 'I suppose,. the obvious candidate must be her husband.'

She hated herself as soon as she had said it. She actually did have feelings for John Marsden despite the deception she had played on him, and he seemed to be a really nice down-to-earth guy, but, given the affair, and as the letter was stored in his house, it seemed certain that he must have known about it; he had to be the prime suspect.

The detective leant back once more. 'I suppose, and it is only a possibility, that we could look into John Marsden's movements on the night in question.' He smiled in Baz's direction. 'How would you feel about that?'

'It's a start.' It was out before Baz had properly considered her response.

'A start? A start? Now listen, young lady, I have already made clear that I, sorry, *we* were entirely satisfied with our original conclusion regarding this case. I have offered to look at things once again, albeit on a whim of yours, and you suggest it's just a start.'

'I'm sorry. I didn't mean it that way.' Though in truth she did. 'Thank you so much for listening to me and really I am grateful for your willingness to look at the case again.' She then added, for effect, 'Honestly.'

As she left the office, she remembered an old adage that she had once heard. The secret of success, she had once been told, was sincerity: 'Once you learnt to fake that you could do anything.'

It was just that she wasn't sure who had faked it best in the interview, her or the detective.

chapter twenty-one

When Frankie woke up, he noted the strange surroundings. Everything was white and polished. He wasn't in his own bed and a plastic tube was attached to his arm. He tried to push himself up the bed to better appreciate his surroundings but felt a sudden stab of pain in his back.

He groaned involuntarily.

Immediately he was aware of somebody at his side. It was a young woman, somebody he didn't recognise. She wore a blue uniform and blue plastic gloves. Before he had moved, she had been fiddling with the tube in his arm.

The stranger smiled at him. 'Hello, Francis. Welcome back to the land of the living.'

'Where am I?' he mumbled; his mouth felt dry, his lips cracked and he could taste dried blood.

'You're in the City hospital. You had some kind of accident.'

'An accident? What do you mean?' More pain suffused his body as he shifted position to face her.

'You were found unconscious in the street and brought here by ambulance. That's all I know.' She paused and then continued, 'Your mother's here. She's been very worried about you. She has been sitting at your bedside since you arrived. I had just sent her off for a cup of tea when you started to come round. I am sure she'll be back in a minute.' She touched Frankie's arm reassuringly.

Almost on cue, the door to the small room was pushed open and Frankie's mother appeared clutching two paper cups. 'I brought one for you too,' she said to the nurse. Then, seeing Frankie sitting up, she exclaimed, 'Oh, Francis. I was so worried.' She stepped forward and tried to hug him, forgetting the two cups in her hands. The nurse stepped forward to relieve her of them.

Frankie's mother smothered him in an all-embracing hug.

He groaned as the pressure increased the pain in his ribs.

'Oh, sorry, Francis, am I hurting you? I didn't mean to. It's just I'm so happy to see you come round.' A tear trickled down her cheek.

Frankie looked into his mother's face. 'What happened to me?' he asked painfully.

He caught his mother glancing up at the nurse, now standing a little back from the bed to allow the reunion more space. The nurse in turn returned her look but remained silent.

After a moment's thought, his mother turned back to face him. 'It appears you were attacked, Francis.'

'Attacked?'

'Yes, attacked in the street. Hit over the head and kicked when you were lying unconscious. Then they just left you lying there.' She started to cry more vigorously. 'They just left you there. Lying in the street. Lying in the street,' she repeated, shaking her head as she did so. 'I just can't believe it. How could anybody do that to another human being?'

The nurse leant forward and softly asked Frankie, 'Have you any idea who did this?'

Frankie had an idea, but he decided to keep it to himself and he just shook his head from side to side.

'The police will want to talk to you, Francis.'

'It's Frankie.'

'What?'

He caught his mother looking down disapprovingly at him, but she allowed him to continue.

'It's Frankie, everybody calls me Frankie.' He addressed this remark as much to his mother as the unfortunate nurse.

'Okay, Frankie,' the nurse responded, 'the police have already been here. They left me a number to contact them on when you regained consciousness. Is it okay for me to give them a ring?'

Frankie really didn't feel like talking to the police. He guessed that it was Tommy and his gang that had attacked him, but there was no way he was going to share this with the police, or anybody else, for that matter. He knew he couldn't prove it. He couldn't really remember much of the attack and he certainly couldn't remember any faces as such. To drop Tommy and his gang in it, only for them to get off, was only going to cause him more of the same. Of that, he was convinced.

So he determined to say nothing.

chapter twenty-two

The next day, Baz travelled down to East Brookfield and found herself standing in front of John Marsden's front door. She somewhat apprehensively rang the doorbell.

After what felt like an age, the door was opened by an elderly woman holding a duster in one hand.

'Is Dr Marsden in?' Baz asked, trying to suppress the anxiety in her voice.

'He's out, I'm afraid, at his surgery, I'm just cleaning his house for him. Every Wednesday I come here. If you want to see him about something medical, I'm sure he could fit you in. He's very good that way.'

'No, no, it's something personal. I was just hoping to catch him at home.'

Baz started to turn away and take her leave, but the older woman caught her arm.

'If it's personal, why don't you come in? He'll be back for his lunch. You can see him then.'

Baz hesitated, but only momentarily, before following the cleaner as she retreated down the hallway.

'You sit down at the table.' She pointed to a table in the centre of the kitchen. 'I'll make you a cup of tea while you're waiting.'

As she fussed around the kitchen, filling the kettle, fishing out teabags and mugs, and then searching for a teaspoon. She obviously wasn't used to visitors calling round when she was at work in John Marsden's house.

'He is usually back around one-ish. His surgery is just around the corner,' she explained.

Baz glanced at her watch. It was already ten to one; it had taken her a couple of hours to get down to East Brookfield, notwithstanding the time it had taken her to summon up the courage to actually do so.

As she sipped the warm sweet tea, she heard the front door opening.

'That'll be him now. Always punctual, he is.'

Baz felt her heart rate increase and her palms felt sweaty as she gripped the mug of tea more tightly.

'Hello, Mrs Houston, I'm home,' came John Marsden's voice from the hallway. As he put his head round the kitchen door, he stopped, almost transfixed, to see Baz seated at his kitchen table.

'You've got a visitor,' announced Mrs Houston, somewhat unnecessarily.

'Ah, hello… again,' stuttered Baz.

John Marsden dropped his briefcase at the doorway and made his way over to where Baz was sitting. He pulled out a chair and sat down opposite her. 'I didn't think I'd see you again. You just left without even saying goodbye.'

167

Mrs Houston hovered in the background, now clearly intrigued by the meeting. John Marsden seemed to recover his composure as he turned to face the cleaner. 'I think you can probably go now, Mrs Houston. I'll settle up with you next time if that's okay.'

'But I still have the upstairs to do,' she opined. It was obvious to Baz that she wasn't going to go quietly. Mrs Houston clearly felt there was a lot of village gossip to be gleaned by this improbable meeting.

'No, it's alright, Mrs Houston. I think I can manage the upstairs,' he said kindly but firmly, before adding, 'Baz and I have a lot of catching up to do.'

He turned to Baz again.

Reluctantly, it seemed, Mrs Houston gathered up her things and made her way out of the house.

As the front door closed behind her, John Marsden was first to speak. 'Why did you sneak away? Was it something I'd done?' He sounded self-reproachful, fully believing it was his fault that they'd parted.

Baz felt truly sorry for him. The guilt burnt into her chest.

He smiled. 'It is good to see you again.' He appeared genuine in this sentiment.

It only served to make Baz feel even worse. 'It's a long story,' she replied.

'Well I have all the time in the world, well, at least until my afternoon clinic at two o'clock. Why don't you start at the beginning?'

Baz shuffled her feet and lowered her head, avoiding eye contact. This wasn't going to be easy, but she had known that before she had come down to the village, so she started to confess the whole sorry tale of her deception of him.

John Marsden had sat silently through Baz's confession. His expression had hardly changed throughout. Finally, he spoke, 'So you came here for the sole purpose of investigating my wife's death?' He seemed to physically diminish in stature as he spoke. 'So what was that night together all about? More deception?'

Baz was horrified, not only by her own behaviour, but because she actually felt something for him.

'I didn't plan for this to happen.' She reached for his hand only for him to withdraw it quickly.

'I came down here in the first place simply to see if I could glean any details about her death. Then I met you and… well, I enjoyed your company and one thing led to another.'

She moved towards him and knelt at his feet.

He looked down at her, a disapproving look on his face.

'You've got to believe me, John. I didn't plan any of this… Honestly.' She was almost pleading. 'I do care for you, I really do. I apologise for the deception. It was stupid, I know that now.'

John Marsden's facial expression seemed to soften a bit. 'So what did you hope to find out, then?'

Baz hesitated then went on to explain the detail of her research and the anomaly she had unearthed.

'Baz.' He interrupted her before she could finish the explanation. 'There isn't anything more than what you told me the police explained. Cathy died peacefully in her sleep. I got back late from a conference; the fire crew had already rescued her from the bedroom. I jumped in and tried everything I could to resuscitate her.' His head dropped and Baz detected small tears well up in the corner of his eyes. 'But… she was dead. She was already dead.'

He looked down into her face.

'Do you understand what I'm saying? I did everything I could, everything within my power. But I couldn't do anything, she was already gone.'

Baz looked away, ashamed at her own actions and of the grief that she had inflicted on him.

After a few minutes of silence between them, he went on to explain that the firemen had told him exactly the same details that the police had given Baz surrounding how Cathy had been found apparently asleep in bed and that there were no suspicious circumstances.

'I would have done anything to stop it happening, to have saved her. Don't you think I've been over this a million times in my own mind? What if I hadn't gone to that bloody conference? What if I'd just left earlier? What if I'd rung her on the way home to tell her I was on my way? She might have been awake and able to escape.' The tears now ran freely down his face.

'But what about the affair…?' Baz bit her lip, but it was out before she could stop it.

John Marsden slowly lifted his head. He stared at her quizzically. 'What… What did you say?'

There was no going back now for Baz. 'I-I saw a letter that you'd kept. It suggested that Cathy was having an affair.'

He got up shrugging her aside. He walked over to one wall, striking it with his fist and then paced around the room, shaking his head. 'You were sneaking about my house? Looking at things that don't concern you?' He could no longer look her in the face.

Baz felt a little frightened by his new demeanour. 'I'm sorry. It was stupid of me. I know that now,' she pleaded.

John Marsden continued to walk back and forth in silence for what seemed to Baz an eternity.

Finally he seemed to come to a decision. He sat down opposite her once more. 'I really liked you, Baz, I really did. But you have deceived me… and worse, you seem to be implying that I actually had something to do with my wife's death. Nothing, nothing, could be further from the truth.'

He leant in closer to Baz's face.

She pulled back a little, still frightened.

'Let me tell you why you are so wrong.' He engaged her gaze.

'I loved Cathy and she loved me, she really did. Yes, she had an affair, but it was my fault, I know that now.' He stared hard down at the floor.

'Let me explain.' He looked up and made eye contact. 'She was a city girl, at least at heart, but we moved down here to the country because of me. Me and my job. I didn't take to hospital medicine and it was always my dream to be a country GP. As I told you, this practice came up and I jumped at it. I didn't discuss it with Cathy, I just presented it as a done deal, she had no choice in the matter. She had to give up the job she loved to move down here with me. She lost touch with her city friends and found it hard to relate to the people here. Her brother had actually moved near here some years ago but that was only a small comfort to her.

'I was too busy to notice her unhappiness. I worked very hard, too hard probably, to establish myself here in East Brookfield. I was such a good doctor helping everybody else that I couldn't even spot my own wife slipping into depression. I was just so preoccupied that I ignored Cathy and didn't appreciate nor accept all that she had given up for me. I know that now. So, bored as she was, and I firmly believe that was all there was to it, she had an affair, but I found out and confronted her.'

'That was the letter I saw,' added Baz, reluctant to admit that she had been rifling through his things before coming upon it.

'There were other clues as well.'

Baz looked at him questioningly.

'The way she acted, that she got mysterious phone calls, all the usual stuff. The point is, I was aware of things, I was starting to wise up, to get things properly into perspective. Work/life balance and all that. I had come to realise what I had been doing to Cathy and how unhappy she was.'

Baz moved a little closer.

'So yes, she had an affair. She admitted it. But she broke it off. We decided to start again and to get things right this time. We had a real heart to heart. We told each other things that we had never spoken about before until finally we even came to a decision together, a decision that could change our lives dramatically.'

Baz looked at him, initially puzzled by this revelation.

'It was to do with our past, something from our past lives that could have come back and altered our future. But I'm not going to talk about it.' He raised his hand in a stop signal to reinforce his reluctance to elucidate any further.

Baz though immediately thought of Frankie but decided not to pursue that line of questioning as it was likely to prove fruitless in any case, at least at this time.

So instead she asked, 'Did you know who the affair was with?'

'I never met him. To be honest, I didn't want to. I didn't ask and she didn't tell me. It was over, that was all I knew.'

He stopped and lowered his head into his hands momentarily before looking up again. 'He didn't like it, though.' He almost smiled at the recollection.

'How do you mean?'

'He kept pestering her. Ringing her up. He even called round once when I was out, but she didn't let him in. I think, though, he finally did get the message.'

Baz gripped both of his hands in hers before getting to her feet. She felt genuinely sorry for him and her own guilt weighed even more heavily on her shoulders after his explanation.

'I'd better go.' She turned and, letting his hands go, started to make for the door.

As they stood in the hall saying their tearful goodbyes, his from the story he had related, hers from her genuine remorse and feelings for him, there was a knock at the door.

John Marsden eased past Baz to open the door, only to find Detective Sergeant Brown standing in the porch.

Baz and the policeman exchanged puzzled looks over the doctor's shoulder.

'Dr Marsden?'

'That's me.'

'DS Brown, Bridgetown Police.' He said matter-of-factly, raising his identification card in front of the doctor's face.

'I know, I think we've met before, at the enquiry into my wife's death?'

'Perhaps so, Sir. May my colleague and I come in?'

The detective and a uniformed officer pushed past John Marsden as he flattened himself against the wall in the narrow hallway. William Brown and Baz exchanged puzzled looks as he passed her on the way to the living room. Neither spoke.

Standing in the living room, the detective was the first to speak.

'Dr Marsden, we would like you to accompany us to the station to answer charges relating to the death of your wife.'

Baz was at first struck dumb and then horrified by the turn of events; she tried to intervene.

'No. I think there's been some mistake. John had nothing to do with his wife's death. I'm sure of that now.'

At the word 'now', John Marsden wheeled round to look quizzically at Baz.

'I'm sorry, John, I'm sorry. Really I am.'

'Could you get your jacket, Dr Marsden? We have a car waiting outside.'

Nobody said anything further; they all simply filed out. John Marsden locked the front door of his house before being eased by the uniformed constable into the backseat of the police car.

As the car drove off, Baz stood at the front gate of the house, watching it travel down the small road before turning right and disappearing from view.

Tears streamed down Baz's face.

chapter twenty-three

Baz was sitting alone in her flat, knees drawn up to her chest, cradling a cup of tea that had already gone cold because she hadn't made any attempt to drink it. She just sat motionless, going over and over recent events in her head. One minute she was sure John Marsden must have murdered Cathy, the next that he couldn't have done it. She tried over and over again to rationalise things but was failing miserably.

Her mobile buzzed on the table beside her; she reached down and retrieved it. Glancing at the screen, it was a number she didn't immediately recognise.

'Hello,' she answered tentatively.

'Oh, hi, Baz. It's me, Frankie.'

'Frankie, how are you? I was going to ring you to bring you up to speed. Where are you?'

'Uhh... Actually, I'm in hospital. I borrowed this phone to ring you.'

Baz nearly dropped the phone. 'Are you okay? What happened?'

'I was attacked. Hit over the head and—'

'Attacked. By who?' Baz interrupted.

'Long story. Don't worry, I'll tell you later.'

'Are you okay?' Baz couldn't conceal the concern in her voice.

'That's just it. I'm fine, really. In fact, they want to discharge me.'

'That's good news at least.' Her relief was palpable.

'That's why I'm ringing you, actually.'

'Yes?'

'I don't want to go home, not straightaway at least. Could you come and pick me up and then…' he hesitated, 'could I stay with you?'

Baz remained silent.

'Just for a few days… honest.'

'What about your mother?'

'I'll talk to her, I'm sure she'll understand.'

Baz was less sure. But she agreed to his request on the condition that he did clear it with his mother.

A couple of hours later and Baz stood beside the nursing station watching as Frankie leant over the bed he had occupied for the last twenty-four hours, packing his pyjamas and toiletries into a plastic bag that the ward had provided.

His packing completed, he gathered up the bag and made his way slowly and painfully over to where Baz stood waiting.

'Are you sure your mother is okay with this?' she asked.

He nodded.

'Absolutely sure?'

'Honestly, I am. I told her I needed a little time and she has accepted it. That's not to say she won't be on the phone every ten minutes.'

He attempted a smile but winced when he did so, as his face still hurt from the bruising he had sustained.

The drive back to Baz's flat was done in silence. Baz didn't know what or how to ask what had happened and Frankie seemed reluctant to share.

Arriving home, Baz helped Frankie out of the car and, one hand supporting him and the other clutching the hospital bag, she eased him up the stairs to her small flat. She threw the plastic bag containing his things onto the sofa as she pushed the front door open.

'There's not much room, I'm afraid.'

Frankie could see that for himself. The door opened directly onto a small living room with an open plan kitchen on one side; on the other side of the room there was a partially open door, through which was a bathroom. Another door at the far end of the room was, he guessed, the bedroom.

'I wasn't expecting visitors.'

Another understatement. The living room was cluttered with books, papers and discarded clothes, and a wastepaper bucket overflowed beside the small television set in the corner of the room.

Letting go of Frankie's arm, Baz hurried to try to shuffle a few of the papers and books into larger single files in order to create a bit of space for Frankie to sit down.

A space cleared, Frankie slumped onto the sofa.

'You'll have to sleep on the sofa as well, I'm afraid. I don't have a spare room.'

'That's fine, honest. Just for a day or two till I figure out what to do.'

Baz left him to unpack the bag and make himself comfortable. She busied herself making them both a cup of coffee. 'How do you like it?' she asked.

'White two sugars, please.'

After the coffee and a couple of rich tea biscuits, Baz felt emboldened to ask Frankie what had happened. It took a bit more probing, but finally the whole sorry story of his mother and Tommy Hardcastle's gang poured out.

Baz felt genuinely sorry for him. 'Look, Frankie, you can stay as long as you want. We will figure a way around this, okay? But you must promise me one thing.'

'Anything, what?'

'You must ring your mother every day to let her know you are alright. Agreed?'

'Agreed,' he muttered somewhat reluctantly.

Then she brought him up to date with all that had happened to her since they had last met. Naturally leaving out the bedroom details.

When she had finished, Frankie's spirits seemed to have lifted considerably.

'So that was why she wrote to my mother? They did want to see me again?'

'It does look that way, Frankie, but let's not get too carried away.' Baz was acutely aware the Cathy Marsden was dead and therefore any future hope of any sort of reconciliation had long since disappeared.

chapter twenty-four

As John Marsden emerged from the police station, he noticed the driver's door of a small red Fiat opening ahead of him.

Baz emerged, waving in his direction.

He stopped, then turned and started to walk the opposite way.

'John! John!' He heard the clatter of her steps as she jogged after him. She reached out and grabbed his arm. 'Please, John, give me a chance to explain.'

He wheeled around and held her in a cold stare. 'What you did was unforgivable.'

'I know, I know. I am so sorry. Please let me explain.'

'What is there to explain? You think I killed my own wife and then you told the police as much.'

'No I don't… okay, yes, I did, but I don't now. I am genuinely sorry. Can we go for a coffee or something and I'll explain everything.'

John Marsden considered his options, but then reluctantly agreed.

They sat across the small wooden table in the café nearest the police station. Conversation was unsurprisingly a bit stilted at first.

'At least they let you go.' Baz tried a reassuring smile.

'Not exactly, I'm on police bail,' he answered curtly.

'They don't still think you killed her? Do they?'

'Thanks to you, yes, they do.' He leant forward over the table towards her. 'It's just that they haven't got sufficient evidence to hold me, that's all.'

Baz slumped in her seat. 'I am so sorry, John. I really didn't mean to drop you in it.'

'Drop me in it? Drop me in it?' He had raised his voice and other customers had looked round questioningly in their direction.

Baz glanced about self-consciously, but then decided to defend herself. 'Look, John, there are some unanswered questions. I got it wrong, but I still do genuinely feel that Cathy's death was not as straightforward as it seemed.'

John Marsden leant back and seemed to recover his composure. They sat silently for a few minutes, both mutually avoiding any eye contact.

Finally, he looked up and spoke, 'Alright then, explain yourself.'

'Explain myself?'

'Tell me exactly why you think Cathy's death was suspicious.'

When the waitress came, Baz ordered two coffees. After they had arrived and more, importantly, any other customers remaining in the café had lost interest in the earlier arguing couple and were no longer eavesdropping, Baz tried as succinctly as possible to explain her studies and the anomalies she had unearthed in the post-mortem.

'It's all a bit circumstantial, isn't it?' he replied, although he did seem to be thinking about it.

'That's what the police said too.'

'I bet they did,' then added, 'I did have some misgivings myself.'

'Misgivings?'

'It wasn't like Cathy to get so drunk she would crash out, as they implied she did. She was a bit upset and anxious, but I still found it hard to believe that she could have set the house on fire the way it was portrayed.'

Baz listened intently but then seized upon the words 'upset and anxious'. She queried, 'Why was she upset and anxious?'

'All to do with that dammed affair of hers,' he answered almost absentmindedly.

'Her affair? What about it?'

'Well, it was over. I told you that. It was a mistake on her part, she could see that. She had just been flattered by the attention, that's all. She told me it was nothing serious and she ended it as soon as I found out.'

'So?'

'So, the guy didn't see it that way. By all accounts he wanted the relationship to continue, wouldn't take no for an answer, started to badger her, even stalk her, she said. I think she was genuinely afraid of him.'

'Afraid of him?'

'Maybe that's too strong a word. I don't know, maybe she was, again, my fault for not paying sufficient attention. I was too caught up in my job, making plans trying for the future, trying to change our lives.'

Baz's mind started to work overtime. If Cathy's death wasn't an accident and John Marsden was innocent, then who was to blame? And who was this possessive lover? Could he have something to do with it?

She decided not to air these thoughts with her companion, at least, not at the moment, but she couldn't quite let it go.

'Who was this guy?' she asked.

'You know as much as I do. You've seen the letter. He's called Liam, apparently he was an old school friend of hers, but she hadn't seen him again until relatively recently before the affair began.'

'Where did she meet him?'

'Again, I don't really know.' Then, as an afterthought, 'Actually, maybe I do. She told me that she'd bumped into him, quite literally, as it turns out. Cathy had a car crash sometime around early 2015, April, I think. Someone bashed into her at the crossroads just outside the village. The chap, Liam, he was involved in some way. It was then that they realised they knew each other from school and arranged to meet up, I guess to reminisce, at least at first. It probably spiralled from there.' Then he stopped and fixed her with a look of realisation. 'Oh, no. No you don't. Don't even think about it. Do you hear me?'

chapter twenty-five

Baz stood in front of the desk that had become so familiar to her at the police station. After, what seemed like an eternity, Detective Sergeant Brown appeared from a door behind the constable seated at the desk.

'Miss Clifford, what a surprise.' He could not hide the annoyance in his voice. 'What can I do for you?' he said, indicating a bench on the far side of the waiting area where they both moved over to and sat down.

Baz proceeded to impart the new information about the mystery lover that she had gleaned from John Marsden.

The policeman, while at first appearing totally disinterested in hearing what she had to say, seemed to pay more attention to her as her narrative proceeded.

After she had told him all she knew, William Brown paused, reached for his notebook which was inside his jacket and took some notes.

'April 2015, you say?'

Baz confirmed the date.

'The crossroads near East Brookfield?'

Again, a confirmatory nod.

'Which one? There are several in the area.'

'Ah, I'm not really sure, but there can't have been too many car crashes around that area in April 2015.'

'Possibly not.'

'You would have a record, wouldn't you?'

'Only if the crash was reported to us. Many are so minor we wouldn't even hear about them.'

'But you will have a look, won't you?'

'If we have a file, I'll pull it and have a look at it. See if there is anything relevant in it.'

'You will let me know, won't you?'

'This is a police matter now. Do you understand? You keep out of it, mind your own business and let us get on with it.'

Reluctantly, Baz rose to her feet, bade William Brown goodbye and left the police station, not at all convinced that he would really follow up on the lead she had given him.

Having returned to her flat and discussed everything that had happened with her new flatmate, she and Frankie mulled through things over a cup of coffee.

'So you don't think he will do anything?'

'I'm not sure, but I don't trust him, that's all.'

'Well, if he won't do anything, why don't we have a go?'

'Where would we start?' She hung her head in her hands despondently.

Frankie got up and paced up and down the apartment. Then he came to a realisation. 'I know,' he said. 'We have two leads.'

'Two leads?'

'Yes, the car crash, which may or may not be relevant, and the fact that they were old school friends.'

'I'd forgotten about that. I'm not sure I actually told the police about the school bit.'

'Don't worry, we can do a bit of research ourselves.'

She looked at him quizzically.

'Who else would have a record of the car crash?' he asked, mainly to himself. 'Apart from the police?'

Baz thought for a minute or two and then answered, 'The insurance company. Of course.'

Frankie nodded. 'Yes, if there was a crash, she is bound to have informed her insurance and they would have the other driver's details.' He paused to let this information sink in. 'Let's at least start there.'

Baz nodded her agreement but knew that this meant contacting John Marsden again.

John Marsden had, at least at first, been annoyed that Baz appeared to be still pursuing her investigations. But having explained things over the phone to him, albeit somewhat reluctantly, he had agreed to hunt out the details of the car accident.

She was grateful that he had admitted he was pretty fastidious about keeping paperwork. *Probably something to do with being a doctor*, she thought.

He came back to her after about fifteen minutes. 'Okay, I have it all here, but I'm still not convinced, Baz, that you should be getting involved at all. Why not leave it to the police?'

'I will, I promise, just let me follow this lead first. Okay?'

There was a pause, as if he was thinking about it, then, 'The insurance company report details the crash. It happened at a crossroads near here. Do you want to know exactly where?'

Baz considered the question. 'No, probably not. Just the people involved, that's all.'

She heard the turning of pages on the other end of the phone. 'It looks like it was Cathy's fault. She pulled out of the smaller road straight across the main road without looking; the other driver didn't see her coming and he T-boned her.' A pause. 'Our car was a write-off.'

'But is there any record of the other driver?' asked Baz a little impatiently. She regretted it immediately and hoped the impatience in her voice hadn't been picked up at the other end of the phone.

It had.

'I'm doing my best here, Baz, and against my better judgement.'

'Sorry.'

'Okay, here we are then. The crash was quite a bad one from the reports I have here. The police and an ambulance both attended, but happily no-one was badly injured. They took Cathy to hospital and kept her in overnight, but it was just shock, really.'

'Who was the other driver?'

'Let me look again… A Mr L Thompson.'

Baz punched the air. L Thompson. 'L' for 'Liam'. *Got him,* she said silently to herself.

Trying to fight back her excitement, she asked, 'Have you any other details about him?' and then, hardly able to contain the anticipation, 'Like his address?'

Another pause at the other end of the phone. 'I have it here. Have you got a pen handy?'

chapter twenty-six

The next day, Frankie and Baz sat in Baz's car in a small street lined with nondescript terrace houses on either side. They were, in fact, just down the road from the address that had been obtained from the insurance company for the driver of the car that had been involved in Cathy's accident.

They had knocked at the door, but there had been no answer. So the two of them sat in silence, trying to decide what to do next.

However, their decision was made for them when an elderly man, looking frail and slightly stooped, limped along the pavement past them and then stopped at the front door of the house they had been watching. He reached into his trouser pocket and after some effort, produced a bunch of keys. He shuffled through them and then, satisfied he had the right one, he reached up and inserted it into the lock of the front door.

As he pushed the door open and was about to enter the house, Baz swung her car door open and leapt out, pausing only momentarily to bend back into the vehicle and tell Frankie in no uncertain terms to stay where he was.

She would handle it alone.

'Mr Thompson!' she yelled, just as he was starting to disappear inside the building and the front door was swinging shut.

The door stopped and a heavily lined face appeared around it. The man must have been in his sixties at least. 'What do you want?' he asked rather grumpily, obviously expecting some sort of sales patter.

'May I have a word? It's about a road traffic accident about three years ago.'

'Road traffic accident?' He paused as if in thought for a moment. 'Oh, the one near East Brookfield? I thought you police had given up on that?'

'Actually, I'm not from the police, but might I have a word?'

He looked at her suspiciously.

Baz tried to appear at her charming best.

It clearly worked, as he looked her up and down and although still suspicious, realised that Baz was of no real threat, so he relented.

'Can I come in?'

Again, there was a certain reluctance, but once again, he gave way and ushered her in.

This man was clearly too old to have been an old school friend of Cathy Marsden, but she sat down in his living room, which, as Baz observed, did not have a women's touch and probably hadn't changed since the nineteen-eighties. So she asked, 'Is Liam in?'

'Liam? Who is Liam?'

Baz had presumed that Liam Thompson must be the elderly man's son, but maybe she'd got that wrong, nephew, perhaps?

Before she got to explore the options, he continued, 'There's no Liam here, young lady. You must have got the wrong address.' He started to get up as if to show her out.

Baz stood her ground. 'The road accident, surely that was him. Some relative of yours?'

The older man looked at her incredulously. 'What are you talking about?'

'The road traffic accident near East Brookfield.'

'That was the accident that I was involved in. My name is Leonard, Leonard Thompson. You must be barking up the wrong tree altogether.'

'Leonard, Leonard Thompson. "L" Thompson, that was you?'

'I just said so, didn't I?'

Baz slumped back in the chair, completely taken aback by the turn of events. She sat silently for a few more minutes, trying to think what to say next.

She didn't have to, as her older companion embarked on a tirade. 'I thought you wanted to see me about that accident. Bloody disgrace, if you ask me.'

'What do you mean?' Baz looked at him quizzically.

'She just shot out of that side road. Didn't even look. I had no chance, didn't have time to swerve or anything, I hit her, fair and square, I'll admit that, but it was entirely her fault. My car was wrecked and me, well, I was shaken up at the time, but I didn't realise the consequences.'

'Consequences?'

'The next day I couldn't move. All stiff and sore. Whiplash, the doctor called it. But I tell you, I was laid up for weeks, I was.'

Baz struggled to take in the new information and make sense of it.

He continued, 'I complained to the police, over and over. She should have been prosecuted. Dangerous driving, I called it. But no, nothing.'

'They didn't pursue it?'

'No, nothing.'

'Any reason?'

'I blame that policeman.'

'Policeman?'

'Yes, the one that attended the scene. The one that seemed to be in charge of things then and after.'

'Any reason you can think of why nothing happened?'

'She was a young and attractive woman, that's what.'

'Surely it wasn't just because she was a woman that he didn't pursue it?'

'Oh yes, I believe so.'

'Why do you say that?'

'Well at first, he acted all cool and impartial, but then it seemed to change. She was crying and he took pity on her, I guess.'

'But they took her to hospital?'

'Well, yes, that might have accounted for his behaviour, but, honestly, you could see she wasn't badly hurt. It was later that they even tried to say it was my fault. I was going too fast, he said. But that wasn't going to work, it was obvious what had happened. But it just got written up as an accident. Nobody, apparently, was at fault and that was that.'

'What happened next?'

'I complained and complained to the police. Wrote letters and everything. I wasn't to blame in any way and I wasn't accepting any of it.'

'So...?'

'With the police, nothing, but she, the other driver, she did admit responsibility to the insurance company and I got my car fixed. Later they even paid out compensation for my injuries. So, I just gave up, accepted the money and got on with things. It wasn't right, though.'

'I can appreciate that.'

'I heard that policeman even got a promotion, you know. Despite me saying he was in the wrong. There doesn't seem to be any justification in that, does there?' He paused, though the question didn't need an answer. Then he continued, 'So what have you to do with it anyway?'

Now Baz was a bit flustered, especially what to say next to try and explain herself. 'I was in touch with the insurance company, they… Err… just wanted to make sure you were okay now.'

'Bit late, if you ask me.'

'Yes, sorry.'

Baz stood up and made her way to the front door.

'I'll let myself out,' she mumbled over her shoulder. He remained seated, staring at her empty chair, trying to make sense of her visit.

As she opened the car door and eased herself in, Frankie looked at her expectantly.

'Don't. Not yet. I'll explain later,' she said as she revved the engine and pulled away from the kerb.

Frankie and Baz travelled back to town without a word being spoken between them. Frankie was clearly desperate to know what Baz's meeting had revealed, but she obviously was not ready to discuss it.

Baz mulled things over and over in her mind. She really didn't quite know now how to proceed, where to go next. The accident seemed to be a blind alley. 'L' Thompson was blatantly not 'Liam' after all.

Her thoughts were interrupted by her phone ringing in her handbag. She pulled the car over to the kerb just as Frankie had retrieved it and was handing it to her. There was a loud blast on the horn from the vehicle behind her, obviously not appreciating her sudden manoeuvre. A disgruntled driver gesticulated at her as he passed. Baz waved submissively.

'Hello?' she answered, simultaneously swiping the screen just in time before it rang out.

'Miss Clifford,' the familiar voice asked.

'Oh, hello, Sergeant Brown. Any news?'

'Not much, I'm afraid. Doesn't seem to be any record of the car crash you told us about.'

Baz was confused but said nothing.

'Probably just one of those incidents that didn't get reported to us. As I said, happens all the time.'

Baz waited, deciding what to say next, then blurted out, 'But the police did attend. There was even a complaint afterwards, so there must be a paper trail.'

There was silence at the other end of the line, then, 'Do you mind me asking, just how do you know this, Miss Clifford?'

'I've just talked to the other party involved in the crash.' It was out before she could stop herself.

'What?' he almost screamed down the phone. 'I told you not to interfere. You have no right—'

'Look.' She became defensive. 'If you had done your job right, you'd have discovered everything that I've found out. There clearly is something on file somewhere. I suggest you go back and look again or I'll ask your detective inspector to do it.'

With that she hung up and switched her phone off.

Frankie stared at her. 'What just happened there?'

'Bloody policeman, he just can't be bothered, that's all. Obviously thinks it's all a waste of time.'

Frankie looked at her, crestfallen.

Baz turned to face him. 'Well, I for one am not giving up.'

chapter twenty-seven

Baz sat in her flat, staring at the television screen. The news was on, but she really wasn't taking any of it in. Thoughts were flying around in her head and she was trying to make sense of it all. Most importantly, she was trying to think of what to do next.

'What are you thinking?'

'What?' She looked up and then over at Frankie seated on the sofa opposite her.

'I just asked what you were thinking about. You were miles away.'

'I'm just frustrated, that's all.' She shifted in her seat, reached for the remote and flicked the television off.

'I know, I am too. What can we do now?'

'Those are my thoughts exactly. There must be something we can do. Even if the police won't do anything.'

'But what?'

Baz snapped back angrily, 'I don't bloody know, do I?'

Frankie winced at the outburst.

She regretted it immediately. 'Sorry, Frankie. I'm sorry I didn't mean to snap at you. It is just that bloody policeman's attitude, that's all.'

Frankie accepted her apology. He understood exactly where she was coming from.

'Wait a minute,' she brightened up, 'maybe there is another lead we can follow.'

Frankie straightened up expectantly. 'What lead?' he asked.

'There was something else John said about the guy that Cathy was seeing.'

'What did he say?' Frankie was all ears now.

'He said she met him at the car crash, we know it wasn't the other driver, but we don't know who else was there. There could have been other witnesses, bystanders, she was taken to hospital, so ambulance crew, doctors, etcetera, etcetera.'

'But without the police helping, we aren't going to able to trace them anyway, are we?'

'No, but John Marsden did tell me that Cathy and this bloke were old school chums.'

'So how does that help?'

Baz sat back and thought for several minutes. Then she seemed to brighten up. 'We try and trace Cathy's school records, old photos, roll calls, that sort of stuff. Then we see if we can find other Liams and then see if any of them are still local and might have been at the scene in one capacity or another.'

'Okay, sounds a bit complicated, but yes, okay.'

Baz smiled self-satisfactorily, pleased at having come up with the idea.

'So what school did Cathy go to?' Frankie asked.

'Ahhh...' Her smile faded, but then after a minute it returned. 'I think I can find out, though, easily enough. I'll ring her husband, he's bound to know.'

She paused for another minute before saying, almost to herself, 'But before we do that, there's another call I'm going to make.'

chapter twenty-eight

Detective Sergeant Brown had barely sat down at his desk the next morning when the detective at the desk behind him attracted his attention and told him that the DI wanted to see him.

'He doesn't seem to be in a good mood,' he warned him as DS Brown rose back to his feet. 'Good luck.'

DS Brown headed in the direction of Denis Warlow's office, slightly puzzled by the invitation. Reaching the office, the door was partially ajar, but he knocked it anyway.

'Come in, come in,' came the rather tetchy reply.

DS Brown stuck his head round the door. 'You wanted to see me, boss?'

'Yes, I did.' His voice still betrayed some irritation. 'Come in and sit down.'

William Brown did as he was told, if a little apprehensively. He suspected that Warlow's irritation was due to something he had done, hence the summons. 'What's it about, boss?' he asked.

'What's it about? What's it about? I'll tell you what it's about.' Brown could see that he was trying to suppress his anger. 'It's about this Marsden case.'

'What about it?' he asked with genuine bewilderment.

'I told you to co-operate with that Clifford woman. Or at least go through the motions.'

'Yes, and…?'

'Well, you tell me exactly what you have done, because I had her on the phone first thing this morning threatening to go to police complaints.'

'I reopened the investigation as you asked, but there didn't appear to be anything new, so I told her so. I suspect she just won't take no for an answer.'

'And what about the RTA? Did you follow that up?'

The junior detective shifted uncomfortably in his seat, clearly thrown off balance by the question. 'She told me about that, yes, but there didn't seem any mileage in it.'

'Miss Clifford told me on the phone that you told her there was no record of that crash, yet it was attended by both police and ambulance. So there has to be paperwork. She said you just couldn't be bothered. Is that true, DS Brown?' Warlow had addressed him by his formal title to emphasise to him his displeasure at the turn of events. 'If you ask me, Sergeant, it's your investigation that is the car crash.'

DS Brown nodded defensively. 'I just don't think there is anything in this at all. In my opinion, it's a waste of time, especially when we have so many other things to be getting on with.'

'I am not interested in your opinion, DS Brown. I gave you an order and I expect you to carry out a proper investigation. There may not indeed be anything in what Miss Clifford says and I expect there may indeed not be, but she, and I, will not be satisfied if and until the issues she has raised are examined in a clear and competent manner and proven to be of no substantive importance.'

DS Brown looked sheepishly at the older man and again nodded his compliance.

'Right, you have heard what I've got to say. Now get out and get on with it.'

William Brown rose slowly to his feet, turned and headed for the door. He was reaching for the door handle when Denis Warlow spoke once more. 'Just get that bloody woman off my back. Do you understand?'

DS Brown turned slightly and over his shoulder affirmed that he understood.

Reaching his desk in the detective's room, he thumped it loudly and swore, somewhat to the amusement of his colleague still seated at the desk behind his.

chapter twenty-nine

Slightly reluctantly, Baz had contacted John Marsden and, after a few platitudes, had broached the real reason behind her call.

'What school did Cathy go to?

'Just what are you up to, Baz? Whatever it is, I wish you'd just drop it.'

There was a slight pause, but then Baz continued, telling him of her investigations around the car crash and now the need to look in another direction and then, if possible, tie the two up.

'I'm really not sure about this, Baz. Okay, if her death was not exactly as we believe it was, I don't know that after all this time I really want it all raked up again anyway.'

'Please, John, humour me. I know this is painful for you, but if Cathy was murdered, surely we owe it to her to prove it and catch the culprit?'

There was silence at the other end of the phone. The silence seemed to last an eternity. Baz was beginning to think that they had somehow been disconnected.

'St Malachy's.'

'What?'

'St Malachy's. That was the secondary school she went to. It's actually fairly local to here.'

'I thought Cathy was from London?'

'Yes, I mean, no.'

'What?'

'Sorry. Cathy's family was from around here, she grew up not far from where I'm standing. Her parents moved to the city when she was about twelve. They are dead now, but as I think I told you, her brother moved back here and still lives here.'

'You did,' she confirmed, remembering that he had.

'Cathy left here when she went to university, moved up to London. That's where we met and then I dragged her back down here kicking and screaming when this job came up. Foolishly, I actually thought she might have liked returning to her roots.'

'She didn't?'

'At first everything seemed alright. But then she got bored and the rest is history.'

He hung up.

chapter thirty

The young woman behind the desk replaced the receiver and looked up to address Baz.

'Miss Clifford, Mrs Williams just called. She apologises, she has been delayed in the parent-teacher meeting. She says she won't be long if you don't mind waiting. Can I get you a tea or a coffee?'

'No thanks. I'm okay, honestly. I'm happy to wait.'

The younger woman returned to her keyboard. Otherwise there was silence in the small waiting area outside the headmistress's office.

St Malachy's hadn't been hard to find; it was the only mixed comprehensive school in the area. As she had driven through the impressive wrought iron gates, Baz had been impressed by its formidable red brick façade, even boasting a reproduction medieval-type tower at one end of the building, atop of which she spotted a flagpole, though no flag flew today.

However, it was clear that the school had seen better days: lumps of plaster hung off the walls in places and the windows appeared to be those that were common in the sixties with painted metal frames.

Throughout the playground, children milled about, seemingly split up into smaller groups. Some boys were playing football quite noisily across the central area. Around the edges other smaller groups stood and chatted idly, whiling away the time before the next lesson.

Both boys and girls wore similar uniforms of identical colour: dark blue blazers, grey trousers or skirts, white shirts, but ties of a variety of knots or length, which were the only expressions of individuality within the dress code.

With directions from one of the pupils, she had found her way into the main building and after an occasional wrong turn, had located the headmistress's office.

'You said on the phone it was a police matter?'

Baz wheeled around at the voice.

A middle-aged woman with grey streaked hair and, perhaps surprisingly, friendly and welcoming features, had entered the anteroom. It was she that had spoken with, as Baz noted, a hint of a Yorkshire accent.

She extended her hand. 'Mrs Louise Williams,' and then added, somewhat unnecessarily, 'Headmistress.'

Baz shook her hand; the headmistress's grip was strong and firm. A trait that probably reflected the rest of Mrs Williams's personality, despite her warm exterior, Baz mused.

'Yes, sort of,' Baz replied. 'It concerns the death of one of your former pupils.'

'My goodness!' exclaimed the headteacher, clearly shocked by the revelation. 'A death, you say?'

'I'm afraid so.'

'Do come into my office. We can talk more privately there.' She ushered Baz through the door behind the secretary's desk and into her inner sanctum.

As she passed the secretary, Baz detected the disappointment in the young woman's face, presumably upset to miss out on a juicy story.

'Sit down, please.' Mrs Williams indicated a chair in front of a formidable dark wooden desk, behind which the headmistress herself squeezed past and sat down on the far side. 'A death, you say? Can you elucidate?' Then she paused as if in thought. 'Actually, maybe we should do this more formally.'

'Formally?'

'Yes. Firstly, can I see your warrant card and know your rank and station's location?'

'Ahhh… I'm not actually in the police as such,' admitted Baz.

The headmistress seemed somewhat taken aback by this revelation. Regaining her composure, she leant forward, placing both forearms on her desk and asked, 'So you'd said on the phone that this was a police matter. Then you tell me it concerns the death of a former pupil, but then you reveal that you yourself are not actually in the police.'

'It's a long story,' Baz mumbled somewhat defensively.

'Then you better begin before I have you ejected from the school.'

There was a steeliness to the teacher's voice, one Baz guessed had emerged many times before in this woman's career.

Taking her time, Baz tried to explain as succinctly as possible but consciously omitted some of the facts surrounding her own investigations that she deemed irrelevant or damaging to what she wanted from the school.

Mrs Williams listened patiently. When Baz had finished talking, she looked over the desk at the older woman and awaited her response.

After a few minutes' reflection, the headmistress spoke, 'I am not sure we can help you, Miss Clifford. I personally have not been here long enough to remember the individual who has sadly died. I was only appointed headmistress here five years ago, having previously taught at a different establishment.'

Baz noted the controlled tone with which she spoke.

'From what you are saying, you are actually more interested in someone she knew at the school, rather than the deceased herself?'

Baz nodded in agreement.

'To be frank, Miss Clifford, I really don't know how you expect to find this person. No school keeps records of friendships among pupils.' She sat back, not expecting there to be any comeback to that revelation.

But Baz had been expecting her to say that; it was obvious. 'I understand that, of course, but if I could have look through school records, old classes, school photos, perhaps I could find some link to the person Cathy met at the car crash, who, by all accounts, did attend this school.'

Baz noted a dark expression come over the headmistress's face. 'Now look, young lady. You come here, to my school, under false pretences, you give the impression that you are a policewoman—'

'I never meant to deceive you,' Baz pleaded, trying to retrieve the situation.

'That's as may be. But you did, and now you ask to be granted permission to have access to this school's confidential records?'

'Only old roll calls and photos.' Baz realised she was rapidly losing the argument.

'Well, I'm afraid the answer is no.'

Baz slumped in her seat; she'd lost and she knew it.

'Tell me, young lady, just who did you say was leading the police investigation?'

'Detective Inspector Warlow.' It was out before it occurred to Baz why the other woman had asked the question.

'I shall be contacting him directly.' She had just confirmed Baz's worst fears. 'I will be alerting him to your intervention and your impertinence. If he, or anyone from his team, want to view the files, then they would be most welcome. You, Miss Clifford, are not. Do I make myself clear?'

'Crystal,' Baz replied a little flippantly as she rose to her feet to leave.

The headmistress remained seated behind her desk.

Baz didn't look back as she somewhat sheepishly exited the office.

As she passed the secretary's desk, she could see the puzzled look on the young woman's face. If she had been about to ask something, she was interrupted by the phone on her desk buzzing. As she lifted the receiver and pressed it to her ear, Baz was just leaving through the outer door when she heard the start of the conversation.

'Certainly, Mrs Williams. Inspector Warlow, Bridgetown Police. No problem, I'll get him for you now.'

chapter thirty-one

The bedroom was dark, but moonlight steamed through a gap in the curtains, lighting the wall across the room from where she lay. She tossed and turned, unable to sleep, the events of that day and before racing around in her head. She had no doubt that she would get a further telling off from the police for interfering in their enquiries, but she was upset, and, more particularly, annoyed that nothing had been forthcoming. She was now convinced that it was unlikely that anything more was going to be revealed regarding the circumstances of Cathy's death. The police in general and DS Brown in particular had been most unhelpful and even dismissive of many of her concerns. Eventually she had slipped into a fitful sleep, only really doing so when she had resolved, at least in her own mind, the way forward.

Finally, after many hours of tossing and turning repeatedly, she reached a conclusion. It wasn't really a conclusion that she liked or even fully endorsed but was one that at least allowed her to return to the laboratory and resume the rest of her PhD.

She had resolved to discard Cathy Marsden's sample from the main analysis, only including it in the appendix to the thesis, explaining it as an anomaly. Now she only had to come up with a rational alternative explanation for the anomalous GABA result.

Could lack of oxygen itself raise neurotransmitter levels without the subject being conscious?

Could Cathy have woken up even momentarily before she succumbed to the fire?

Could Cathy have had some undetected brain anomaly which secreted GABA prior to her demise?

As she lay awake staring at the darkened features of her small bedroom, she had to admit that all of these theories could be correct but would require further research, principally ploughing through the published medical literature in order to see if anybody had previously put forward such theories or had even produced actual clinical findings that supported them.

These thoughts seemed to settle her, at least to a small degree. She felt herself slowly drifting off to sleep. Satisfied for the first time in a long time that she may actually be able to produce some sort of explanation that might satisfy the venerable Jennifer Ashfordly. More importantly, she could step back from any further involvement with the police, though, she thought, she might like to see John Marsden again. This time without any hidden agenda.

Certainly, she thought, she owed him that at least.

She definitely felt more relaxed, more at ease than she had felt for a while. Not since she had become involved in the fruitless investigations surrounding Cathy Marsden's death.

As her eyes slowly closed and she snuggled down below her duvet, she heard a noise. Her flat was in an old building and sometimes extraneous noises happened with slight temperature changes.

But this noise was different.

There it was again.

It sounded like her bedroom door being slowly opened.

Then a footstep.

She sat up, startled. There was a figure in her room approaching her. Someone was in her room, but she couldn't make out any features because of the gloom. Now the figure pushed the bedroom door behind them and appeared to be heading directly to where she lay.

Baz sat up and reached for the bedside light. But before she could switch it on, the intruder had grabbed her by the shoulders and pushed her roughly down on the bed. He held her there. She struggled to free herself, but he was strong, too strong for her.

She was about to scream when, anticipating it, the intruder pulled the pillow out from under her head and pushed it down firmly on her face.

She kicked and bucked to try to dislodge it, but now the assailant had sat down on top of her, restricting her ability to free herself.

The pressure increased as the pillow was pressed down powerfully, enveloping her head and restricting her breathing. Baz realised that she was suffocating under the pressure on her face. She squirmed and tried to punch with her hands, now freed as her assailant concentrated on applying more pressure on the pillow.

Baz knew she could hold her breath longer than most, but this was different. She was burning off vital oxygen in trying, and failing, to struggle. She was coming to the realisation that further resistance was futile. The downward pressure continued, the pillow blocking her airways and slowly choking her.

Baz felt herself slipping into unconsciousness. Her kicking and struggling abated. Her life was ebbing away and there was nothing she could do about it.

As her thoughts slowed and a blackness swept over her, suddenly, there was a loud crash.

The pressure on the pillow lifted.

She reached up and grabbed the pillow, throwing it quickly to one side.

She swung her legs over the side of the bed, grabbed the bed on either side of her for support and slumped over her knees. She gagged and retched but, more importantly, sucked in air.

After a few minutes she felt sufficiently recovered to look around her. She tossed aside her hair, which had hung over her face and, tears streaming down her face, looked about her.

A figure stood over the bed. She retreated, pressing back into the headboard, but then she realised that this was not the figure that she had glimpsed, albeit briefly, before being grabbed and assaulted. This figure was small and thin and shook slightly as it stood looking downwards at the floor beside Baz's bed.

It took Baz a few moments to realise that this second figure was Frankie. Then there was another crash. This one not as loud as the one a few minutes earlier. Baz, now recovering her senses but still gasping for breath, looked over in the direction of the crash. She was instantly relieved to discover that it was simply the remains of a broken bottle that Frankie had, almost unconsciously, dropped from his grasp, which now rolled harmlessly back and forth on the bedroom floor.

Looking down at where the remnants of the bottle had landed, Baz saw that her attacker was now also lying on the floor face down, near to where the bottle had landed. Blood was oozing visibly from a head wound. There was no movement. The attacker was clearly unconscious.

'He's not dead, is he?' Frankie's voice quivered as he spoke.

'What happened?' Baz spoke shakily too. She flicked on the bedside light. As she glanced down at the fallen assailant, it was obvious that it was a man.

'I was asleep on your sofa. I didn't hear him break in and I guess he didn't see me, or even know that I was staying with you.' He paused. 'Then I heard the struggle from your bedroom. I got up and looked in.'

'Thank God you did.' Baz stood up and reached for him. She hugged him tightly. She could feel his small frame trembling at the encounter.

'He didn't hear me come in,' he continued, his voice shaking with emotion. 'I grabbed a bottle from the cabinet and... and... well... I just hit him with it.'

'Frankie, you saved my life.' She hugged him more tightly. 'Thank you, thank you so much.'

Her words seemed to calm Frankie down and the frightened shaking started to abate.

There was a groan from the figure on the floor. He started to move.

'Quick, sit on him, Frankie. Pin him down, I'll get something to tie him up.'

Frankie did as he was bid. Happily, the intruder was still too groggy to offer much resistance.

Baz returned with a couple of leather belts and the two of them secured the man's hands behind his back. As they attempted to secure his legs, he started to struggle, trying to turn himself over. Happily for Baz and Frankie, he remained too weak and too groggy to offer any real resistance. And so it was that they manged between them to immobilise his legs as well as his hands before sitting back and admiring their handiwork.

The intruder continued to recover from the blow that Frankie had inflicted. As he did so he, though still lying on his stomach and face down, strained at his bindings and grunted furiously.

Recovering from the shock and the effort, Baz turned breathlessly to Frankie. 'You okay?' she asked.

'I'm fine,' he confirmed.

'Thank you again, Frankie, you are a hero.'

It was the first time in his life that Frankie had ever been called a hero. He smiled from ear to ear.

'You call the police, Frankie, I'm going to see if I recognise this guy and try and find out he attacked me.'

Baz tossed Frankie her phone from the bedside table. 'The PIN is 1234,' she told him, re-examining the man's bindings as she spoke.

'Original,' mocked Frankie, now also clearly recovering from the ordeal.

'Just get on with it,' she snapped, worried that their captive might loosen his bonds and escape, or worse.

Frankie did as he was told, then put the phone down. 'They said they'll be here ASAP.'

'Good. Now shall we see if either of us recognise him?'

Between them they managed to turn him over, despite his unwillingness and his struggles to defy them. They sat him up against the bed, his arms still securely bound behind him. He tried to kick out at them, but his legs too remained tethered and the kick was ineffectual.

'Now, now. Just sit still,' Baz scolded him.

With that she reached up and turned on the bedside light so that it shone directly onto his face.

The intruder glared up at her, snarling as he did so.

Baz recoiled in shock.

'You know him?' Frankie stared at her in puzzlement.

Baz had moved back a few feet, still staring at their captive.

He strained against his bonds. But to no avail; they held strong.

Eventually Baz had recovered sufficiently to speak. 'Yes, I know him.' She still had not removed her gaze from the man seated on the floor in front of her.

'Who is he?' Frankie almost shouted at her.

'He's a policeman,' Baz's voice quivered as she spoke.

'A policeman?' Frankie asked incredulously.

'Yes, a policeman.'

'And you know him?'

'We've met before.' She directed the next question directly to their prisoner: 'Haven't we…? Detective Sergeant Brown.'

It seemed like an age that the three of them sat in Baz's small bedroom waiting for the reinforcements to arrive. Apart from DS Brown's ineffectual attempts to free himself, they sat in silence, not knowing what more to say.

A million questions buzzed around in Baz's head, but she didn't know where to start, or what she could hope to achieve by asking them. She hoped the police would be able to determine the reasons why this detective sergeant had broken into her apartment and tried to kill her. At the moment she was just too overwhelmed by what had happened in the last few minutes.

Finally Baz heard police sirens in the distance, getting louder by the minute. As Frankie moved himself over towards the bedroom window to watch their approach, Baz noted that his figure was being lit up by flashing blue lights from the street below.

The relief she felt was immense. As they had waited all that time, she had feared that William Brown would break free and either make a run for it or worse, attack her again. The doorbell rang and Frankie rushed down the stairs to open the door for the police.

Baz heard heavy footsteps approaching rapidly up the staircase. Her bedroom door was roughly pushed wide open and a couple of armour-clad and helmeted police officers stood in the doorway, each brandishing a baton. They surveyed the scene around them. A frightened young woman stood in the middle of the room, visibly shaking with relief as she greeted their arrival. Seated on the floor, his back resting against the bed, was a man dressed in a black sweater and trousers, a small pool of blood on the floor beside him. The man's head hung limply down, exposing only the top of his head, his hair by now matted with blood.

'You reported a break-in?' the first policeman asked somewhat breathlessly; the question was posed to Baz.

'He tried to kill me.' Baz pointed at the man tied up beside the bed.

'He did. I can confirm that.' Frankie had followed the two policemen up the stairs, leaving a third guarding the front door. 'He was trying to suffocate her with that pillow.' He pointed at the pillow that lay on the floor beside the bed.

The taller of the two policemen nodded at Frankie and then turned back to Baz. 'Okay, Miss. You're safe now, just you leave this scumbag to us.' He turned around to face his colleague.

'Get him up, Geoff. We'll take him down to the station.' Then, to Baz, 'You follow along later, Miss, and give a statement. There's no rush. I think we can see what's happened here.'

The second policeman moved across the room and started to pull the intruder to his feet. As he did so, he caught sight of the man's face. He released his grip almost immediately and stepped back, leaving the prisoner standing in the centre of the room.

'Allister, you better look at this.'

'What?'

'Sorry, I mean him.' He pointed at the now-dishevelled figure standing unsteadily, his arms and legs still bound.

'What the—'

Baz intervened. 'I know. He's a policeman. I take it you know him?'

Still recovering from the shock, the first of the officers confirmed that they did. 'We used to work with DS Brown when he was in uniform, that is before he was promoted to CID and moved to a different station.'

'He still attacked me,' Baz asserted.

'There must be some mistake, surely?'

Frankie stepped forward. 'No mistake, officer. Baz is absolutely correct. He attacked her here in her flat.'

'And if it hadn't been for Frankie, I'd be dead.' She started to cry.

'Okay, Miss. We'll take him down to the station right away. You wait here, I'll call another car to bring you and your friend down and I'll also send a forensic team round. Then we can sort this out.'

They undid the straps that restrained William Brown and replaced them with a pair of handcuffs. Then they led him down the stairs.

Baz and Frankie watched through the window as one of the officers placed his hand on DS Brown's head and guided him into the back of the waiting police car.

'Do you think they believed us?' Baz asked despondently.

'They bloody better,' was Frankie's retort.

chapter thirty-two

B az and Frankie sat in the waiting area of the police station for what seemed like an age. At one point, Baz was taken to a small room equipped with rudimentary clinical equipment. There she was asked to strip to bra and pants and subjected to a cursory medical examination by a young woman who had introduced herself as a police medical examiner. By the time she returned to join Frankie, early-morning light was already starting to permeate through the small window above the desk sergeant's counter.

Finally a young police officer dressed in plain clothes popped his head around the door and motioned to Baz.

'Can you come with me, please, Miss Clifford.' It was more a command than a question.

Baz and Frankie both rose to their feet.

'Sorry, just Miss Clifford.' He pointed at Baz.

Frankie sat back down.

Baz glanced and gave him a reassuring look. 'I'm sure I won't be long.'

'I'll wait,' replied Frankie.

'Make sure you do. The superintendent will probably want to talk to you after Miss Clifford,' growled the police officer.

The young detective ushered Baz out of the waiting area and down the corridor that she recognised from her last visit. He opened the door to the office that she had seen Inspector Warlow in on her last visit. Her guide followed her in and then stood behind her at the door after he had closed it behind her. There was another policeman that Baz didn't recognise seated behind the desk this time. Baz reckoned it was probably too late, or in fact too early, for the rotund Inspector Warlow to have gotten himself out of bed and come to work.

The man behind the desk introduced himself. 'I am Detective Superintendent Cartwright, this...' he indicated the other man still standing behind her, 'is Detective Constable Butler.'

The superintendent didn't bother to get up as he made the introductions. He simply briefly raised his head from the file in front of him to register her presence. *A superintendent,* thought Baz, *at least they are starting to take things seriously at last.*

The senior man continued, 'For the purpose of the interview, Miss Clifford, we intend to record all that is said. So firstly, could you state your full name, date of birth and current address?'

'Am I some kind of a suspect?' she said, alarmed, her previous optimism dwindling.

'If you wouldn't mind, Miss Clifford,' the senior man stated, pointing at the microphone on the desk between them.

Baz stated her name and address as she was asked.

'And your date of birth, please.'

She quickly complied and then somewhat tetchily spoke again, addressing the superintendent directly. 'Can you tell me exactly what is going on? My friend and I are the innocent parties here.' She continued, 'That man broke into my apartment and tried to kill me.'

'I'm sorry we kept you waiting, but we wanted to interview Sergeant Brown first.'

'To get his side of the story, you mean.' Baz was getting angry now.

'He does have a slightly different view on things, yes.'

'Look, this man, Detective Brown—'

'Detective Sergeant Brown,' the superintendent corrected her.

'Whatever. He broke into my apartment and attempted to kill me. Frankie will tell you exactly the same story.'

'I'm sure he will, Ms Clifford. Attacking a police officer is a serious offence.'

'What !' Baz screamed across the desk. She made to stand up, leaning forward, her hands on the desk and her face now directly in front of the senior policeman. 'You are not serious!'

The constable behind her stepped forward to intervene but was waved back by his superior.

'Sit down Miss Clifford,' he spoke forcefully, using the full authority that went with his rank.

Baz, her anger a little assuaged, did as she was bid. Though she still glared across the desk.

'Right, Miss Clifford, if we may begin again. Tell me your side of the events of early this morning and we will try to sort this out as quickly as we can.'

Baz took her time and relayed all that had transpired in her apartment in the early hours of the morning. Superintendent Cartwright listened carefully, making short notes from time to time. When Baz had finished speaking, he asked, 'Tell me,

Miss Clifford, why do you think, as you allege, Detective Sergeant Brown would break into your flat and attempt to assault you?'

Baz took her time in answering the question. After a little thought, she replied, 'I guess he may have something to hide. I put in a complaint about him, you know.'

'Are you seriously suggesting, Miss Clifford, that because you put in a complaint against a fellow officer, that he would try to murder you?' He smiled somewhat condescendingly in Baz's direction whilst glancing at his colleague behind her for confirmation.

'I don't believe this.' Baz was exasperated by the way the interview had proceeded.

'Detective Sergeant Brown has a slightly different version of events, Miss Clifford.'

'And what might his version be?'

'He tells us that he was upset by your complaint. He went around to visit you to discuss it and explain his enquires. He said you and your "friend" got angry and hit him, rendering him unconscious. Then you concocted this story that you have just told me, to try to justify your actions.'

'This is just unbelievable,' stuttered Baz. 'Okay then. It was the middle of the night. Just how does he explain that?'

'Apparently DS Brown has been having some marital difficulties, as well as other personal problems. He says he's not been sleeping well over the last few weeks. Apparently has been getting up and getting in his car and just driving aimlessly around at night, basically I think just trying to work things out in his head. Your complaint was apparently the final nail in the coffin, it was hanging over his head and causing him further upset. He says that in the course of one of his nocturnal drives he found himself in your area and just decided, on the spur of the moment, to call in and try and work things out with you.'

'And what? I just let him in?'

'He says, yes, but then in the course of discussion you got angry. He tells me that's when your "friend" intervened and things got heated, resulting in Mr Walker hitting him over the head with a bottle.'

'I don't believe this,' snapped Baz. 'He attacked me, tried to kill me, for Christ's sake!'

'I have to tell you, Miss Clifford, the results of the clinical examination did not reveal any bruising or cuts, etc., to your body that would support your accusations that he did indeed try to injure you.'

'He used a pillow to try to suffocate me. Tell me, what sort of marks would that leave?'

There was a pause. The superintendent reclined in his chair. After a few minutes, to allow Baz to compose herself, he resumed speaking: 'Detective Sergeant Brown has generously, in my opinion, decided not to press charges against you or your companion. He has graciously said that it was simply a misunderstanding and to leave it like that.'

Baz could feel her face flush, but she bit her tongue to stop herself from replying.

'Think yourself fortunate on this occasion, Miss Clifford.' He rose to his feet from behind his desk and offered his hand to her. 'Goodbye.'

Baz looked at the proffered hand, ignored it and him and stormed out of the room.

As she joined Frankie who was still seated in the waiting area, she was visibly shaking. She wasn't sure herself whether it was from anger, frustration or even fear as to what might happen next, given that the police appeared to be closing ranks against her.

Frankie, noting her distress, put his arm around her and asked needlessly, 'How did it go?' Baz just looked at him with a blank stare. 'That well, eh?' Frankie wasn't accustomed to acts of affection, but on this occasion, he made an exception and hugged her more tightly.

She looked up at him, realising that tears were now starting to well up in the corners of her eyes. 'Let's just get out of here.'

They rose simultaneously to leave; Frankie's arm remained around her shoulders.

As they took their first step towards the outer door, another inner door opened and out stepped DS Brown. His head sported a bandage and he was rubbing at it as he approached them. He looked as if he was going to say something to them when the desk sergeant intervened. He put his arm across the other officer's chest and held him back.

'You shouldn't be here, Liam,' he spoke softly to the detective and then ushered him back through the door through which he had entered the waiting area.

Baz stopped in her tracks, dislodging Frankie's arm as she did so. She turned and made her way over to the desk sergeant. 'What did you just say?'

'I told him he shouldn't be here, Miss, not with what's going on. I'm sure you understand?'

'Yes… but what did you just call him?'

'DS Brown?'

'Yes, of course DS Brown,' she snapped; she was getting annoyed again.

'William?'

'No, you didn't. You called him Liam.'

'So, so what if I did. Liam, that's short for William, isn't it?' The policeman looked smugly at her. 'His friends all call him Liam, William's a bit formal, don't you think?'

'I want to see that superintendent again. Now!'

chapter thirty-three

Some time passed and it was already late afternoon, early evening by the time Baz and Frankie pulled up outside John Marsden's cottage. Both were exhausted by the long day they had just been through.

'You coming in?' Baz asked Frankie.

'Of course I am,' he replied as he unbuckled his seatbelt and moved to open the car door.

'Just let me do the talking. Okay?'

Frankie made a zip sign across his lips.

The front door opened before they had made it all the way up the path. John Marsden eyed up Frankie and then returned his gaze to Baz. 'I heard the car,' he explained. 'So what now?'

'Can we come in, John?'

He seemed to think for a moment then stepped aside and bade them entry.

Baz led the way, making for the sitting room where she and the doctor had spent the evening which now felt like so long ago. They sat down and declined the coffee that was offered. Baz and Frankie glanced at each other. Baz introduced Frankie as Frankie Walker and stated simply, 'He's been helping me.'

'So, to what do I owe this unexpected visit?' John Marsden asked somewhat curtly.

'We've just come from the police station. In fact, we've been there all day.'

'So?'

'So, we and the police themselves now believe that Cathy was murdered.'

John Marsden recoiled in exasperation. 'Oh, Baz. Why can't you just drop it? It was over a year and a half ago and I am really just now starting to put my life back together.' Then he added, a little unnecessarily, 'As you know.'

Baz flushed. Frankie noticed it and looked at her quizzically. Baz ignored Frankie inquisitive stare and continued, 'We've found out who Liam is.'

John Marsden sat bolt upright, his attention now piqued.

Baz then went to explain how she had continued with her quest to determine exactly what had happened to Cathy, despite John's reluctance for her to do so, and as to why the police had not uncovered anything suspicious about her death. Principally, she told him because the investigating officer, DS William Brown, and 'Liam', Cathy's former lover, were in fact one and the same.

'So how on earth did you discover this?' asked the doctor, almost not really wanting to hear the answer.

'We overheard one of his colleague's call him Liam rather than William. Liam is actually one of the shortened versions of William, you know.'

'Of course I know that,' he snapped, but then apologised immediately when he realised that he hadn't actually picked up on it himself in his own meetings with DS Brown.

'His friends all call him Liam, apparently.'

'But are you sure it's the same Liam?'

'Obviously, we couldn't be sure at first, but it did seem a hell of a coincidence, you have to admit.'

'But you're sure now.'

'Yes, we are.' Baz and Frankie nodded in unison.

'Okay, explain.'

Baz sat back in her seat; she realised this might take a while firstly to relate her story and then for John Marsden to digest it.

'You remember that you told me you thought that Cathy had met Liam because of a car accident that she had.'

'Yes.'

'Well, I tried to follow up on that lead. It wasn't the other driver.'

'How do you know that?'

'Because I've met him.'

John Marsden sighed.

'Then I went to the police to try and find out who else might have been present at the crash scene. Police, ambulance, witnesses, etc. etc. That's where I first came across DS Brown.' She paused, ensuring that she had John's full attention. 'He informed me that there was no paperwork regarding the accident. Given the circumstances, I found that very strange.'

'Actually, that is strange. I remember Cathy told me the police, at least, did attend the scene. Maybe the file just got lost or mislaid or something.'

'That's what I thought... at first.'

'So what changed your mind?'

'Well, it was only later, after I had put two and two together and then brought my suspicions to Brown's superiors, that they opened their own investigations. Guess what they found when they searched his desk?'

'Details of Cathy's crash?'

'Yep. He had secreted the file away.'

'Why did he do that?' John asked, but then a light seemed to switch on in his brain. 'He was there, wasn't he?'

'The police officer who attended the scene was no other than one Sergeant William Brown, then a uniformed officer. It was a little while later that he was moved to CID.'

It was quite a lot to take in.

John Marsden got up, paced the room for a while and then leant up against the fireplace.

'It's still a bit of a step from him being Liam, meeting Cathy, then starting a relationship with her, to him actually killing her.'

'He's confessed to the murder,' Baz stated bluntly.

'What? How? Why?' John Marsden was flabbergasted.

Baz held back for a few minutes to regather her thoughts but also to let John Marsden regain his composure. 'You may recall that there were a few anomalies around Cathy's death.'

'Anomalies?' He seemed to be still struggling to take it all in.

'There was evidence of a head injury, albeit mild and probably not the actual cause of her death.'

'No, no. That was nothing to do with it.'

'How do you know? The killer could have forced his way in, hit over the head and then set the house on fire before she could do anything about it.'

'Didn't happen,' John Marsden asserted positively.

'Why couldn't it?' asked Baz once more.

'Because,' John stated, 'Cathy had rung me before she went to bed and she told me about hitting her head. She said that she had had a visitor but had tripped in the hall or something, she said that she had hit her head on a cabinet. I asked if she was okay and she said it had been a bit sore at the time but she was fine now. I told the police about it anyway. So they did know about the head injury and that it was irrelevant.'

'Okay, that's as may be, but, and more importantly,' Baz continued, not allowing herself to be distracted, 'there was no smoke in Cathy's lungs. You as a doctor must have thought that a little strange?'

'Yes, but sometimes a fire just sucks all the oxygen out of a building and so one suffocates without actually inhaling any fumes.'

'That's exactly what the pathologist said.'

John Marsden turned to face her square on. He shrugged his arms in a questioning manner.

'Unless, there is an alternative explanation,' Baz replied.

'What alternative explanation could there be?'

'Well, what if he suffocated her, say with one of her pillows and then started the fire to cover things up? Wouldn't that result in the same post-mortem findings?'

'I suppose so.' He shook his head. 'But how could you prove that?'

'He has confessed to doing exactly that.'

'Why on earth would he confess? He was in the clear.'

Again Baz paused, this time to compose herself. 'He was caught in the act of repeating the exercise.'

'What?! I don't believe you.'

'Well, if he was, then maybe he would have had no option but to come clean. Prison is not a good place for former policemen. It didn't prove too difficult to persuade him that a full confession might mean the authorities going a little easier on him, providing him anonymity, isolation from other prisoners and the like.'

'So he did kill Cathy.' The truth was slowly sinking in. 'But why?'

'She was bored, then she meets a childhood sweetheart. Liam. She embarks on what she regards as a fling. He, though, makes more of it. Apparently he never forgot her from all those years ago. I suppose in his own way he loved Cathy.

'As you know she, on the other hand, quickly realised her mistake and wanted nothing more than to make it up with you, John. He didn't want the affair to end, and just couldn't let go, hence the letter you saw. Apparently he just kept on writing to her, leaving messages, texting her, phoning her up out of the blue. Admittedly, he was going through a bad period himself: his marriage had hit the rocks, his wife had left him, demanding a divorce settlement and had taken their children to live with her mother.

'He became so obsessed with Cathy and their supposed relationship that he actually started to sit in his car outside your house. He would follow her and he would even manufacture "accidental" meetings. Cathy put up with it for a while, assuming that he would just give up and go away. When he didn't, she confronted him, told him she'd report him to his superiors for stalking her.'

'Did she?'

'No, but she hoped the threat would stop him.'

'But it didn't?'

'No, but he was worried about it. He realised that if she did report him to his colleagues it could be the end of his career, he might even be prosecuted or even barred from seeing his kids again.'

'So what did he do?'

'He called at your house. He knew you were away, he'd been sitting in his car watching the house once more, despite Cathy's threat. He saw you leave. Once you were out of sight, he went up to the house intending to ask Cathy not to report him, and probably once again to try and win her back.'

'But he couldn't persuade her?'

'She wouldn't even let him in. Wouldn't open the door. Just shouted at him through it for him to go away and leave her alone.'

'What happened next?'

'He told them that he took himself off to a bar and decided to get drunk and drown his sorrows.'

'And did he?'

'Apparently, though the drunker he got, the more morose he became and unfortunately, the more irrational. By the time he left the bar, or rather was thrown out, he said that he didn't really know what he was doing but he found himself outside your house again. It was night-time by now and the house was in darkness. Despite his drunken state he knew that Cathy wasn't going to let him in. So, stupidly, he did the only thing he could think of... He broke in.'

'How?'

'He broke one of the windowpanes, opened the window and simply clambered inside.'

'But... But—'

'I know what you're going to ask. But bear with me for a minute.' Baz raised one finger to emphasise the point. 'Cathy was in bed, but she woke up when she heard the noise of someone entering the bedroom. Apparently she screamed, flicked the light on and reached for her phone. It was the action of reaching for her phone that proved the mistake.'

'Why?'

'Because, even in his drunken state, Liam quickly realised that if she rang the police, he'd had it. His life apparently flashed in front of him and a red mist descended. That was when he pounced on her and pulled one of her pillows over her face and... well, you know the rest.'

'Okay, as I was about to ask: why did no-one realise that there'd been a break-in?'

'As I said, the only damage he'd caused was one broken window, nothing had been taken, obviously, and a number of other windows had been broken simply by the heat of the fire and again, others by the firemen themselves trying to gain entry or in trying to extinguish it. So nobody really thought anything of the one window he had broken.'

John Marsden sat silently trying to take it all in, then he asked, 'You said he tried to smother somebody else, that was how he was caught?'

'He did,' Baz confirmed. Frankie nodded in the background.

'So who did he try to kill this time?' His voice tailed off.

Frankie glanced over at Baz, whose gaze was resolutely fixed on the floor.

John Marsden fixed Baz with a searching stare. 'Not you? Surely not?'

Baz nodded slowly.

'Oh my God,' he exclaimed as he sunk his head in his hands. Recovering, he asked, 'What happened?'

Baz went on to explain how Liam had become concerned that she wouldn't give up her enquires and had then set out to silence her.

'How did he find you? I mean, how did he know where you lived?'

Baz looked at him and smiled a little condescendingly. 'He was a policeman, you know. They have their methods of tracing people.'

'Sorry, sorry, of course, I just wasn't thinking straight.' Then, recovering his train of thought, 'So what happened? Did he hurt you?' He did appear genuinely concerned.

Baz went on to relate the events of the night when William Brown had broken into her apartment and attempted to suffocate her.

'I thought I'd had it. Really I did.'

'Oh my God, I'm so sorry, Baz. I would never have wanted any of this to happen.'

'I know that.' She knew that he really meant what he said.

'How did you escape? What happened?'

'Frankie saved me.' She pointed at Frankie, who had remained silent throughout. John Marsden had almost forgotten that he was there.

Baz then described how Frankie had intervened and then about the events at the police station. She quickly moved on in these recollections to the point where she was finally being believed by Brown's senior officers and he had been left with little option but to confess to everything.

'You are a hero.' John Marsden gripped Frankie's hands in his. 'Well done, young man.' But then, letting his grip loosen, a puzzled look came over John Marsden's features once more.

'So how did you get involved in all of this in the first place?'

Frankie looked embarrassed; he shuffled his feet and stared at the floor. This was his moment to confront the truth, but he was almost too frightened to do so.

'Tell him,' Baz encouraged Frankie to speak. 'What harm can it do now?'

Frankie looked up and then whispered, 'I think Cathy was my mother.'

'What?' John Marsden recoiled in disbelief. 'What did you say?'

A little louder this time around, Frankie repeated, 'I think your wife was my mother.'

There was a general silence in the room. Baz looked at Frankie, Frankie stared at the floor and John Marsden regarded Frankie in disbelief.

'Explain, Frankie,' Baz chided him. 'Tell him what you know. Tell him about the letter.'

'Letter, what letter?' John Marsden now turned to Baz.

'He got a letter from Cathy. Show it to him, Frankie.'

Frankie reached into his pocket and produced the now-crumpled piece of paper. He offered it to John, who snatched it from him.

As John Marsden read the letter, Frankie explained to him that he had only found out about his adoption from the letter and how his adoptive mother had tried to hide it from him.

Having digested the contents of the letter, John Marsden slowly and carefully handed it back to Frankie, who immediately stuffed back into the safety of his pocket.

Again, silence descended on the room.

Finally, John Marsden came over to Frankie and put his arm around him. 'I'm sorry, Frankie, you've got it wrong. Cathy wasn't your mother. Your real mum's dead. She died shortly after giving birth to you sixteen years ago.'

Frankie was suddenly enraged. 'You're lying. That's what *she* told me.' He shouted the words and jumped up to start pacing back and forth across the room.

'She? Who is she?'

'My other mother. The one I've run away from.'

Baz looked at John Marsden, pleading for him to sort the situation out and appease Frankie in some way.

John Marsden didn't appear to want to rush into any further explanation of the letter from Cathy, though he did confirm that it was her signature and that she had written it.

Given John Marsden's silence, Baz felt compelled to take up Frankie's case. 'So, John, can you explain the letter? I think Frankie deserves at least that.'

Again, John hesitated. Then, slowly, he reached forward and gripped each of Frankie's hands in his and then spoke slowly, directly into his face. 'Frankie, I am so sorry but your mother, your birth mother, really is dead.'

Frankie tried to squirm out of his grip. But John Marsden held on too tightly for him to succeed.

He continued, 'Cathy couldn't have children. She had endometriosis, a condition which usually results in infertility. As, unfortunately, it did in Cathy's case. I am so sorry, Frankie, but Cathy was not your mother,' he repeated. 'Your real mother died many years ago. As I said.'

Baz looked at John with a puzzled expression.

'But, but…' Frankie spluttered. 'The letter says—'

'I know what the letter says, Frankie, but Cathy was not your mother.'

'Explain,' interrupted Baz.

John Marsden turned to her and then back to Frankie.

'You were the result of a childhood romance. Your mother was only sixteen when she had you.'

'You said she died? Are you sure?'

'I'm sure.' He stopped talking for several minutes, then resumed, 'After she gave birth to you, she suffered a complication.'

'A complication? What do you mean? What sort of complication?'

'She got a clot in her leg, a DVT, or deep vein thrombosis, to give it its proper medical name. It's quite a common occurrence in pregnancy, actually. It also happens with the contraceptive pill. The hormonal changes make the blood clot more easily.'

'How does a clot in the leg kill you?' Frankie asked.

Baz looked away; she already knew the answer.

'Normally it doesn't but sometimes, just sometimes,' John Marsden tried to explain, 'a piece of the clot breaks off and travels up to the lungs, that's called a pulmonary embolus. Then it lodges in one of the main arteries and so it stops blood circulating around the lungs and getting back to the heart. Often then the sufferer has a cardiac arrest and dies. That's what happened to your mum. I'm sorry, Frankie, but that is the truth.'

Seeing that Frankie was getting visibly upset by this explanation, he quickly added, 'Death, though, is usually very quick and painless.'

He leant forward and embraced Frankie in both arms.

Baz could hear Frankie softly sobbing.

After a few moments, Baz asked, 'How do you know all this? Were you her doctor or something?'

John Marsden appeared taken aback by Baz's question. 'God, no, I was only seventeen myself at the time.'

'So how do you know all this stuff?' It was Frankie now who asked looking directly into the older man's eyes.

'Because, Frankie... I'm your father.'

Some time passed before the full sequence of events sixteen years ago were shared. John Marsden and Frankie's mother, Anne Best, had a teenage romance. Anne got pregnant. It was a different time then. The families were scandalised.

Anne's family wanted nothing to do with John, or indeed, his family. Anne and he did try to maintain a relationship through the pregnancy, but it was never going to last.

Later, after Anne died, her family couldn't cope, so they put the baby up for adoption. John, though the father, was too young to do anything about it. Especially, as his own family had drummed into him repeatedly, he had a career ahead of him. There was no way they were even going to contemplate him or anyone in his family adopting the unfortunate child.

'What about what the letter says?' Frankie asked.

'The letter, yes, if you read it carefully, you'll see that Cathy doesn't actually say that she is your mother, just that one of us was your biological parent. She knew about you. I'd told her a number of years back and she knew I regretted not having you in my life. So I guess, given the trouble that the two of us had just gone through and the fact that we couldn't have children ourselves, she must have decided that bringing you back into our lives would help us cement to our own relationship as well as enhance yours. I'm sure that's what she meant.'

Tears now streamed uncontrollably down Frankie's face. Baz and John were uncertain whether they came from despair or happiness.

After all this time and all his efforts to find his real mother, he still didn't have one.

But now he had a father.

chapter thirty-four

Mary Walker sat in the rear seat of John Marsden's car. Frankie reclined beside her. After John Marsden had picked Mary Walker up, they had had a full and frank conversation about Frankie's future and how John Marsden did indeed want to play a part in it. He did reassure Mary that as far as he was concerned, she had raised him all these years and she was to all intents and purposes his 'mother' and would remain so. He would not usurp her authority in any way.

Frankie nodded dumbly, accepting the compromise.

Mary Walker, for her part, had not divulged her meeting with Cathy and had decided that it was probably best not to. After all, if Cathy had simply told her husband that she had just tripped and fallen and had the good grace not to mention Mary's part in it, then, she reasoned, it would only cause unnecessary upset to both John Marsden and Frankie to rake it up.

The car was now parked in a side street not far from Frankie's school. One hundred yards up ahead of them at the top of the narrow street, Baz was reclining against the gable wall of the end house. She had on a pair of faded torn jeans, a long woollen sweater that hung limply on her, her hair was tied back in a ponytail and she wore no make-up. She looked much younger than her twenty-eight years.

Two young men crossed the road ahead of them, heading in Baz's direction. 'That's them,' exclaimed Frankie. The two young men were deep in conversation. So engrossed that they didn't notice John Marsden's car headlights flicker.

At the signal, Baz stepped forward, stepping into the path of the two strangers.

They stopped, a little startled by the sudden interruption to their deliberations.

'Got any gear, boys?' she asked.

'What do you mean by that?' the older of the two, stepping in front of the other, replied.

'Gear. Smack, coke, you know.'

'What makes you think we do drugs, then?'

'A little bird told me. Told me you were the two to see around here.'

'A little bird?' the younger one sneered.

'Okay, if you don't want to sell my anything, I'll find someone who will.' She made to move off.

'Not so fast.' The first boy grabbed her arm. 'We might be able to help you out.'

They looked from one to the other and nodded simultaneously. The older one reached into his pocket and pulled out a small clear sachet containing a white powder.

'It's good stuff,' he reassured her. 'No messing about.' He looked suspiciously over his shoulder but couldn't see anybody else in the street. 'Half a gram, that'll do five or six lines. Twenty quid to you.' He paused, replacing the sachet in his pocket. 'Let's see your dosh, then.'

Baz reached into the back pocket of her jeans and pulled out a small bundle of five-pound notes. She held them out in front of her but snatched her hand back when the younger man reached forward to take the notes from her.

'You hand over the coke first.'

'That's not the way it works, love.'

Baz waited a few seconds as if in thought. 'Look there are two of you, one of me. What do you think I'm going to do? Beat you up? Make a break for it? Come on, guys, give me a break.'

The two looked at one another, then the older one nodded at the other. He handed over the sachets and Baz held out the money.

The younger one took it quickly from her and stuffed it into his pocket.

At that moment, two older, somewhat larger and well-built middle-aged men wearing virtually identical suits leapt out of a nearby car and ran towards the trio.

Hearing the rapidly approaching feet, the two younger men standing in front of Baz wheeled around. Their expressions changed to fear; they glanced at each other before deciding to make a run for it in the opposite direction of their pursuers and towards John Marsden's parked car.

'Police! Stop!' The shouted command simply confirmed their worst fears.

Before he had taken more than a single step, Baz had kicked out at the retreating foot of the boy who had passed over the drugs. This action caused his rear foot to catch on back of his other leg and resulted in him tripping and falling painfully to the ground. One of the policemen jumped on top of the boy lying on the pavement. He knelt over the figure, one leg on the pavement and the other in the small of his prisoner's back, securing him from further attempts to escape. Then, happy that the youth couldn't get back to his feet, he leant forward and forcefully pulled both his prisoner's arms up and behind his back before producing a pair of handcuffs and fastening his hands together.

The younger of the two, though, appeared more agile and was starting to outdistance the other policeman. As he careered down the street, he looked over his shoulder and smiled, realising he was indeed escaping. In doing so, he failed to notice the parked car with the three people in it sitting at the kerb in front of him. As he was about to sprint past the car, Frankie thrust open the back-passenger door directly into the fugitive's path. Being so close and going so fast, there was no time for Tommy Hardcastle to take any avoiding action and he careered into the door and then fell back crashing to the ground, clutching his chest where it had struck the top of the door.

As he lay on the ground writhing in agony, the second policeman arrived and, slightly breathlessly, handcuffed the former fugitive and wheezed at him, 'Thomas Hardcastle. I am arresting you for being in possession of illegal substances and with intent to supply. You have the right to remain silent, but anything that you do say will be taken down and may be used in evidence against you. Do you understand?'

Tommy Hardcastle looked up; a small trickle of blood oozed from his nose. He sheepishly nodded his affirmation and was led back down the road to where his fellow prisoner stood similarly handcuffed and restrained by the other police officer.

A moment later a marked police car rounded the corner and two uniformed officers got out and helped the two detectives push their two captives into the backseat.

Before the detective could close the rear door, shutting them in, Baz leant into the car and said directly to the younger of the two, 'Detective Inspector Warlow says thanks for the tip-off, Tommy. It will go in your favour.'

Tommy Hardcastle looked at her in bewilderment.

At the words, the older of the two boys immediately swung and fixed Tommy in a malevolent stare. Baz slammed the car door closed and it drove off, disappearing around the corner at the end of the street.

Baz climbed into the car parked beside John. 'A job well done, I think,' she said over her shoulder in Frankie's direction. She noted that Mary Walker was hugging him tightly despite his half-hearted attempts to escape and John Marsden was grinning widely.

'I'm glad the police agreed that they owed us one after DS Brown. I don't think Tommy Hardcastle will be bothering you for a while, Frankie.'

'He's in big trouble,' agreed Frankie.

'Double trouble actually,' said Baz. 'After what I said to him, I don't believe his partner in crime is going to be too happy with him either. I think Tommy's going to be too busy watching his own back from now on.'

John Marsden started the car and delivered Frankie and Mary Walker back to their house. As agreed, Frankie would continue to live with Mary, but John would start to play a big part in Frankie's future. Everyone, especially Frankie, seemed happy with this proposed solution.

Having dropped off Frankie and Mary Walker, Baz turned to John and rested her hand gently on his leg as he continued to drive. 'John, I'm really sorry about the deception. I do care about you, honestly, I do.'

'I know, Baz, and I'm actually quite grateful you did come into my life the way you have.'

'Then, maybe,' she continued, 'we could go right back to the start and try again.'

'Maybe we can do just that.' He smiled.

about the author

James I. Morrow has been a Consultant Neurologist based at a major teaching hospital in Belfast. During his career he has been involved in and supervised a number of clinical trials, principally examining the safety of medicines. He has written and published a number of medical books as well as another novel *Slainte*.